The Sovereignty
of Quiet

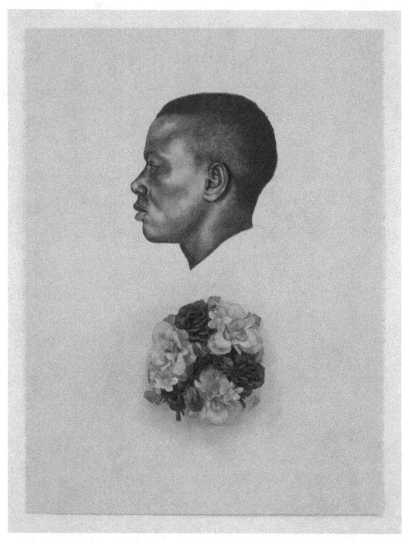

Frontispiece. Whitfield Lovell, *Kin VII (Scent of Magnolia)*, 2008. Conte crayon on paper with attached wreath. 30 × 22½ × 3 inches. Courtesy of the artist and DC Moore Gallery, New York, N.Y.

The Sovereignty
of Quiet

Beyond Resistance in
Black Culture

KEVIN QUASHIE

RUTGERS UNIVERSITY PRESS
NEW BRUNSWICK, NEW JERSEY, AND LONDON

Library of Congress Cataloging-in-Publication Data

Quashie, Kevin Everod.
   The sovereignty of quiet : beyond resistance in Black culture / Kevin Quashie.
      p. cm.
   Includes bibliographical references and index.
      ISBN 978-0-8135-5309-2 (hardcover : alk. paper) — ISBN 978-0-8135-5310-8
   (pbk. : alk. paper) — ISBN 978-0-8135-5311-5 (e-book)
      1. American literature—African American authors—History and criticism—
   Theory, etc.   2. African Americans—Intellectual life.   3. African Americans—Race
   identity.   4. Identity (Psychology) in literature.   5. Group identity in literature.
   I. Title.
      PS508.N3Q83   2012
      810.9′896073—dc23

                                                                    2011035602

A British Cataloging-in-Publication record for this book is available from the British
Library.

Visit our website: http://rutgerspress.rutgers.edu

Manufactured in the United States of America

Contents

Introduction: Why Quiet   1

1   Publicness, Silence, and the Sovereignty
    of the Interior   11

2   Not Double Consciousness but the Consciousness
    of Surrender   27

3   *Maud Martha* and the Practice of Paying
    Attention   47

4   Quiet, Vulnerability, and Nationalism   73

5   The Capacities of Waiting, the Expressiveness
    of Prayer   103

Conclusion: To Be One   119

Acknowledgments   135
Permissions   137
Notes   139
Bibliography   169
Index   187

The Sovereignty
of Quiet

Introduction

WHY QUIET

The story of this moment has been told many times: It is the 1968 Olympics in a volatile Mexico City, and two male athletes, both black Americans, make an emblematic gesture during the medal ceremony for the 200-meter race. One of them, Tommie Smith, has won the race while the other, John Carlos, placed third. As the U.S. national anthem plays, both men punctuate the space above their heads with their black-gloved fists, Smith raising his right hand, Carlos his left. Their salute is a black power sign that protests racism and poverty, and counters the anthem and its embracing nationalism. The third man on the podium, standing to their right, is Peter Norman, a white Australian who won the silver medal; Norman doesn't elevate his fist but wears an OPHR (Olympic Project for Human Rights) pin in solidarity with Smith's and Carlos's protest.

The power of this moment is in its celebrated details—the clenched fists, the black gloves, the shoeless feet—details that confirm the resoluteness of the action. Since that day, commentators have memorialized the public assertiveness of Smith's and Carlos's gestures. Their paired bodies have become a precise sign of a restless decade and especially of black resistance. But look again, closely, at the pictures from that day and you can see something more than the certainty of public assertiveness. See, for example, how the severity of Smith's salute is balanced by the yielding of Carlos's raised arm. And then notice how the sharpness of their gesture is complemented

Figure 1. Tommie Smith, John Carlos, and Peter Norman, 1968 Mexico City Olympics. Courtesy of AP Photo/File.

by one telling detail: that their heads are bowed as if in prayer, that Smith, in fact, has his eyes closed. The effect of their bowed heads is to suggest intimacy, and it is a reminder that this very public protest is also intimate. There is a sublime balance between their intentional political gesture and this sense of inwardness, a sublimity that is often barely acknowledged. In truth, the beauty of the protest is enhanced by noting the intimacy, in reading Smith and Carlos not only as soldiers in a larger war against oppression but also as two people in a moment of deep spirituality, in prayer, as vulnerable as they are aggressive, as pensive as they are solidly righteous. In this reading, what is compelling is their humanity on display, the unexpected glimpse we get of the inner dimensions of their public bravery.[1]

And yet this interior quality of Smith's and Carlos's protest is rarely discussed, even as their gesture has earned a long life as one of the most iconic moments of resistance of the twentieth century. Why is this so? There is certainly no question that their action was an intentional and public demonstration, the most significant of the OPHR's attempt to organize athletes toward a boycott of the Games. And still, what is moving about seeing them is as much the quality of graceful, lithe surrender in their posture as it is the awareness of the politics that are at stake. Like many other moments from the civil rights movement, their protest is an exquisite balance of what is public and what is intimate. How is it, then, that the intimacy of their fists-in-protest can be overlooked or deferred in our reading, such that the breadth of this moment is commented on only for its publicity? How is it that they are largely icons of resistance, and that vulnerability and interiority are not among all the things we are encouraged to read on their image?[2]

———

This book explores what a concept of quiet could mean to how we think about black culture. The exploration is a shift in how we commonly understand blackness, which is often described as expressive, dramatic, or loud. These qualities inherently reflect the equivalence between resistance and blackness. Resistance is, in fact, the dominant expectation we have of black culture. Indeed, this expectation is so widely familiar that it does not require explanation or qualification; it is practically unconscious.

These assumptions are noticeable in the ways that blackness serves as an emblem of social ailment and progress. In an essay from his 1957 collection

White Man Listen!, Richard Wright captures this sentiment, noting that "The Negro is America's metaphor" (109). Wright's comment might be hyperbolic, but it also summarizes the exceptional role that black experience has played in American social consciousness: Blackness here is not a term of intimacy or human vagary but of publicness. One result of this dynamic is a quality of self-consciousness in black literature, a hyperawareness of a reader whose presence—whether critical or sympathetic—shapes what is expressed. Such self-consciousness is an example of the concept of doubleness that has become the preeminent trope of black cultural studies. The result is that black culture is celebrated for the exemplary ways it employs doubleness as well as for its capacity to manipulate social opinion and challenge racism.

This is the politics of representation, where black subjectivity exists for its social and political meaningfulness rather than as a marker of the human individuality of the person who is black. As an identity, blackness is always supposed to tell us something about race or racism, or about America, or violence and struggle and triumph or poverty and hopefulness. The determination to see blackness only through a social public lens, as if there were no inner life, is racist—it comes from the language of racial superiority and is a practice intended to dehumanize black people. But it has also been adopted by black culture, especially in terms of nationalism, but also more generally: it creeps into the consciousness of the black subject, especially the artist, as the imperative to represent. Such expectation is part of the inclination to understand black culture through a lens of resistance, and it practically thwarts other ways of reading. All of this suggests that the common frameworks for thinking about blackness are limited.

Resistance is hard to argue against, since it has been so essential to every black freedom movement. And yet resistance is too broad a term—it is too clunky and vague and imprecise to be a catch-all for a whole range of behaviors and ambitions. It is not nuanced enough to characterize the totality of black culture or expression. Resistance exists, for sure, and deserves to be named and studied. And still, sometimes, when the term "resistance" is used, what is being described is something finer. There is an instructive example of this tension in Stephanie Camp's *Closer to Freedom: Enslaved Women and Everyday Resistance in the Plantation South*, a compelling work on the lives of black women during slavery. As Camp's title suggests, the frame for the book is resistance, the ways that black women's everyday lives ("private, concealed, and even intimate worlds" [3]) constitute a defiance of the vagaries of enslavement. Like Deborah Gray White and others before her, Camp notices how black women's acts of resistance appear in day-to-day activities as much as (if not more than) in formal planned rebellions or revolts. And yet even Camp realizes that the meaning of black women's everyday lives was not shaped entirely by their engagement with and resistance to the institution of slavery—that black women and men who were enslaved grew gardens and decorated their living spaces and organized parties in the woods (the chapter "The Intoxication of Pleasurable Amusement: Secret Parties and the Politics of the Body" is beautifully imagined and written). The point here is not to dismiss the intensity and vulgarity of slavery's violence on black people, but instead to restore a broader picture of the humanity of the people who were enslaved. Under Camp's careful eye, these women's everyday lives are brought into fuller relief, and even if Camp reads these lives as moments of resistance, their aliveness jumps out beyond that equation to offer something more.[3]

The case for quiet is, implicitly, an argument against the limits of blackness as a concept; as such, this book exists alongside many others that have questioned the boundaries of racial identity. These include recent scholarly work by Robert Reid-Pharr, Paul Gilroy, Thomas Holt, Michelle Wright, Gene Andrew Jarrett, Kenneth Warren, Kimberly Nichele Brown, Hazel Carby, Trey Ellis, Thelma Golden, and especially David Lionel Smith, whose essay "What Is Black Culture?" is dazzling and indispensable. There is also a large body of work by black women scholars, especially since the 1970s, that has posed consistent challenges to the singularity of race. The specific concern about the dominance of resistance as a framework, however, is exposed by black artists who have always struggled with the politics of representation. From Zadie Smith, Afaa M. Weaver, and Rita Dove, to Zora Neale Hurston, Langston Hughes, and Ralph Ellison, the black artist lives within the crosshairs of publicness and, if she or he is to produce meaningful work, has to construct a consciousness that exists beyond the expectation of resistance. Inspired by these artists, this argument for quiet aims to give up resistance as a framework in search of what is lost in its all-encompassing reach.[4]

Resistance, yes, but other capacities too. Like quiet.

The idea of quiet is compelling because the term is not fancy—it is an everyday word—but it is also conceptual. Quiet is often used interchangeably with silence or stillness, but the notion of quiet in the pages that follow is neither motionless nor without sound. Quiet, instead, is a metaphor for the full range of one's inner life—one's desires, ambitions, hungers, vulnerabilities, fears. The inner life is not apolitical or without social value, but neither is it determined entirely by publicness. In fact, the interior—dynamic and ravishing—is a stay against the dominance of the social world; it has its own sovereignty. It is hard to see, even harder to describe, but no less potent in its ineffability. Quiet.

In humanity, quiet is inevitable, essential. It is a simple, beautiful part of what it means to be alive. It is already there, if one is looking to understand it. An aesthetic of quiet is not incompatible with black culture, but to notice and understand it requires a shift in how we read, what we look for, and what we expect, even what we remain open to. It requires paying attention in a different way.

This point about how we read is especially relevant to the image in the frontispiece, Whitfield Lovell's *KIN VII (Scent of Magnolia)*. Lovell is a giant in contemporary art, a 2007 MacArthur fellow whose work has been showcased at the Smithsonian, the Whitney, the MOMA, and in various other locations in the United States and abroad. His most well-known exhibits, Whispers from the Walls and Sanctuary, consist of a series of tableaux and full-room installations that display the daily lives of anonymous African Americans. In these installations, charcoal drawings of posed studio photographs found at flea markets or town archives (largely from the 1900s to the 1940s) are paired with various objects (boxing gloves, a knife, barbed wire, a bucket). The drawings are made on pieces of wood—parts of fences or walls—and seem to bring domestic scenes to life. More recently, in a stunning collection entitled Kin, Lovell has continued drawing portraits of anonymous black people, though this time on paper; these figures are made from identification photographs (headshots from passports or mug shots, for example) and are often paired with an object. Critics note the dignity of Lovell's figures, which is a tribute to his skill in drawing: His portraits render their subjects in terrific clarity (the intensity in the eyes, the defined neck and cheek, the textured quality of the hair). His use of shadow is astute, and the result is images of people who look like people—not symbols of a discourse of racism, but people in the everyday, wary and resolute, alive. They look familiar to us even if it is rare to see black faces represented in such a studied, elegant way.

But the dignity is related also to the pairing of image and artifact, the clean juxtaposition of locating each near the other without abrasion or overlap. This doesn't really create a sense of doubleness because the portrait is intended to be prominent; still proximity is contagion, and the artifact insinuates itself on the portrait. In *KIN VII (Scent of Magnolia)*, the cloth wreath becomes part of the male figure's body, marking the place where one might expect a shirt collar, a piece of jewelry, the outline of a chest. Localized and domesticated, the wreath's randomness becomes specific to this bold beautiful black face.

And the subject is clarified by the artifact: Are these flowers from his room, a private and unusual explosion of color? The flowers he gave to a date or the ones he brought to a funeral? A sign of his desire to visit all the world's spectacular gardens? We might pick up the title's reference to Billie Holiday's thick voice on "Strange Fruit" ("scent of magnolia sweet and fresh/the sudden smell of burning flesh") which might lead to a more ominous reading—his killed body marked by a wreath—but it is unsatisfying to be so singular and definitive with this image. Because of the flowers, he can be a subject more than an emblem; we can wonder if he loved pink and purple tones, without ignoring the possibility of racist violence. Whatever the story, the flowers are a surprise that interrupt the dominant narratives that might be ascribed to the profile of a black man of that age.

The foreboding is there to be read in some of the objects in Lovell's work—chains, barbed wire, targets, rope—which is as it would be, often is, for a black person in the United States. And still, foreboding is only part of one's life story, and it should not overwhelm how we think of the breadth of humanity. Lovell seems to aim for a balance between the social or public meaning of a person or object, and its intimacy, its human relevance. Where his earlier work created tableaux using full-bodied figures, the aesthetic of juxtaposition in these more recent pieces is what evokes narrative, as if we are seeing the unfolding of a scene of human life, as if more and more of the image will manifest if you look long enough. (This is especially true of Lovell's drawings that lack a corresponding artifact.) The key is to let the unexpected be possible.

We might want to read a narrative of resistance on *KIN VII (Scent of Magnolia)*, but there is something else there: a ravishing quiet.

Quiet is antithetical to how we think about black culture, and by extension, black people. So much of the discourse of racial blackness imagines black people as public subjects with identities formed and articulated and resisted in public. Such blackness is dramatic, symbolic, never for its own vagary, always representative and engaged with how it is imagined publicly. These characterizations are the legacy of racism and they become the common way we understand and represent blackness; literally they become a lingua franca. The idea of quiet, then, can shift attention to what is interior. This shift can feel like a kind of heresy if the interior is thought of as apolitical or inexpressive, which it is not: one's inner life is raucous and full of expression, especially if we distinguish the term "expressive" from the notion of public. Indeed the interior could be understood as the source of human action—that anything we do is shaped by the range of desires and capacities of our inner life.

This is the agency in Lovell's piece, the way that what is implied is a full range of human life: that we don't know the subject just by looking at him or noticing the artifact; that his life is wide-open and possible; that his life is more than familiar characterizations of victimization by or triumph over racism. For sure, the threat and violence of racism is one story, as is the grace and necessity of the fight. But what else is there to black humanity, this piece seems to ask. The question is an invitation to imagine an inner life of the broadest terrain.

It is remarkable for a black artist working with black subjects (and in a visual medium) to restore humanity without being apolitical. It is remarkable, also, to make the argument that Lovell makes so well with his work—that what is black is at once particular and universal, familiar and unknowable.

This is challenging territory to navigate, given the importance of resistance and protest to black culture. But the intent here is not to disregard these terms, but to ask what else—what else can we say about black culture, what other frameworks might help to illuminate aspects of the work produced by black writers and thinkers? How can quiet, as a frame for reading black culture, expose life that is not already determined by narratives of the social world? After all, all living is political—every human action means something—but all living is not in protest; to assume such is to disregard the richness of life.

In humanity, quiet is inevitable, essential. It is a simple beautiful part of what it means to be alive. It is already there, if one is looking to understand it.

There are many books on black expressiveness and resistance; there will be—and should be—many more. This, however, is not one of them. This book is about quiet.

————

The first chapter explores the way that public expressiveness has become the dominant framework for understanding texts or moments in black culture. Specifically, the chapter considers the concept of doubleness through a close reading of W.E.B. Du Bois's notion of double consciousness, Paul Laurence Dunbar's characterization in "We Wear the Mask," and Zora Neale Hurston's representation of signifying in *Their Eyes Were Watching God*. In noticing the limits of these idioms, the chapter offers quiet as a metaphor for the interior and as a more capable expressiveness. In making this case, the chapter distinguishes between quiet and silence, and discusses Let Your Motto Be Resistance, the inaugural exhibit at the National Museum of African American History and Culture; it also revisits the image of Smith and Carlos.

At the heart of the second chapter is the concept of quiet as surrender—the idea that human subjectivity is not tethered to fighting the social world, but instead could be imagined as the agency to be had in surrendering to the wildness of one's inner life. The discussion here uses Marita Bonner's little-known essay from 1925, "On Being Young, a Woman and Colored," a poetic 1,679-word treatise that serves as a counterpoint to Du Bois's famous idiom: not a consciousness that is irrevocably doubled, but one of surrender. The third chapter considers this consciousness of surrender through Gwendolyn Brooks's slim novel *Maud Martha*. The chapter wonders what quiet looks like in an everyday life, and engages these questions: How does interiority inform interactions with other people? How does the quiet subject negotiate moments of subjection and power? What is the action that quiet motivates, or how does it shape behavior? Simply, what does a quiet life look like? The chapter also studies Rita Dove's "Daystar" from *Thomas and Beulah*.

The fourth chapter moves away from the consideration of quiet through constructs of individuality, as in the second and third chapters, and wonders if quiet is possible in collectivity. Necessarily, the chapter looks at nationalism and its centrality to black culture, as well as its perils to a notion of interiority. Thinking through representations of the civil rights movement, especially James Baldwin's *The Fire Next Time*, the chapter tries to understand how the terms of quiet—surrender, interiority, and especially vulnerability—can be meaningful to collectivity. In this exploration, the chapter revisits Elizabeth Alexander's reading of her inaugural poem, "Praise Song for the Day," and engages Alice Walker's definition of "womanism" and Marlon Riggs's documentary on black identity, *Black Is . . . Black Ain't*.

The last two chapters are closely connected in that they take on quiet's expressiveness. In the fifth chapter, the concepts of prayer and waiting are used to expose expressiveness that is not public and that is not only urgent. The chapter also considers the importance of form to understanding the figurative capacities of language. Key texts here are poems by Natasha Trethewey and Dionne Brand, and Lorna Simpson's visual piece *Waterbearer*. The concluding chapter relates quiet to the notion of "oneness," the energy of the inner life that constitutes a person's being. Conceptually, quiet is the subjectivity of the "one" and is equivalent to wandering. This case is made by reading two key scenes from Toni Morrison's *Sula* as well as the title poem from Ruth Ellen Kocher's *When the Moon Knows You're Wandering*. Finally, the chapter considers the particular contributions that black women have made to the ideas that inform quiet, and offers brief snapshots of other examples and dimensions of quiet that are not explored in this book. The chapter closes with a reconsideration of the ineffability and essentiality of quiet.

Inevitable, essential, sovereign; expressive and lush; a little foreign to our thinking on black culture, but there all the while: quiet.

CHAPTER 1

Publicness, Silence, and the Sovereignty of the Interior

Look again at that image of Tommie Smith and John Carlos from the Mexico City Olympics: Part of what limits our capacity to see their fuller humanity is a general concept of blackness that privileges public expressiveness and resistance. More specifically, in most regards, black culture is overidentified with an idea of expressiveness that is geared toward a social audience and that has political aim; such expressiveness is the essence of black resistance. That public expressiveness and resistance are definitive of black culture is an effect of the role the public sphere has played in making, marking, and policing racial difference. Indeed since ideas about white racial superiority are formulated and articulated in public discourse (literature, art, science, medicine, law) and are enacted in public spaces (neighborhoods, schools, parks), it makes sense that publicness, as both an act and a location, would be integral to the struggle for racial equality. As a result, black culture has been characterized largely by its responses to racial dominance, so much so that resistance becomes its defining feature and expectation. In this context, black culture is or is supposed to be loud, literally as well as metaphorically, since such loudness is the expressiveness that articulates its resistance. These notions inform how we think about black subjectivity, which is necessarily contrarian and seemingly lacking an inner life.[1]

Resistance, then, is the dominant framework for reading black culture. One result of this dominance is that the major concepts used to discuss black culture (for example, doubleness, signifying, the mask) are engaged largely for their capacity to support the idea of resistance. In this light, these concepts say less and less about the interior of black subjectivity, and leave us without a general concept that can characterize the inner life.

Consider closely the example of doubleness, one of the central idioms of black cultural studies: In terms of articulations of doubleness, there is perhaps no concept more notable than that of W.E.B. Du Bois's notion of double consciousness. A psychological term codified in the opening chapter of his *The Souls of Black Folk*, "double consciousness" describes the experience of having two conflicting identities. In Du Bois's formulation, this split identity is the definitive impact that oppression has on the black subject, who sees himself through the revelations of the dominant world. Double consciousness is descriptive of the general notion that selfhood is achieved through interactions with other people, but when the term is used in specific regard to black identity, it suggests something more: a black subject whose being is conscripted not only by race but also by a racist discourse. In short, double consciousness conceptualizes black subjectivity as conflict with whiteness and imagines black agency only as/in resistance.[2]

From the first sentence of the first chapter, even before he uses the term "double consciousness," Du Bois's argument pivots on the idea of a subject ensnared in a racialized discourse: "Between me and the other world there is ever an unasked question . . . How does it feel to be a problem?" (9). In this sentence, the narrator, Du Bois himself, suggests that this question is the one that is always on the minds and lips of white people when they engage a black person, though the directness of the question changes from moment to moment. Writing at the turn of the twentieth century and in the midst of profound questions about race and the implications of the end of the Civil War, Du Bois rightly contextualizes the black subject as a problem in the white imagination. His black subject is defined by race, and particularly by this racial formulation of being a problem.

Though the narrator claims to offer no response to the question, his refusal is not characteristic of interiority, since he is already overdetermined by the unasked and unanswered (perhaps even unanswerable) question: "At these [the questions that are posed] I smile, or am interested, or reduce the boiling to a simmer. . . . To the real question, How does it feel to be a problem? I answer seldom a word" (9–10). Notably, Du Bois represses whatever he is feeling, performs a smile, but does not engage the question explicitly. Instead, the "answer" seems to come in a reverie that describes a young Du Bois's early encounter with race and racism:

> In a wee wooden schoolhouse, something put it into the boys' and girls' heads to buy gorgeous visiting-cards—ten cents a package—and exchange. The exchange was merry, till one girl, a tall newcomer, refused my card,—refused it peremptorily, with a glance. Then it dawned upon me with a certain suddenness that I was different from the others. (10)

This memory of coming to consciousness is offered, in some ways, as an emphasis to and clarification of the unasked question in the opening paragraph of the chapter; that is, this is the articulation of the interior that is repressed or silenced in the adult Du Bois. But the interior here is not a place of surrender and exploration where Du Bois can engage a range of feelings and thoughts and desires. Instead, this interior is under the command of rejection that comes from the outside. Having experienced rejection, the young Du Bois develops a growing contempt for his white peers: "That sky was bluest when I could beat my mates at examination-time, or beat them at a foot-race, or even beat their stringy heads" (10). It is not only the competitive aspect that is fascinating here, or even that Du Bois imagines himself to be singularly consumed by this moment, but also that the elegant and studied language of his prose gives way to the vernacular "beat their stringy heads." Of course, the narrator recovers from this eruption of the repressed and starts the next sentence with a statement of composed resignation: "Alas, with the years all this fine contempt began to fade." What does not fade, however, is the sense of being shaped by race and racialization; the Du Boisian subject is "overdetermined from without," as Franz Fanon might say, compelled to either accept or defy the prognosis of white culture. In short, Du Bois depicts a subject who is haunted and animated by doubleness.

The narrator describes his determination to resist the idea that the best of the world belonged only to white people; he resolves to achieve success by "reading law, by healing the sick, by telling the wonderful tales that swam in [his] head,—some way" (10). But even this determination does not temper the reality that he is irrevocably tethered to what white culture says of him. This is, in essence, double consciousness, and Du Bois captures it perfectly when he describes the impact of racism on other boys like him: "With other black boys the strife was not so fiercely sunny: their youth shrunk into tasteless sycophancy, or into silent hatred of the pale world about them and mocking distrust of everything white; or wasted itself in a bitter cry" (10). This description reiterates the sense of black identity as "strife," of being in an unending struggle with racism. In this regard, the options are few—accept the racist characterization and become all the inferiority it imagines you to be, or resist it fiercely.

What follows next is the passage where Du Bois uses the term "double consciousness," though he has already described the context for understanding the black person as one "born with a veil, and gifted with secondsight in this American world,—a world which yields him no true self-consciousness, but only lets him see himself through the revelation of the other world" (10–11). One could read the possibility of agency in Du Bois's ironic phrase "gifted with second-sight," though it is clear that whatever additional insight the black subject has is linked to his being the other—this subject who is revealed via the consciousness and imagination of the world around him, as well as via his response to and resistance of such imagining. In double consciousness, the twoness of black subjectivity does not represent another consciousness that is free and wild; instead, the twoness is a kind of pathology, a fractured consciousness that is overdetermined by a public language of black inferiority. The black soul is measured "by the tape of a world that looks on in amused contempt and pity" (11). In this characterization, agency is limited to resisting public discourse, and the black subject seems to possess no interior worth speaking of.

That Du Bois would conceive of black subjectivity in such bleak terms is unsurprising, not only because of the era in which he wrote but simply because racism is a profound phenomenon—it has material and psychological impact, and it is institutionally and individually unrelenting. Indeed, Du Bois's overall thesis is intended to give attention to the unique profundity of racism. But what is striking is that his notion of double consciousness does not characterize the inner life of the black subject, at least not an interior that has its own sovereignty—that is, Du Bois does not offer a description of the black subject as having access to his selfhood beyond the public discourse of race, access that is unfettered and unrestricted, even if only in his own mind. Instead, the argument of double consciousness imagines that black subjectivity is without escape from the publicness of racialization—that blackness is always faithful to or in resistance of the projections of white culture. This description over-privileges race as a part of subjectivity and, in this regard, as much as double consciousness is a contemplative idiom, it does not fare well as a concept of interiority.[3]

Du Bois's double consciousness is similar to Darlene Clark Hine's notion of dissemblance, which Hine coined to characterize black women's ambivalent relationship to public exposure. Hine argues that in response to how they were negatively constructed in the social imagination as racial, gendered, and classed subjects, "Black women, as a rule, developed and adhered to a cult of secrecy, a culture of dissemblance, to protect the sanctity of inner aspects of their lives. The dynamics of dissemblance involved creating the appearance of disclosure, or openness about themselves and their feelings, while actually remaining an enigma" (915). She goes on to assert that "in the face of pervasive stereotypes ... it was imperative that they collectively create alternative self-images" (916). Such use of duplicity as a politic of resistance has been well documented by Hine and others.[4]

Although neither double consciousness nor dissemblance explicitly dismisses the idea of the interior, each nonetheless suggests that its presence is suppressed and disavowed because of the public dimensions of race and racism (and, in the case of dissemblance, gender and sexism). As concepts of doubleness, both idioms forgo the wild vagary of the inner life for what is calibrated and sensitive to the exterior world. The withholding or silence that is implied in both concepts celebrates a kind of artifice or performance, and reiterates the centrality of publicness in black cultural identity. The irony here is that, conceptually, rather than reinforce artifice as an essential practice, dissemblance and double consciousness seem primed to help us scrutinize the suppressed textualities of black identity, to touch greater depths of the subjectivities that are flattened by the broad sweep of racism. Yet, more often than not, what is gained in using these tropes is not the subtlety of the human subject, but the nuances of the act of concealment.[5]

These claims about the aesthetics of doubleness are evident in looking at Paul Laurence Dunbar's poem "We Wear the Mask," a tour de force of signifying and concealment, and an example of another celebrated idiom of black culture—the idea of masking. First published in 1895, the poem reads:

> We wear the mask that grins and lies,
> It hides our cheeks and shades our eyes,—
> This debt we pay to human guile;
> With torn and bleeding hearts we smile,
> And mouth with myriad subtleties.
>
> Why should the world be overwise,
> In counting all our tears and sighs?
> Nay, let them only see us, while
> We wear the mask.
>
> We smile, but, O great Christ, our cries
> To thee from tortured souls arise.
> We sing, but oh the clay is vile
> Beneath our feet, and long the mile;
> But let the world dream otherwise,
> We wear the mask!

The poem is a technical marvel, sustaining perfect singular rhyme with every line echoing the same final assonance, except in three places—the repetition of the word "mask" at the end of stanzas two and three, and the use of the word "subtleties" to end stanza one. What is striking about the rhythmic disruption that "subtleties" causes is that visually, the word seems to fit the rhyme scheme—it looks like it should rhyme with "lies," "eyes" or "cries." This is a poetic sleight of hand where Dunbar seems to play on the tendency of the mind to want to follow the poem's sing-song rhythm (it is perfect iambic tetrameter, except for this disruption), and thereby force "subtleties" to sound like the words that end the lines before it. Further evidence of the poem's cunning is the slowly revealed truth that the near-perfect rhyme actually turns on the approximate rhyme between two sets of words that have the same long vowel sound but do not rhyme in their consonants: "lies" and "eyes," on one hand; "guile" and "smile" on the other. The poem's mask is not only its subject but its form; for example, its fifteen lines is one line longer than a traditional sonnet, a fact which reads like a performance of formlessness. Furthermore, the playfulness in Dunbar's manipulation of the rhyme is applicable also to his careful diction—cheeks, shades, grins, lies, guile, smile, hides, subtleties, all words that connote doubleness.

Dunbar's poem is brilliant in its technique and powerful in its general theme, but what is notable is how little it says about the interior of the masked subject. Other than bold declamations about "tortured souls" and "bleeding hearts," one knows nothing about the "we" whose selves are masked, about the depth or quality of their desires or fears. (Part of this is the use of the plural first-person, the way the pronoun "we" flattens as much as it unifies.) For sure, we learn about the aesthetic of the mask and its value as a ruse against oppression, about the masked persona's awareness of audience and the perils of publicness . . . but nothing of the subject. Even as the poem suggests that there is agency in the act of withholding one's true self from being revealed—a claim punctuated by the emphatic repetition of the title in the poem's last line—the agency does not allow the poem's masked subject to express selfhood beyond the surface of a furtive smile. There is little quality of an inner life to be found in the poem's response to racism and, at best, one can infer only that the wearer of the mask is either pained and rageful, or deceiving. This does not diminish the brilliance of Dunbar's poem, which is peerless for its marriage of form and content, and which, like Du Bois's double consciousness, imagines doubleness as subjection but also agency. And still, the poem illustrates that an aesthetic of guile is inept at rendering the inner life. Indeed, Dunbar's poem could have used the trope of masking to tell us something about the edge and pasture of one human's experience, a telling that would have expanded the archive of black subjectivity; instead the poem defers to a broader, less intimate view and characterizes a subjectivity that, in its sketchiness, feels caricatured.[6]

The limitations of masking and doubleness are a consequence of the way those terms have become part of a larger notion of black resistance, such that the intent of black subjectivity is always toward a political discourse of oppression, and never toward its own human vagary. This overlooking of interiority in favor of what is publicly expressive is also applicable to the idea of signifying: Based on the "verbal art of ritualized insult in which the speaker puts down, needles, or talks about someone, to make a point or sometimes just for fun," the concept of signifying celebrates the use of humor, indirection, and word play (Smitherman, *Black Talk*, 207).

Conceptually, verbal signifying has three rhetorical components—what is said, what is unsaid, and the relationship between the two. The piece that is said is often demonstrative and dramatic, and it plays to the listening audience; this contrasts with the silence of what is unspoken. The power of signifying as a rhetorical act lies in the third component—the dialectic produced between what is spoken and what is not—as irony, indirection, and juxtaposition coalesce to create meaning that is complicated and subtle, even surprising. In fact, it is never assured that the act of signifying will yield, for the reader or listener, the desired expression. In this regard, signifying is extraordinary expressiveness, relying unreliably on interplay between said and unsaid, public and not; one cannot appreciate it by only paying attention to what is explicit. And yet the general discussion of signifying as verbal exchange tends to focus on its demonstrative quality rather than its capacity to reflect what is unsure and interior. This emphasis suggests that the meanings of signifying are only legible through publicness (for example, audience).[7]

That signifying is considered primarily as a demonstrative idiom confirms how ingrained publicness is to black cultural discourse. Still, because signifying is complicated and nuanced, it is worth trying to understand its expressiveness beyond the limits imposed by publicness. An articulate example can be found in Zora Neale Hurston's masterful *Their Eyes Were Watching God*, a novel that represents Janie's longing for self-revelation as a meditation on interiority. One of the most studied examples of signifying in black literature is the argument between Janie and her husband Jody in the county store after Janie makes a mess of cutting a piece of tobacco for a customer. The customer, Steve Mixon, uses this moment to tease Janie and women as a whole, a teasing that causes great laughter from the other customers. But Jody does not laugh; instead he gets up, re-cuts the tobacco and then proceeds to curse at Janie in the presence of everyone. In particular, he comments on her aging body—her "rump hangin' nearly to [her] knees." The customers, accustomed to spirited teasing, laugh at first and then, as they notice the mean-spiritedness of Jody's comment, they go quiet. Janie, however, for what feels like the first time, speaks back, and the two get into a quick exchange of words, Jody cautioning Janie to watch her words, repeating his belief that it is inappropriate for Janie as a woman to talk back to him, especially in this public place. Besides Jody's patronizing warning, the rest of the argument consists largely of insults about aging, and it ends with a hot final word by Janie:

> Naw, Ah ain't no young gal no mo' but den Ah ain't no old woman nei-
> ther. Ah reckon Ah looks mah age too. But Ah'm uh woman every inch of
> me, and Ah know it. Dat's uh whole lot more'n *you* kin say. You big-
> bellies round here and put out a lot of brag, but 'taint nothin' to it but yo'
> big voice. Humph! Talkin' 'bout *me* lookin' old! When you pull down
> yo' britches, you look lak de change uh life. (75)

This indictment is followed by two quick comments from men in the group that essentially give the verbal victory to Janie, and the narrative notes that "Then Joe Starks realized all the meanings and his vanity bled like a flood."

Janie's response to Jody's verbal assault goes to the heart of his perceived power, his manhood, and it has such weight that it marks the beginning of his declining health and then his death a few pages later. This act of signify-ing in the novel has been read for its public demonstrativity—for the deep laughter it brings to the crowd in the store, for the retributive shame Janie has brought on Jody in a definitive moment of one-uppance. But the novel seems to suggest that the meaning here extends beyond the sparring and the laughter: Earlier in the chapter, the narrative was careful to describe not only Janie's sense of her repressed voice, but her noticing Jody's aging body. In fact, to this point, the whole story has privileged Janie's interior—we largely learn about her through the representation of her thoughts, as would be the case given her marriage to a man who believes deeply sexist ideas about the minds of women. The meaningfulness of the interior to Janie is amplified in an earlier scene when, after Jody demeans her intelligence and slaps her for ruining dinner, "Janie stood where he left her for unmeasured time and thought. She stood there until something fell off the shelf inside her. Then she went inside there to see what it was" (67). This is her interior, this place where time is without measure and where change and stillness cohabitate; as she explores it, she finds "that she has a host of thoughts she had never expressed to him, and numerous emotions she had never let Jody know about . . . She has an inside and an outside now and suddenly she knew how not to mix them" (68).

This heightened awareness of her interior—and the repressive, demand-ing exterior—is the defining idiom of Janie's journey in the novel. It is, then, in this context that we should read her signifying moment, since her harsh verbal blow to Jody is less about a public performance that is attuned to audience, and instead is an expression of her long-brewing thoughts about herself, her dreams, her freedom. The deeper value of Janie's signifying is found in its connection to this meditation in her interior. When the customers laugh and applaud Janie's comments, they are responding to the certainty and explicitness of what they hear in Janie's words. But this clarity is in contrast to the absence of control, the waiting and listening, suggested by the novel's description of Janie's sense of self. In fact, after that riotous scene, which Jody predictably concludes by slapping Janie again, the narrative returns to Janie's interior: "So new thoughts had to be thought and new words said. She didn't want to live like that. Why must Joe be so mad with her for making him look small when he did it to her all the time?" (77). This comment could be read as if it were a part of the signifying moment in the store, and the paragraph's narrative voice appropriately slips from omniscience to Janie's, to the intimacy of her interior where these "new thoughts" and "new words" are in process.

Not what is sure and singular and public, but what is interior and complicated and dynamic: Reading Janie's signifying as a compilation of moments of consciousness transcends the focus on public drama and reinforces the importance of the inner life as a part of expressiveness.[8] This rethinking of signifying is important because it points to what is lost in understanding expressiveness only through a discourse of publicness. The concern here is that the ways we interpret these central idioms of black culture—doubleness, signifying, dissemblance, double consciousness, masking—assume that black expressiveness is exclusively public. This assumption is troubling because it ties black expression to the discourse of resistance; that is, without other concepts with which to understand expressiveness, resistance becomes the lingua franca of black culture. And in the face of the inviolable relationship among publicness, expressiveness, and resistance, black cultural studies lacks a metaphor for characterizing the inner life, a metaphor capable of noticing the beauty and intimacy of Smith and Carlos.[9]

———

What, then, would a concept of expressiveness look like if it were not tethered to publicness? The performative aspects of black culture are well noted, but what else can be said about how we understand blackness? Could the notion of quiet help to articulate a different kind of expressiveness, or even to stand as a metaphor for the interior?

In everyday discourse, quiet is synonymous with silence and is the absence of sound or movement, but for the idea of quiet to be useful here, it will need to be understood as a quality or a sensibility of being, as a manner of expression. This expressiveness of quiet is not concerned with publicness, but instead is the expressiveness of the interior. That is, the quiet of a person represents the broad scope of his or her inner life; the quiet symbolizes—and if interrogated, expresses—some of the capacity of the interior.[10]

As a concept, the interior is slippery, but it can still be useful to our understanding of quiet. Most simply, interiority is a quality of being inward, a "metaphor" for "life and creativity beyond the public face of stereotype and limited imagination" (x). This latter description is from Elizabeth Alexander's collection *Black Interior*, and it captures precisely the value of the concept of the interior—that it gestures away from the caricatures of racial subjectivity that are either racist or intended to counter racism, and that it suggests what is essentially and indescribably human. The interior is the inner reservoir of thoughts, feelings, desires, fears, ambitions that shape a human self; it is both a space of wild selffullness, a kind of self-indulgence, and "the locus at which self interrogation takes place" (Spillers, *Black, White, and in Color*, 383). Said another way, the interior is expansive, voluptuous, creative; impulsive and dangerous, it is not subject to one's control but instead has to be taken on its own terms. It is not to be confused with intentionality or consciousness, since it is something more chaotic than that, more akin to hunger, memory, forgetting, the edges of all the humanness one has. Despite its name, the interior is not unconnected to the world of things (the public or political or social world), nor is it an exact antonym for exterior. Instead, the interior shifts in regard to life's stimuli but it is neither resistant to nor overdetermined by the vagaries of the outer world. The interior has its own ineffable integrity and it is a stay against the social world.[11]

There is, in trying to describe the interior, a predicament of expression, since the interior is not really discursive—it cannot be represented fully (or even fully accessed) and is largely indescribable. Furthermore, the interior is mostly known through language or behavior, through exterior manifestations, and is therefore hard to know on its own terms. For sure, the interior can be approximated, hinted at, implied, but its vastness and wildness often escape definitive characterization. And yet the interior *is* expressive; it is articulate and meaningful and has social impact. Indeed, it is the combination of the interior's expressiveness and the inability to articulate it fully that makes interiority such a meaningful idiom for rethinking the nature of black expressiveness.

Quiet, then, is the inexpressible expressiveness of this interior, an expressiveness that can appear publicly, have and affect social and political meaning, challenge or counter social discourse, yet none of this is its aim or essence. That is, since the interior is not essentially resistant, then quiet is an expressiveness that is not consumed with intentionality, at least in regard to resistance. It is in this way that the distinction between quiet and silence is clearer. Silence often denotes something that is suppressed or repressed, and is an interiority that is about withholding, absence, and stillness. Quiet, on the other hand, is presence (one can, for example, describe prose or a sound as quiet) and can encompass fantastic motion. It is true that silence can be expressive, but its expression is often based on refusal or protest, not the abundance and wildness of the interior described above. Indeed, the expressiveness of silence is often aware of an audience, a watcher or listener whose presence is the reason for the withholding—it is an expressiveness which is intent and even defiant. This is a key difference between the two terms because in its inwardness, the aesthetic of quiet is watcherless.[12]

The interest in quiet arrives because of the trouble posed by public expressiveness, particularly the assumption that black culture is predominantly resistant. This characterization is so commonsense, so totalitarian, that it ends up simplifying blackness. Furthermore, because the characterization is supported by the political and historical reality of black people—for example, the important role expressiveness plays in the struggles for civil rights—it goes largely unchallenged. The problem here is not expressiveness per se, but that black expressiveness is so tethered to what is public and to a discourse of resistance. As it is engaged, this concept of public expressiveness presumes to know and to say everything, clearly and definitively. This is why it is useful to political discourse, because it can allow a group to speak with a sense of singular purpose. In this regard, public expressiveness is the workhorse of nationalism, and is vital to any marginalized population. And perhaps this is as it should be, since there is no question about the meaningfulness of race and especially racism to black life; there is also no question that resistance, as individual or collective action or as an aesthetic, is a meaningful part of black culture. But there is, still, an important question about the other qualities of black culture that are overwhelmed by resistance's status as the predominant or even solitary cultural framework. Simply, what else beyond resistance can we say about black culture and subjectivity?[13]

The quarrel is with the way publicness has a chokehold on black culture. It is hard to imagine a conceptualization of blackness that does not already envision itself—and the humanness of its struggle to be free—within the context set by publicness: as a subjectivity whose expressiveness is demonstrative and resistant. Hortense Spillers is right when she notes that "every feature of social and human differentiation disappears in public discourses regarding African-Americans" (*Black, White, and in Color*, 224). This is precisely the need for a concept of interiority, that it can support representations of blackness that are irreverent, messy, complicated—representations that have greater human texture and specificity than the broad caption of resistance can offer. We should be wary of the dominance of expressiveness as a black aesthetic, and the easy conclusions that it makes possible.[14]

This interior expressiveness is already present in Smith and Carlos's protest, if we can remember to ask questions about their hearts in excited flutter, their heads bowed, the inwardness of their bodies in prayer. Part of what makes their protest so striking is its stark contrast with another iconic image of black publicness—the black body hanging from a tree. The magnitude of the contrast is heightened by the compositional similarity between photographs of their 1968 protest and images of lynched bodies. But at its horrible best, the image of the lynched body is one of silence and speaks through the alphabet of violent repression. Smith and Carlos's image, on the other hand, is alive, is articulate in its quiet; though they do not speak, their language is a generous vocabulary of humanity. In this context, Smith and Carlos are a triumphant, beautiful alternative.[15]

But there is also a danger in only reading their moment for the way it counters the violence of white supremacy (as an "alternative")—to do so is to disregard the evidence of their humanity for its own sake, to disavow that they are strong but also vulnerable, two people in a moment of grace, all thrill and tremble and loveliness. It is not only the explicit public argument that they are making about racism and poverty that should be important to us—or even their implied contrast with countless killed others—no, what must also matter is the argument announced in their posture of surrender, the glimpse of their exquisite interior. Their protest is more fluent because of this expressiveness that is not dependent on publicness; they are compelling as much for their quiet as for the very publicity of their expression.[16]

———

Quiet is the expressiveness of the inner life, unable to be expressed fully but nonetheless articulate and informing of one's humanity. As a concept, it helps us explore black subjectivity from beyond the boundaries of public expressiveness. That image of Smith and Carlos in Mexico City is in need of a framework that allows us to see it more fully. For sure, they make a gesture of resistance, but the meaning of their bodies, standing there, is not captured entirely by a notion of resistance. They are resistant in context, but not in essence.

The idea of an aesthetic of quiet might seem foreign or counterintuitive to black culture, but it is not. In fact, there is a strong contemplative tradition in black culture, a tradition inspired by the existential struggle of living with the confines of racial identity. The earliest writings by black Americans exemplify this capacity to question not just the imposition of identity but also the very meaning of human existence; this self-reflexiveness is evident through almost every form of black art. And yet this existential consciousness is often read through the discourse of resistance and therefore is reduced to what it says about the nature of the fight with publicness.[17]

The command (and limits) of resistance as a discourse is evidenced in the inaugural exhibit showcased at the National Museum of African American History and Culture in 2007, an exhibit that has been preserved partially online and in a catalog. A stunning collection of one hundred photographs of African Americans, the exhibit was titled Let Your Motto Be Resistance after an 1843 speech given by Henry Highland Garnet, the abolitionist and clergyman. The photographs cover about 150 years and include every notable figure in black history and many that people would not recognize by name or image. Among these is one of Duke Ellington laughing modestly in a dressing room; Gordon Parks as subject of the camera he wielded so masterfully; Diana Ross with Mary Wilson and Florence Ballard in a Detroit studio, each woman in elegant motion (and Ross signally in the center); Booker T. Washington tall and aware, poised, before a large crowd.

One understands why resistance was chosen for the exhibit's title, not only because of Garnet's powerful words but also because the presence of this breadth of black humanity is in fact a contradiction of the stereotypes of racism. The people in these images are not mammies or jezebels or bucks; they are human beings who worked and laughed and loved and made mistakes and had quirks, and the collection showcases that. Even more than this is the fact that many of the figures in the exhibit were activists, explicitly or by the nature of their willfulness to pursue a particular career or ambition. Many of them were the first African Americans to achieve excellence in a particular arena, which surely meant that conflicts with racism were a part of their lives and careers. In fact, some of the images capture moments of resistance—Jesse Owens in the starting blocks at the 1936 Berlin Olympics; Malcolm X offering copies of a newspaper on the street, the headline telling of seven black people killed in Los Angeles, as a white woman and then a white man walk by undeterred; a headshot of Angela Davis before a single microphone, eyes engaged and directed not to the camera but to whatever audience she was addressing. Even the image of Marian Anderson performing with Leonard Bernstein in 1947 gestures toward her battle with the DAR in 1939 for the right to sing at Constitution Hall. There is the poignant photograph of a slain Martin Luther King, Jr. in an open casket, and the youthful shock of his five-year old daughter, Bernice, as she watches her father's still body; the magnitude of recognition in her face speaks for a whole nation of people.

And still, looking at these images, it is clear that resistance as an idiom is not sufficient to capture the breadth of what is represented here. If we read these images only through the catch-all of resistance, searching for and noting the ways that each person existed in a public battle with white racism, we miss all the other loveliness that is to be had in such a collection of images. We miss the airy, angelic quality of Sarah Vaughn's closed eyes, the way this matches the lightness of her hands; or the dramatic staging of softness in James Baldwin's image, an almost campy rendering of him as a religious icon with his head nearly covered in cloth and his hands nearly prayered . . . and how gentle and fiery his eyes look. Resistance alone is not capable of taking the viewer through all one hundred images, of pointing attention to the shape of Anderson's mouth as she sings, the sureness in her eyes that seem to speak both of utter mastery and deep pleasure. As a concept, resistance is not capable of helping a viewer to notice all this beauty, all this heart-stirring loveliness. Even the very medium of the exhibit, photography, is compromised by the idea of resistance. That is, photography is, in a way, quiet—its expressiveness is always a little more ambivalent and less definitive than prose, for example. Rare is the photograph that offers a single, sure narrative; instead the medium flourishes on the tension between definitiveness and uncapturability, how what cannot be captured is and then, as one looks beyond the frame and image, is not.[18]

Resistance may be deeply resonant with black culture and history, but it is not sufficient for describing the totality of black humanity.

———

In humanity, quiet is our dignity. This quiet is represented by our interior, that "place in us below our hip personality that is connected to our breath, our words, and our death" (Natalie Goldberg, *Wild Mind*, 28). In its magnificence, quiet is an invitation to consider black cultural identity from somewhere other than the conceptual places that we have come to accept as definitive of and singular to black culture—not the "hip personality" exposed to and performed for the world, but the interior aliveness, the reservoir of human complexity that is deep inside. Quiet compels us to "explore the beauty of the quality of being human," not only our "lives weighed down by the suppositions of identity."[19] It is this exploration, this reach toward the inner life, that an aesthetic of quiet makes possible; and it is this that is the path to a sweet freedom: a black expressiveness without publicness as its forbearer, a black subject in the undisputed dignity of its humanity.[20]

CHAPTER 2

Not Double Consciousness but the Consciousness of Surrender

In an 1892 essay, Anna Julia Cooper noted that black people "are the great American fact, the one objective reality on which scholars sharpened their wits, at which orators and statesmen fired their eloquence" (136).[1] At the heart of Cooper's comment is the idea of black publicness, the reality of race as a concept formed and sustained in public discourse. Black people can be "the great American fact" because their presence as racial subjects influences and reflects the country's ambition; as a group, black people are essential figures in the national narrative. This equation of blackness and publicness shapes our understanding of black culture as a whole, and the notion of resistance in particular. And yet, as argued in the previous chapter, resistance is too limited an idiom to adequately characterize black humanity. Which leaves the question, is it possible to engage the public discourse of black identity beyond the imperative of resistance? What might it look like to write about race and identity in the context of an aesthetic of quiet, to write about race using the capacities of the interior?

———

Of all the qualities that could characterize an aesthetic of quiet, it is the idea of surrender that is most compelling. In common usage, "surrender" is a passive term, the counterpart to being conquered, dominated, or defeated, which is how we would think of it given the prevalence of war. But surrender can also be expressive and active, as in some religious uses or in the surrender to love: It is a deliberate giving up to another, the simultaneous practice of yielding and falling toward what is deep and largely unknowable. Though surrender is not only a conscious process, it does require a certain faith in one's human capacity. As a term that suggests bounty and unsureness as well as a quality of inwardness, surrender is an apt synonym for quiet.[2]

The consideration of surrender brings us back to the shortcoming of Du Bois's double consciousness, and to another writer, Marita Bonner, whose description of black consciousness uses a rhetoric of surrender as a means for engaging the inevitable fact of black publicness. Bonner is not well known today, but she was a celebrated writer in the Harlem Renaissance. Born and raised in New England, she received an undergraduate degree from Radcliffe College in 1922, and though she never lived in Harlem, she was a force in its artistic explosion. Like Langston Hughes, Zora Neale Hurston, and Nella Larsen, Bonner gained early recognition for her writing, winning *The Crisis* magazine's short fiction competition in 1924 for the story "The Hands." She went on to publish three plays as well as at least twenty short stories and essays, the last coming in 1941. She died in 1971, having spent the latter years of her life as a high school teacher, mother, and Christian Scientist.

Her best known essay is the brilliant "On Being Young, a Woman, and Colored," published in *The Crisis* in December 1925, when she was still an up-and-coming writer. The essay is brief—only 1,679 words—but still manages to offer a thoughtful meditation on the consciousness of the black woman in a new era. The title is audacious and bold in its philosophical posture, and in this regard, Bonner's piece parallels Du Bois's first chapter of *Souls*, "Of Our Spiritual Strivings." In fact, Du Bois himself was editor of *The Crisis* at the time Bonner's essay was published, and he must have been taken with this young woman writer whose learned prose seemed to reflect his own dreams about black intellectualism.[3]

Hence Bonner and Du Bois are contemporaries, which makes her distinct consideration of black consciousness an interesting read. Like Du Bois, Bonner's essay addresses the aspirations that a young educated black person—in her case, a woman—might have: the desire to be free and to revel in both the thrills of the modern world and the spoils of her education and youth. The essay begins with this eclectic flourish:

> You start out after you have gone from kindergarten to sheepskin covered with sundry Latin phrases.
>
> At least you know what you want life to give you. A career as fixed and as calmly brilliant as the North Star. The one real thing that money buys. Time. Time to do things. A house that can be as delectably out of order and as easily put in order as the doll-house of "playing-house" days. And of course, a husband you can look up to without looking down on yourself.
>
> Somehow you feel like a kitten in a sunny catnip field that sees sleek, plump brown field mice and yellow baby chicks sitting coyly, side by side, under each leaf. A desire to dash three or four ways seizes you. (3)

This opening introduces the idea of a young woman poised to build a life rich in freedom and describes this ambition as a conflict between the demands of the exterior world on one hand, and the willfulness of the self's desire on the other. While the first sentence speaks to the exterior world, represented here via education, the next sentence turns immediately to the interior: "At least you know what you want life to give you." The use of "at least" implies that something is amiss, that there is a disconnect between the aspirations that education is supposed to inspire and the yearnings of one's inner life. It is almost as if before the meditation gets too far, the narrator puts a governor on the expectations of the social world. Notice, for example, how the description of career, house, and husband is rendered in whimsical language that is about excitement and agency—intimate language. The passage is remarkable for how much it privileges the interior. For sure, Bonner's narrative recognizes the encroachment of the world outside, represented in the rules of gender and domesticity that prepare young girls for the limits of womanhood. But these expectations are tempered by the exuberance of the interior, which is characterized as wild, predatory, and boundless; indeed, even the potentially sexist connotation of "a kitten in a catnip field" is transformed into an idiom of female interiority, as a desire to dash wherever pleasure may be found.

Bonner's meditation on black female consciousness starts, then, from a position that recognizes, even reveres, the interior above all else. This reverence is emphasized by the rhetorical intimacy that is created by the direct address of the essay, the use of the second person. It is as if the essay were a letter of advice from one woman to another, or even a diary entry as a woman speaks to herself about herself in the most private of ways. The speaker never names her addressee, and there is no explicit salutation to substantiate that this essay is a letter, but the direct address certainly assumes a kind of familiarity and suggests a manner of engagement that is consonant with the nature of letters. The intimacy here is essential to how Bonner is able to manage what is essentially a description of double consciousness—the conflict between one's interior and the world outside—differently from Du Bois. That is, because the narrator's comments are housed in the intimacy of direct address, the ideas have an aura of privacy, as if they are precious exchanges between speaker and reader. Instead of rehearsing familiar historical or sociological facts about black people and/or women's oppression—the facts of black publicness—the essay reads like it is exploring the quirky, energetic musings of a beloved.[4]

This is not to imply that the essay is apolitical or ignores the challenges of racism and sexism that may be presumed from its title; in fact, the opposite is true in Bonner's nimble engagement of the racial and gendered expectations that impose on the freedom that a young black woman might imagine for herself. The speaker moves easily between the assumptions of cultural nationalism ("All your life you have heard of the debt you owe 'Your People' because you have managed to have things they have not largely had") and the prejudices of patriarchy and white supremacy as she outlines the limits—rather than the possibilities—of the modern world. She warns the reader that her ambitions are likely to be shunted aside by the intersecting nature of racism and sexism. But in Bonner's language, even the warning is engaging stuff:

You hear that up at New York this is to be seen; that, to be heard.

You decide the next train will take you there.

You decide that next second that that train will not take you, nor the next—nor the next for some time to come.

For you know that—being a woman—you cannot twice a month or twice a year, for that matter, break away to see or hear anything in a city that is supposed to see and hear too much.

That's being a woman. A woman of any color. (4–5)

The effectiveness of Bonner's prose is not only its brevity, but the way the short sentences mimic the quick progression from excitement to disappointment. In having each sentence stand as a paragraph, Bonner recreates the landscape of the speaker's thinking, a kind of stream-of-consciousness as the mind flits from one thing to another. It is a dramatic and poetic presentation of the speaker's most intimate thoughts.

The consequence of Bonner's syntax is that her argument about racism and sexism—essentially, an argument about the facts of black publicness—is embedded in interiority. In the whimsy of its examples, the essay avoids the language and posture of resistance, and the consciousness it describes acknowledges but is not overdetermined by the exterior world. Unlike Du Bois's chapter, which is in a tussle with the white world from the first sentence, Bonner's essay begins by establishing the potency and meaningfulness of the interior.

Key to Bonner's rhetoric of interiority is her willingness to question the usefulness of race as a social category, a willingness that implicitly demotes the equation of race and publicness from the singular place it holds in how we understand black subjectivity. This is a delicate undertaking, not only because of the broad impact of race in black life but also because of the race-conscious era in which Bonner is writing. For this young woman writer to suggest that the terms of racial publicness were anything other than paramount might be perceived as naïvety at best, heresy at worst. But Bonner's intellectual skill is up to the challenge: In an early example, the narrator addresses residential segregation, though rather than use this as a moment to recite sociological or legal data, the narrator instead considers how the conversation around living among "one's own" reflects the heavy burden of racial identity imposed both from within and from outside of the race:

> And one day you find yourself entangled—enmeshed—pinioned in the seaweed of a Black Ghetto.
>
> Not a Ghetto, placid like the Strasse that flows, outwardly unperturbed and calm in a stream of religious belief, but a peculiar group. Cut off, flung together, shoved aside in a bundle because of color and with no more in common.
>
> Unless color is, after all, the real bond. (3–4)

The diction here is exquisite as the narrator notices a distinction between a community of people whose relationship is "unperturbed" and "calm" and shaped by their shared beliefs; and a community "flung" together on the basis of nothing but color. The sarcastic tag, "Unless color is, after all, the real bond," accentuates the point that she has made—that color alone is not sufficient to determine humanity or kinship; certainly, color does not equate to desire and ambition and interior subjectivity. The narrator suggests that the idea of racial difference, which is produced by a racist discourse, is adopted by black cultural nationalism, and that both the racist and the nationalist conventions impinge on freedom. At the heart of this critique is her longing to experience a world, "where you can marvel at new marbles and bronzes and flat colors that will make men forget that things exist in a flesh more often than in spirit. Where you can sink your body in a cushioned seat and sink your soul at the same time into a section of life set before you on the boards for a few hours" (4). It is a lush and human desire the narrator has for herself and for the reader to whom she imparts this advice, a desire that is not merely a naïve rejection of the realities of social inequity but one that holds firm to the right to be human. In moving beyond the social and political implications of the body toward a celebration of spirit and feeling, Bonner's essay makes a plea for interiority: not a consciousness that is doubled and encumbered, but a consciousness that is free, full of wander and wonder, where surrender—not resistance—is an ethic.[5]

It is important to notice that this argument for a consciousness of the interior is built on an intersectional analysis of identity. That is, unlike Du Bois's double consciousness which accepts race as the singular and definitive aspect of black life, Bonner's idiom of consciousness engages both race and gender, and also implicitly addresses age and class. In her narrator's worldview, the struggle for subjectivity is broader than just a contestation with whiteness, and her arguments challenge racism and cultural nationalism ("shoved aside in a bundle because of color and with no more in common . . . [as if] color is, after all, the real bond" [4]) as well as patriarchy and sexism ("For you know that—being a woman—you cannot . . . break away . . . That's being a woman. A woman of any color" [5]). Indeed given her gender, the narrator could not merely articulate, uncritically, the tenets of cultural nationalism, just as, given her race, she could not only engage sexism and patriarchy. She must consider all these and in doing so, her argument recognizes the limits of identity politics and moves closer to the larger issue of humanity that is always at stake.[6]

This commitment to what is human is not an easy achievement, and even Bonner's poised narrator falls into a moment of ranting, cataloguing her frustrations with the resilience of the "old . . . outgrown and worthless" stereotypes that affect black women. In response, the narrator exclaims "Every part of you becomes bitter." When white friends "who have never had to draw breath in a Jim-Crow train" counsel her to be more understanding, the narrator's anger is especially clear: "You long to explode and hurt everything white; friendly; unfriendly" (6). Here, the speaker imagines, even embraces, what she has been cautioning against—letting the exterior world encroach on one's interior, orienting one's self against the world since it is seemingly already and always against you.

But the moment does not hold and in the very next sentence the speaker reminds the reader that "you know that you cannot live with a chip on your shoulder even if you can manage a smile around your eyes" (6). This is a warning against internalizing the dynamics of oppression, and the phrasing is reminiscent of Du Bois's response to the unasked question, how does it feel to be problem—to smile or nod or say nothing, even as his blood boils inside. For Du Bois, this suppressed frustration is the "prison-house" that corrupts the youthful agency of his peers, who give into "tasteless sycophancy, or into silent hatred of the pale work about them . . . or wasted in a bitter cry" (Du Bois, *Souls*, 10). (Notably both writers describe the experience as being tasteless: Bonner writes that "Everything you touch or taste now is like the flesh of an unripe persimmon" [5]). By and large, Du Bois's notion of consciousness accepts racial blackness as a prison house of struggle that is internalized. Bonner's interior consciousness, however, is explicit in its refusal of such imprisonment:

But you know that you cannot live with a chip on your shoulder . . .

    For chips make you bend your body to balance them. And once you bend, you lose your poise, your balance, and the chip gets into you. The real you. You get hard.

    . . . And many things in you can ossify . . . (6; third and fourth ellipses in original)

This is a gentle caution about the futility and danger of fighting against the exterior world and having one's whole selfhood shaped—hardened—by the imperative of resisting ignorance and insults. For Bonner's narrator, the solution is not to privilege racial identity and community; the problem itself is gender and race as social categories, the way they can undermine one's humanity when they are embraced as sites of resistance.

It is surrender that Bonner's speaker values, since surrender evidences the agency and wildness of the inner life and is at least as human and as sustaining as any act of protest. At the end of the essay, the speaker says as much in a closing flourish that must be quoted at length:

> You see clearly—off there is Infinity—Understanding. Standing alone, waiting for someone to really want her.
>
> But she is so far out there is no way to snatch at her and really drag her in.
>
> So—being a woman—you can wait.
>
> You must sit quietly without a chip. Not sodden—and weighted as if your feet were cast in the iron of your soul. Not wasting strength in enervating gestures as if two hundred years of bonds and whips had really tricked you into nervous uncertainty.
>
> But quiet; quiet. Like Buddha—who, brown like I am—sat entirely at ease, entirely sure of himself; motionless and knowing, a thousand years before that white man knew there was so very much difference between feet and hands.
>
> Motionless on the outside. But inside?
>
> Silent.
>
> Still. . . "Perhaps Buddha is a woman."
>
> So you too. Still; quiet; with a smile, ever so slight, at the eyes so that Life will flow into and not by you. And you can gather, as it passes, the essences, the overtones, the tints, the shadows; draw understanding into your self.
>
> And then you can, when Time is ripe, swoop to your feet—at your full height—at a single gesture.
>
> Ready to go where?
>
> Why . . . Wherever God motions. (7–8; ellipses in original)

This breathlessness is an argument for the pleasures and agency of the interior. The subjectivity the speaker offers is that of the black woman as an infinity of understanding, poised in her knowing and beyond reach or sight of the public's limited imagination. She is sure of herself, at ease, aware, in the full consciousness of her voluptuous interior rather than choked by a consciousness in persistent conflict with the world and its expectations.

In this closing passage, the narrator is deliberately engaging the sexist idea of the feminine interior—the image of a woman in her sitting room, silent, in waiting while the world happens around her and decides who and how she can be. Bonner's speaker reforms this notion of waiting, first in claiming it as a woman's particular condition and agency ("So—being a woman—you *can* wait"), and then by arguing that waiting is a location of intelligence and insight. This second argument is achieved by the speaker's suggestion that the black woman, in her waiting, refuses to waste "strength" learning the boundaries put in place by the ideologies of white supremacy, male patriarchy, or black cultural nationalism. Instead, she has an insight older and deeper and wilder than these. Her waiting looks, as it would to a casual eye, as if it has no motion and no intellect, as if it was provincial, but she knows differently: She, this woman who is also black, waits like Buddha. She is not merely oppressed from the outside but is also humble and knowing from the vastness within. In this context, waiting is not passivity but instead is patience, the thoughtful attentiveness of one who is wise. Waiting is the surrender to the interior. The narrator goes one step further in suggesting that it is women, and in particular black women, who realize this consciousness of surrender through their consideration of the futility of publicness.

In describing this consciousness, Bonner uses the word "quiet" as well as "silent." As noted in the previous chapter, the two terms are sometimes used synonymously, though the idea of quiet as the expressiveness of the interior is distinct from the general connotation of silence as an absence. Bonner's "silent" seems interchangeable with the notion of quiet, especially when the narrator asserts that the motionlessness on the outside is not reflective of the activity of the inner life. In keeping with the idea of quiet, the silence here is not performative, not a withholding, but instead is an expressiveness that is not entirely legible in a discourse of publicness.[7]

Also key to Bonner's description of a consciousness of surrender is the notion of Buddha as a metaphor for the idealized black woman. Buddha is an icon of thoughtfulness, a man whose quiet changed the world as we know it, and in this regard he is representative of a subjectivity of surrender. Bonner's argument makes the case that the concept of being a "woman" is also emblematic of surrender, that a woman's categorical agency is her capacity to wait . . . as if the word "woman" literally means one who waits with knowing grace. It is in this sense that phrase "Perhaps Buddha is a woman" makes full sense, since Buddha's exemplary mindfulness is compatible with Bonner's notion of woman. Indeed, the narrator's identification with Buddha, which transgresses racial, gendered, national, and historical boundaries, is in keeping with the overall argument about the futility of identity. Buddha could be a woman, a black one even, since to be a woman is a habit of consciousness and a practice of a kind of human wisdom. Bonner's use of identity here is ambivalent and, in its concluding moment, the essay embraces a selfhood that is found in an icon of spirituality (Buddha) and in a practice (waiting). Importantly, neither of these is a category of identity; instead, they represent a state of being and a habit of self.[8]

If the end of the essay is a grace note on waiting, it is also a rejection of publicness. The very form of the essay—poetic and wandering and elliptical—is askew from the argumentative or polemical rhetoric one might expect. Bonner doesn't offer a call to arms or a private rant; she doesn't present her narrator as bothered and bothersome. In this way, the essay does not entirely fulfill its title, in that it does not set forth grievances to elicit guilt or pity. The refusal of the public moment is striking especially because the essay remains feisty and critical. That is, Bonner's speaker does not back down from the challenges of a racist and sexist culture. But neither does she take up the gauntlet as it is thrown down or fight in the terms that are outlined. Rather than an essay of resistance, Bonner offers a slim, poetic essay, a letter really, that describes subjectivity as a surrender to the interior. In doing so, she constructs the black subject as possessing a consciousness of imagination rather than a consciousness that is doubled. Her essay does not plea for freedom but instead suggests that the freedom worth having is already always present: the freedom of being, innately and complicatedly, a human being.[9]

That Bonner's essay so staunchly avoids using the first person, except for one brief clause at the end ("brown like I am"), is an important feature of its quiet. In fact, this choice of narrative voice is notable because it is contrary to the conventions of the essay genre, for although essays usually speak to readers implicitly—that is, there is always a sense of direct address of the reader—it is the use of the first person that generally gives an essay its rhetorical power. Why, then, would Bonner avoid first-person speech so explicitly, especially in an essay that seems so autobiographical and so personal? Why would she adopt a point of view that sidesteps the power to be had in speaking autobiographically?

The answers might lie in the discourse of autobiography itself, as well as in the kinds of cultural agency first-person narratives can offer black and female subjects. Among the assumptions of autobiography is the expectation of truth and representativeness—that the first-person narrative not only speaks for its narrator but speaks of his or her condition representationally, iconically. This dynamic is especially true for marginalized subjects writing about a topic related to their social identity; for such a writer, the first-person moment is "a public way of declaring oneself free, of redefining freedom and then assigning it to oneself in defiance of one's bonds to the past or to the social, political, and sometimes even moral exigencies of the present" (Andrews, *To Tell a Free Story*, xi). This is how William Andrews describes the convention of first-person voice in his important work on slave narratives, and his description makes clear the anxieties and expectations that are likely to follow any black writer working in the genre. By avoiding the first person, Bonner bypasses the presumption that the narrator is a representation either of herself or of her social group. Her use of direct address allows her to avoid being the autobiographical subject on display as an act of resistance or defiance.[10]

Had Bonner spoken of her own experiences more directly, the essay would have fallen into the kind of public struggle over identity that she herself seems to abhor. It is helpful to remember that the essay was published in 1925, following the suffrage movement and the continued migration of African Americans to northern cities; it is also an era characterized by the literary and social activism of the Harlem Renaissance. Hence the public conversation about women and black people was at a feverish pitch, and discussions of race and/or gender were combative and often pivoted on the issue of representativeness and authenticity. These conversations are antithetical to the idea of interiority, and Bonner avoids them by utilizing the second-person voice to create an insulating intimacy between narrator and reader.

In fact, Bonner's use of the second person is exceptional for the way it imagines the reader. Here the reader becomes the protagonist, and therefore she is committed by (and committed to?) the intimacy of the conversation. The construct of the essay assumes closeness between the narrator and every reader, any reader, which helps to bracket the noise of public discourse, since the exchange is between just the two (narrator and reader). This is all seduction, and the reader is, literally, made to surrender. It also allows Bonner to take certain liberties; for example, she imposes on the reader a set of desires and frustrations without regard for who the particular reader might be. This imposition is based in the assumption of intimacy—as in, I know who you are and what you want—but might also be a way for Bonner to imply that her arguments are, at the end, universal: Every human being knows, to some degree, what it is to want to move without restriction and what it is to encounter the limitations of the social world. The intimacy here is the perfect context for having a quiet exchange about race, gender, and power. Largely because of the direct address, the essay reads as an intense but affectionate conversation of understanding and encouragement, letter-like in its coziness and caution: for example, "You long to explode and hurt everything white; friendly; unfriendly. But you know that you cannot live with a chip on your shoulder" (6). There is a certain tenderness here, the sense that the narrator knows and cares for the reader. In avoiding rhetorical buzzwords in favor of whimsical poetic phrases (kitten in a catnip field; plump brown field mice and yellow baby chicks), Bonner sustains the notion that this conversation is on a different register.

The use of the second person is further notable because it does not reinforce the narrator's sense of authority or increase distance between her and the reader. Indeed, the closeness between the narrator and the reader seems to facilitate the agency of the narrator to make direct reference to herself near the end of the essay. It is as if, in being shielded from becoming the representative of black femininity and establishing a kind of bond with the reader, the narrator is safe to come into subjectivity. When she says "Like Buddha—who brown like I am—sat entirely at ease, entirely sure of himself," the narrator slips herself into the very possibility and wonder of the interior that she has been arguing for. Like her protagonist, the narrator too is poised to go wherever she can imagine. It is a lovely moment of connection, where the reader and narrator—and ultimately, Bonner herself, since the narrator speaks also for her—become bonded through the practice of surrender. If one is inclined to interpret Bonner's interior consciousness as self-indulgent, this connection between narrator and reader suggests otherwise.[11]

Imbedded in this consideration of Bonner's use of the second person and negotiation of publicness is the question of audience that is so critical in black culture. That is, because of the public dimensions of both race as an identity and writing as a profession, a black writer who writes about race is often forced to confront a generic but daunting inquiry: To whom and for whom are you speaking? In regard to this question, a writer experiences a kind of double consciousness where he or she is expected to represent but also transcend race. This ambivalence of representation and transcendence means that the writer has to balance at least three expectations: that she would speak to and about black people, challenge a dominant white audience, as well as stand as evidence of black excellence. Bonner effectively avoids this dilemma of audience by speaking to and about her *protagonist*, who is ultimately herself. This solipsism—the speaking to the self about the self—makes the subject and object of the essay synonymous, and thereby displaces the audience as a factor. Indeed, the dilemma of audience is undermined further by the essay's refusal to approach race as if it has to be singularly preeminent in a black person's humanity.[12] The connection between audience and publicness is an important part of the difference between Bonner's rhetorical approach and Du Bois's. Though both are writing about racial consciousness, Du Bois's position as narrator in the first chapter of *Souls* seems to be shaped definitively by public discourse, by how he is interpellated. The term "interpellation" has been advanced by the theorist Louis Althusser as a way to describe the dynamic of subjectivity. For Althusser, the modern subject is "hailed" or commanded into subjectivity via social discourses. (He famously gives the example of a policeman calling out to a person on the street "Hey you there," where the second-person invocation literally arrests the person and makes him capable of being engaged as a social subject.) What is useful about Althusser's idea of interpellation is the way it explains subjectivity as a social event, as an experience of being legible and identifiable; subjectivity here is the location of a public and exterior consciousness. But Althusser also suggests that interpellation provides agency, since it is in being named in ideology that the individual comes into being as a subject. Literally, it is in being subjected that one becomes a subject.[13] Althusser's notion is Foucaldian in its recognition of the dialectical nature of power and it works well with Du Bois's conceptualization of double consciousness: When Du Bois opens his chapter with the unasked question, how does it feel to be a problem, he acknowledges that the black subject is interpellated via an ideology of negation and inferiority. Though Du Bois the narrator refuses to answer the question, it still serves as the foundation of his anger, resentment, and resolve. This unasked question is a saluation, as is the moment when the young white girl refuses his card—they are the coordinates for his theorization of black subjectivity as doubled.[14]

This is quite different from Bonner's engagement of consciousness, which articulates a subjectivity that seems to extend beyond interpellation. That is, in privileging the interior and avoiding the question of audience, Bonner turns the conversation about her subjectivity as inward as possible, as if she is hailed only by her own interior. When the essay cautions against becoming hardened or wearing a chip, it is discarding the subjectivities that are possible via a racialized discourse. Instead, the narrator encourages the protagonist to wait in quiet, ready to go wherever. The essay imagines a human subject called into being not by a social discourse, but by desire, ambition, dreams, by one's affinity to the "essences, the overtones, the tints, the shadows" of life as one takes it in. Bonner's is a deliberate conceptualization of subjectivity as being called from within.

The grand fault of Du Bois's double consciousness is that it is tethered to the notions that publicness projects onto the racialized subject. As Hortense Spillers writes, double consciousness is about "the *specular* and the *spectacular*—the sensation of looking at oneself and of imagining oneself being looked at through the eyes of the other/another [which] is precisely performative in what it demands of a participant on the other end of the gaze" (*Black, White, and in Color*, 397). What Spillers captures is the anxiety of publicness that is at the heart of Du Bois's idiom. Here, the doubleness of black subjectivity is constituted by resistance, and the imperative of black culture is to engage public discourse to counter the racism created by public discourse. In this way, double consciousness is riddled with the terms of publicness. Bonner's consciousness of surrender is something else, for though it is engaged with the idioms of publicness, it privileges the interior; indeed, it luxuriates in the wild possibilities that the interior offers. These possibilities are not all positive, nor are they without social relevance, as we shall see later on. And still, it is a remarkably different way to orient one's self—surrender as an alternative to the anxiety of double consciousness.

Perhaps the defining difference between Bonner's and Du Bois's idioms of consciousness is in their faithfulness to the politics of identity. In *The Souls of Black Folk*, Du Bois sets out to mobilize race in a way that will serve black political needs. As such, he not only embraces race but also works to articulate—even celebrate—racial differences. For Du Bois, race is a "meta-language," a towering doubled-discourse that requires an awareness of what is exterior to the subject himself.[15] Bonner's consciousness of surrender, on the other hand, seems to work to undermine the meaningfulness of race (in its intersectionality and its critique of cultural nationalism). Indeed, if there is an identity that her narrator seems to engage, it is the notion of a woman's particular capacity. But even here, Bonner's idiomatic use of "being a woman" seems intent to evade essentialism: Starting with the stereotype of women as the second and fairer sex, of women as passive and domestic beings—notions which are already racialized—Bonner fashions a notion of waiting as wisdom and agency. This is her subjectivity of the interior and it is not necessarily exclusive to women, since Buddha himself is referenced as an icon of a consciousness of waiting. Bonner's finessing of the politics of identity is terrific because it refuses to ignore the impact of race and gender but also refuses to give up humanity in the face of stereotypes or the effort to fight them.[16] Whereas Du Bois sees liberation in the idioms of publicness and wants to rehabilitate notions of blackness to this end, Bonner wants to surpass not only racial stereotypes but the dynamics of race itself. And one could argue that with the surrender she proclaims at the end of her essay, she achieves exactly that.

———

So much of Bonner's consciousness of surrender is related to the concept of imagination. The act of imagining is the practice and willingness to dream, speculate, or wonder, and it helps us to move beyond the limits of reality. Imagination is the landscape of such dreaming, what educator Harold Rugg describes as a place and process of magic that is also a particular human capacity (*Imagination*, xii). In this latter context, imagination *is* an interiority, an aspect of inner life that constitutes an essential agency of being human.

The concept of imagination is useful in thinking about the balance Bonner tries to strike between the politics of identity and the wild vagary of inner life. Implicit in Bonner's arguments is the idea that the main goal of cultural nationalism—freedom for black people—cannot be achieved without a consideration of the interior. In his book *Freedom Dreams: The Black Radical Imagination*, the historian Robin Kelley seems to understand how essential dreaming is to achievement of social change—that there is an important need for the whimsy of and surrender to the imaginative interior. Early on, Kelley notices that his mother

> has a tendency to dream out loud. I think it has something to do with her regular morning meditation. In the quiet darkness of her bedroom her third eye opens into a new world, a beautiful light-filled place as peaceful as her state of mind. She never had to utter a word to describe her inner peace; like morning sunlight, it radiated out to everyone in her presence. (1)

This description of seeing with a third eye is emblematic of possibility, of the invention of a world that happens in the interior. But Kelley is clear that the "bliss" of his mother's imagining, though otherworldly, was not bereft of political reality: "Her other two eyes never let her forget where we lived. The cops, drug dealers, social workers, the rusty tapwater . . . were constant reminders that our world began and ended in a battered Harlem/ Washington Heights tenement apartment" (1). And still, the imagination's agency doesn't merely have to succumb to the reality of the exterior world. Its fancifulness engages the overtones of the world outside, but then invents its own habitat:

> Yet she would not allow us to live as victims . . . So with her eyes wide open my mother dreamed and dreamed some more, describing what life could be for us . . . She dreamed of land, a spacious house, fresh air, organic food, and endless meadows without boundaries, free of evil and

violence, free of toxins . . . free of poverty, racism, and sexism . . . just
free. She never talked about how we might create such a world, nor had
she connected her vision to any political ideology. But she convinced my
siblings and me that change is possible (1–2).

There is good balance in Kelley's description between an awareness of the
exterior world, and a self authorized by an agency that extends beyond that
world. His mother's vision is political and is shaped by social realities, but it
also is her own vision of possibility. This is an example of imagination as
"a means . . . of mediating between the domestic and that which lies at
and beyond the limits of knowledge" (Lively, *Masks*, 2). Indeed, Kelley's
characterization of his mother's consciousness highlights imagination
as the capacity to call one's world into being; it is imagining as an act of
deliberateness and self-making.[17]

As a discourse, imagination has played a notable role in black cultural
history, evident by the popularity of literary magical realism as well as the
general colorfulness that characterizes black cultural aesthetics. This imagi-
nativeness is related to the contemplative tradition noted earlier, and can be
seen in iconic examples of enslaved peoples singing spirituals about far-off
lands and experiences of freedom, or in the inventiveness of quilts, or in
culinary adaptiveness. Some scholars have even argued that imagination is
relevant to the achievement of a positive sense of racial identity, especially
in terms of the capacity to envision blackness outside of the binary logic of
racism, where it is aberrant and inhuman.[18]

The meaningfulness of imagination to Bonner's consciousness of surrender is evident in the way her argument is built on hypothesizing and fanciful metaphors; the prose itself is also populated with ellipses, as if to imply
the spontaneity of invention. But it is the relationship between the reader
and narrator, formed via the direct address, that most reflects the quality of
imagination. The intimacy between narrator and reader is hypothetical,
and through it the narrator presumes to speak for the reader's desires.
Moreover, the essay's end is an imagined sequence that includes Wisdom,
Infinity, and Understanding as classical goddesses, and concludes with a
magical invocation to flight. Bonner's narrator is able to balance social realities with the vision of her imagination, and when she cautions the reader
against "wasting strength in enervating gestures as if two hundred years of

bonds and whips had really tricked you into nervous uncertainty" (7), it
sounds a lot like Kelley's comment on his mother. The narrator is well
aware of the legacy of slavery, but this does not override the vision of her
third, creative eye. She dwells in possibility and conjures up a world where
Buddha waits with the agency of a black woman, where waiting is a state of
knowing and grace. The narrator's consciousness of surrender and her
capacity to envision her subjectivity different from the exigencies of the
outer world, is an engagement of imagination. In this way, imagination is
"consciousness as a sphere of freedom" (Collins, *Black Feminist Thought*,
103), rather than consciousness as deficit or imposed doubleness.[19] And
there is a lovely synchronicity between the instruction of the narrator at the
close of the essay and the lesson Kelley remembers from his mother's
dreaming: "She simply wanted us to live through our third eyes, to see life
as possibility" (2).

The notion of imagination helps us to remember the scope and breadth
of the interior, for although the interior is, tautologically, interior, it is not
small; like imagination, the interior is boundless. Such breadth is noted in
Bonner's essay when the narrator warns against misreading motionlessness
or silence, and projects onto her reader a cosmos of an identity: "So you too.
Still; quiet; with a smile, ever so slight, at the eyes so that Life will flow into
and not by you. And you can gather, as it passes, the essences, the overtones,
the tints, the shadows; draw understanding to yourself" (7). Here the narrator envisions the reader as the watcher of life, the perceiver, one who takes
in all its wonders and horrors. One who is in the world, but also of it, and
then, beyond it: "And then you can, when Time is ripe, swoop to your feet—
at your full height—at a single gesture. Ready to go where? Why . . . Wherever
God motions" (8). In this characterization, the quiet subject is active
and embodied, full of agency and capacity; the diction, especially "ripe,"
"swoop," "full height" and "single gesture," implies preparedness but also
potency. The interior, this practice of waiting and stillness, is a vision of a
human being ready to move divinely. Bonner's final characterization dis-
turbs all of the ways that waiting and interiority get rendered as merely
domestic, or feminine, or enfeebled. Instead, waiting is without limit and
is truly cosmopolitan. It is also important that the essay does not end in
triumph, as if the reader or narrator has overcome the exterior world. No,
since this articulation of the interior is quiet, it ends in possibility rather

than achievement. There is no triumph to be had, especially since the self is not calibrated against an external measurement. There is just the work of being complicatedly human. And in this work, the compass for subjectivity is the interior. Even Bonner's construction of the reader to reflect the narrator's ambition and anxieties—that manipulation of direct address—contributes to this sense of self-ordination. For the narrator, there is no other measure but herself, for as flawed as this might be, it is a better compass than to give in to what is exterior. She, this person who is black and female, measures herself by herself, by her capacity for quiet; she surrenders to her interior as a location of agency. "My intimacy is in silence" (81), Trinh T. Minha writes in her elegant *Woman, Native, Other,* and indeed the narrator's intimacy, her awareness of herself, happens in the quiet of her interior and her imagination. This interior self-measure is an articulation of what it is to be sovereign.[20]

The quiet subject is a subject who surrenders, a subject whose consciousness is not only shaped by struggle but also by revelry, possibility, the wildness of the inner life. Quiet is not a performance or a withholding; instead, it is an expressiveness that is not necessarily legible, at least not in a world that privileges public expressiveness. Neither is quiet about resistance. It is surrender, a giving into, a falling into self. The outer world cannot be avoided or ignored, but one does not only have to yield to its vagaries. One can be quiet.[21]

CHAPTER 3

Maud Martha and the
Practice of Paying Attention

Marita Bonner's essay "On Being Young—a Woman—and Colored" helps us to think about quiet as a consciousness that gets beyond conflict with the expectations of the outer world. This consciousness is achieved through surrender to the interior, and it represents the deep value in studying and knowing one's self. But Bonner's essay is too brief to represent what it is to live through quiet in the everyday. How does interiority inform interactions with other people? How does the quiet subject negotiate moments of subjection and power? What is the action that quiet motivates, or how does it shape behavior? Simply, what does a quiet life look like?

There is such a representation in another work by a black woman, Gwendolyn Brooks's slim coming-of-age novel *Maud Martha*. Published in 1953, *Maud Martha* is a quirky story of the title character told in thirty-four short chapters, more vignettes than full chapters. Maud Martha and her family live in Chicago, and the story offers the poetic impressions of her childhood, adolescence, and adulthood. The novel is set in the 1930s and 1940s, and it is remarkable for its emphasis on the ordinariness of Maud Martha's life. That is, we don't learn of her life through definitive moments or conflicts, but through seemingly mundane scenes, each described in its own chapter. While significant events happen—for example, the birth of her daughter, or her marriage—the narrative doesn't treat these moments as if they are more significant than any other. There is no dramatic emphasis in the story, just a rendering of the impressions of thirty-four moments in Maud Martha's life; this is true even when moments in the novel engage issues of racism or the trials of living as part of the working class in urban America.

Maud Martha was an unusual follow-up to Brooks's Pulitzer prize–winning poetry collection, *Annie Allen*, not only because it was a shift of genre but especially because the landscape of black literature in the early 1950s was dominated by three well-regarded novelists, all of them men writing mammoth stories about racial struggle: James Baldwin, whose *Go Tell It on the Mountain* was also published in 1953; Richard Wright, who was the dean of black fiction after the immense successes of *Native Son* (1940) and *Black Boy* (1945), and who published his second novel, *The Outsider*, in that same year; and Ralph Ellison, whose *Invisible Man* was published in 1952 and had just won the National Book Award in 1953. (Though he had less success, one could also add Chester Himes to this trio.) Of course, Ann Petry was also a part of the literary scene, having published *The Street*, a best-seller, in 1946, but the territory of black fiction was largely a man's world. And what is striking is that all of these works, including Petry's, could be characterized as narratives of black existentialism, as stories about an individual's conflict with social institutions. All of them are set primarily in urban contexts, or at least raise questions about the impact of the rise of cities and the migration of black populations from the South to the North. To be sure, each book is distinct and engages its themes in very different ways, but each is also essentially about the struggle between the black individual and society.[1] This is the literary context that has shaped how readers have understood Brooks's novel. And because *Maud Martha* doesn't offer big dramatic action, it has often been read as a study of silence or repression.

But *Maud Martha* is a novel of quiet. That is, rather than focusing on action and decisive moments, the novel privileges the interior sensibility of its title character. It is not the conflicts with the world that Brooks's novel emphasizes, but the wild perceptions and attentiveness of her title character. Quiet is in the daily encounters of Maud Martha as well as in her awareness in the midst of those happenings; it is the agency of paying attention, asking questions, and considering. As we follow the episodic snapshots of the young Maud Martha coming into womanhood, we can understand quiet as a kind of existentialism—not a crisis of doubt about human meaningfulness, but more as an astuteness about living. In Brooks's novel, quiet is the capacity to ask questions about life in the abstract, not merely questions about one's life as it is defined by identity.

The novel opens with a chapter entitled "description of Maud Martha," though the description is more of what she finds beautiful:

> What she liked was candy buttons, and books, and painted music (deep blue, or delicate silver) and the west sky, so altering, viewed from the steps of the back porch; and dandelions.
>
> She would have liked a lotus, or China asters or the Japanese Iris, or meadow lilies—yes, she would have liked meadow lilies, because the very word meadow made her breathe more deeply, either fling her arms or want to fling her arms, depending on who was by, rapturously up to whatever was watching in the sky. But dandelions were what she chiefly saw. Yellow jewels for everyday, studding the patched green dress of her back yard. She liked their demure prettiness second to their everydayness; for in that latter quality she thought she saw a picture of herself, and it was comforting to find that what was common could also be a flower.
>
> And could be cherished! (1–2)

This poetic catalog outlines her specific passions and cues the reader to the broadness of Maud Martha's mind. Objects and colors and sounds are the sensations that animate Maud Martha, and the beginning is a lush presentation of what she finds lovely. By introducing her this way, the novel suggests that Maud Martha, though only seven years old at this point, is aware: She is a careful watcher of the world and has a deep appreciation for certain qualities. She has an interior, a fanciful imagination (the backyard is a dress!), and a particular attachment to dandelions; indeed, dandelions, in their blend of the ordinary and extraordinary, are the discourse on which Maud Martha recognizes and shapes her identity. We don't learn that she is black, or dark-skinned, or poor, or that she hates school or feels ignored by boys; this introductory description of Maud Martha is populated with the wonders of what she loved and a characterization of her keenness.

What is being narrated here is the attentiveness that constitutes the subjectivity of one who is quiet. Though it is not directly in Maud Martha's voice, this passage reflects her search not for her identity in social terms, but for her self in human terms. This is her aliveness, what she longs for and values, what she finds to be beautiful and inspiring. In short, her capacity to notice and appreciate is her agency.

A closer examination of Maud Martha's fondness for dandelions will help to explain this last claim: One of Maud Martha's early struggles in life is being judged as less attractive than her sister Helen, who is fairer-skinned and prettier in a more conventional way (she has graceful eyelashes and feet and hands); this is a very common matter of identity for black girls. In this regard, Maud Martha's affinity for dandelions is a moment where she navigates the politics of beauty without losing herself. She doesn't resent Helen, or long to be beautiful in the way that Helen is; she doesn't develop a sense of self that is reactive or contrarian to the one that deems Helen beautiful. Instead, she locates her consciousness in what she finds compelling. She is active in assessing and redefining the notion of beauty so that it can include her.

Throughout the novel, it is awareness—of color, sensation, vulnerability, possibility—that defines Maud Martha's subjectivity. She has an acute sensibility which is often narrated in aching language, as if the prose were a twin for the bigness of her feeling. In the chapter "home," Maud Martha, Helen, and their mother are on the porch waiting for her father to return from the loan office. The family might lose their home of fourteen years, and the chapter opens: "What had been wanted was this always, this always to last, the talking softly on this porch, with the snake plant in the jardinière in the southwest corner, and the obstinate slip from Aunt Eppie's magnificent Michigan fern at the left side of the friendly door" (28). Though the description is in the narrator's voice, it is told from Maud Martha's perspective. What is notable is how the anxiety of a potential financial disaster is experienced by Maud Martha as a desire to hold on to the exquisite sensations she felt in the home, rather than the house itself. The capacity to be animated by feeling is Maud Martha's agency. It is not so much that she is naïve to the social peril that shapes their waiting; it is more that the beauty of the feeling, the tender and thrill of the moment, is more meaningful to her humanity.[2]

———

Awareness, astuteness, aliveness, attention: these have all been used to characterize the ethic of Maud Martha, but they could also describe existentialism. Indeed, if part of a concept of quiet is the capacity of paying attention and being engaged in one's life, then existentialism is an important part of what quiet means. The term can be unwieldy because it has many points of departure, though generally existentialism is a philosophy that grows from the idea that each human being is "forced to confront the dilemma of existence, to seek infinitude in the face of limits" (Cotkin 3). This is George Cotkin's efficient wording from his book *Existential America*, and it nicely captures existentialism's interest in the experience of the individual and the capacity to live a meaningful life even in the face of obstacles. In existentialism there is no essential identity, and the focus instead is on the struggle to negotiate one's being in the world. And as broad and varied as existentialist thought is, the notion of consciousness is a common thread.[3]

There is no question that *Maud Martha* is immersed in existentialism. Early in the novel, for example, the narrator captures Maud Martha's thinking as she looks at her uncle lying in a casket. The passage reads

> Then just what was important? What had been important about this life, this Uncle Tim? Was the world any better off for his having lived? A little, perhaps. Perhaps he had stopped his car short once, and saved a dog, so that another car could kill it a month later. Perhaps he had given some little street wretch a nickel's worth of peanuts in its unhappy hour, and that little wretch would grow up and forget Uncle Tim but all its life would carry in its heart an anonymous, seemingly underivative softness for mankind. Perhaps. Certainly he had been good to his wife Nannie. She had never said a word against him. (25)

This is an explicit meditation on the meaning of life and what, if any, impact living has on the world. But what is striking about Brooks's engagement of existentialism, at least in comparison to her peers (Baldwin, Ellison, and Wright), is the relative scale of the moments that Brooks's character focuses on. There are no giant or cathartic struggles, no murders or riots or explosive confrontations. In its existentialism, the novel is fascinated with and gives attention to Maud Martha's interior consciousness in the small moments of living. This constitutes all the action in the book, which reads as a study of one person's process of awareness. One might even say that, in concentrating so deliberately on the interior, *Maud Martha* is an exemplary narration of existentialism.[4]

Brooks has her title character proclaim this deliberateness in an early chapter, after watching a famous pop singer perform in a local concert. Maud Martha is aware of the difference between her own work of self, and the public display she's just witnessed. "She had never understood," Brooks writes,

> How people could parade themselves on a stage like that, exhibit their precious private identities; shake themselves about; be very foolish for a thousand eyes.
>
> She was going to keep herself to herself. She did not want fame. She did not want to be a "star."
>
> To create—a role, a poem, picture, music, a rapture in stone: great. But not for her.
>
> What she wanted was to donate to the world a good Maud Martha. That was the offering, the bit of art, that could not come from any other.
>
> She would polish and hone that. (22)

At first glance, Maud Martha's manifesto of self seems to declare a retreat from the world as well as a refusal of creative will, but the exquisiteness of her resolution is in the word "donate": For sure, donate implies simplicity and inferiority, especially when one considers that Maud Martha only wants to be "good," not "great." But donate also implies a gift, as in a gesture of good will that Maud Martha chooses to make. For her to donate her goodness is a profound act; it suggests that she has something to give to the world, a gift so unique and needed that it cannot be purchased—it has to be granted by an act of generosity.

What this represents is an ethic of quiet, the sense that the interior can inform a way of being in the world that is not consumed by publicness but that is expressive and dynamic nonetheless. This scene is a rare characterization of a black subject exploring herself and trying to understand what being human means for her beyond the prescriptions of social identities. This exploration comes from Maud Martha's mindfulness—remember that even when she is at a concert, she is watching, discerning, thinking, feeling, asking questions about her own meaningfulness . . . that she is daring to look at herself on her own terms. The process of consciousness here is not stable and secure, nor does it ignore the world outside; instead it is truly in process, and it leans toward privileging the interior. It is Maud Martha's attempt to mark the meaningfulness of what it means to be alive.

Qualities of existentialism are evident not only in the narrative of *Maud Martha* but also in its structure. For one the book is episodic, written as thirty-four short chapters, some of them as brief as 212 words ("on Thirty-fourth Street"). Each chapter, almost a vignette, poetically describes a moment or anecdote that is unconnected to the previous or succeeding chapter. In this regard, there is a discreteness to each chapter. As a result, the book is not consequential in the way that novels—stories—are. Instead, one scene unfolds, then another, then another, and though all of them are meaningful, no one moment dominates another. In reading and studying the novel, certain scenes stand out because a reader identifies with them, not because the story itself assigns any lasting significance. This is very much in support of the narrator's claim that Maud Martha was "learning to love moments. To love moments for themselves" (78). Rather than evaluating her life as a seamless whole, Maud Martha lives her life through the moments. She does not judge these happenings—she simply inhabits their sadness or joy, their particular lesson or beauty, as well as remembering their specificity. And though these episodes are interesting, they are not strung together as a narrative of consequence. They are just moments, some big, some small, all the breathing lessons of living, all holding something quietly extraordinary, if one is willing to look.[5]

The novel's story appears as a series of moments that constitute the mind of a black woman (it is narrated by an omniscient voice whose perspective often collapses into Maud Martha's interior monologue), and its episodic nature reinforces its existentialism: It refuses to tell, to try to tell, the whole story of a black woman's life in one swoop of significance. After all, it is not possible to illustrate fully any person's life in any representation. This is the exceptional humanity of *Maud Martha*, that it sidesteps the impulse to capture blackness or black femininity, and instead tells of one black woman's thinking on some of the things that happen in her life. The novel is casual, haphazard almost, and in this way it offers more humanity to Maud Martha than if it were more totalizing. Its structure suggests that a black woman could have a full life that is uncapturable, beautiful, human, quiet. When one wonders, for example, why Maud Martha does not leave her stale marriage or longs to see more tender moments with her husband, the structure of the book seems to answer that she might still leave him— that all is not decided—and that they have many tender moments, we just don't see them. And why would we need to assume that they are all representable, or to see them all? Life is too voluminous to be reduced like that.

This absence of consequence is part of the aesthetic of the book, the way each chapter seems to open in mid-thought or scene, as if displacing the reader's desire to be grounded in a narrative with a beginning and end or for a story where things are either cause or have great effect.[6] Indeed, the novel's celebration of existentialism requires suspending the framework of cause and effect that is so essential to the logic of thinking about racism, sexism, and poverty (and the implication that these realities should dominate the experience of being human). In the chapter where the narrator makes the point about learning "to love moments for themselves," Maud Martha and her husband Paul go to the World Playhouse, a theater that is popular among white people and which they regularly avoid because of the social codes of class and race. Entitled "we're the only colored people here," the chapter begins in the middle of the scene that just seems to be happening: "When they went out to the car there were just the very finest bits of white powder coming down with an almost comical little ethereal hauteur, to add themselves to the really important, piled-up masses of their kind" (72). It is on the heels of this invocation from the weather that the couple decides to go to the Playhouse, and when they get there they encounter all kinds of anxieties, real and imagined, as a result of being the only black people in the theater: Maud Martha whispers as they talk in the lobby, for which Paul chastises her even as he himself is whispering; they feel self-conscious about their dress and imagine that their "kit'n't apt" is no match for the "sweet-smelling" homes the white people surely live in; Paul is afraid to approach the white, blonde girl at the candy counter when the box office is closed and as a result, he ends up paying the usher—metaphorically getting in through the back door. At the end of the show, they are starkly aware that they can't turn to any of the other patrons and remark, casually, about the loveliness of the film. And yet in all this, for all of the race- and class-specific action that happens in the chapter, and the frustration it causes and negotiation it requires, the chapter is not significant. That is, what happens here is a scene, intense and beautiful, a site of struggle and learning, but it is not a turning point or a place of hardening. Maud Martha does not become any more or less astute to racial and class politics, any more or less inclined to resist or challenge those politics. It is one moment in her very big life, and the novel respects it as such. This scene, packed as it is with things of social import, just happens. It is a moment, and beyond the moment it is not of consequence, not emblematic or symbolic of something else.

Indeed, another way of thinking of it is that the chapters in the book are not consecutive; this is part of their quiet, that they are chronological but not consecutive. They do not build on each other but instead represent a series of interior moments that characterize Maud Martha's awareness as she engages the world. In the absence of consecutiveness, the book's chapters are an approximation of the interior of a black woman. This is what is so unusual about *Maud Martha*, that it privileges the inner life so unerringly and never falls prey to the tendency to order or organize that life in relationship to the social world, especially discourses of race, gender, or class. These are moments, impressions, and they are significant in the moment but not necessarily beyond it—certainly not conclusively. This is a way the inner life works.

———

Central to existentialism is a consideration not only of power but also of agency—how the force of the world manifests against the will of the individual, and what the nature and meaningfulness of action are in the face of such force. These questions are also important to the notion of quiet, though they might be phrased in a slightly different way: how to live life fully without being trapped by the expectation of resistance, how to engage the agency of the inner life?

Maud Martha is replete with contestations of power, many of them inflected by social identity. A good example is evidenced by juxtaposing two scenes, the first a moment where Maud Martha's second boyfriend, David McKemster, reflects on the opportunities afforded his white college peers who grew up in rich families with learned dinner conversations: "He himself had had a paper route. Had washed windows, cleaned basements, sanded furniture, shoveled snow, hauled out trash and garbage for neighbors. He had worked before that, running errands for people when he was six" (44). Under the weight of this judgment of his life, David's sense of capacity is undermined: "What chance did he have, he mused, what chance was there for anybody coming out of a set of conditions that never allowed for the prevalence of sensitive, and intellectual, yet almost frivolous,

dinner-table discussions of Parrington across four-year-old heads?" (44).
This depressed sensibility is David's agency as it is determined by the world
rather than by his inner life. Indeed, his assessment of his childhood is a stark
contrast to Maud Martha's thinking about the excellence of dandelions.

Later in the book, after a luscious description of Maud Martha's desire to
go to New York (it symbolizes the kind of liveliness she craves), the text
offers this take on her ambitions:

> What she wanted to dream, and dreamed, was her affair. It pleased her to
> dwell upon color and soft bready textures and light, on a complex beauty,
> on gemlike surfaces. What was the matter with that? Besides, who could
> safely swear that she would never be able to make her dream come true
> for herself? Not altogether, then!—but slightly?—in some part?
>
> She was eighteen years old, and the world waited. To caress her. (51)

The passage describes an agency fueled by desire and imagination, so much
so that her work in the world, her "affair," is to dream. It is important that
the sentence says "what she wanted to dream, and dreamed" because the
repetition turns dreaming from a wish into an action: it is something she
does, is part of her act of living. Even the awareness that her dreaming might
not come true is not enough to disturb the strength she gains from understanding that the world is there waiting for her to invent places to go and
things to long for. This sense of agency comes from the deep relationship
Maud Martha has to her interior. And though she never makes it to New
York in this chapter or any of the others, the willfulness of her imagination
inspires living in a way that no trip to the city ever could.[7]

That Maud Martha lives by an ethic of interiority is essential in a story
that involves questions of power, since it is such an ethic—rather than a
politic of resistance—that will guide her. The central question for Maud
Martha is how to act in accord with the notion of quiet. And there are
plenty of moments where power is contested, although, in keeping with the
overall aesthetic of the novel, there are no big face-offs between the protagonist and other characters, or even between the protagonist and oppressive
social forces. There are, instead, small moments where power is at stake,
and where Maud Martha is challenged to respond. One such moment
occurs in a chapter entitled "the self-solace" where an adult Maud Martha
sits in a beauty shop, "waiting" and "quiet. It was pleasant to let her mind

go blank."[8] The narration goes on to note that, amid the noise and perfumes and products of the salon, one "could sit . . . and think, or not think, of problems," that "one was and was not aware" of all the activity of the salon. The ambivalence of this description is a nod to interiority, though Maud Martha's ease is soon challenged by the chapter's central conflict. Of course, the anecdote here is just another moment in the trajectory of the novel, but it is constructive to consider it closely as a study of Maud Martha's engagement of power: A young white saleswoman comes into the salon to offer her products to Sonia, the salon's proprietor. The narrative takes deliberate note of the scene's unfolding snapshot of race:

> Sonia Johnson looked interested [at the lipstick the saleswoman was describing]. She had always put herself out to be kind and polite to these white salesmen and saleswomen. Some beauticians were brusque. They were almost insulting. They were glad to have the whites at their mercy, if only for a few moments. They made them crawl. Then they applied the whiplash. Then they sent the poor creatures off—with no orders. Then they laughed and laughed, a terrible laughter. But Sonia Johnson was not that way. She liked to be kind and polite. She liked to be merciful. She did not like to take advantage of her power. (136–137)

This attention to the dynamic between black proprietors and white salespeople emphasizes the public dimension of racism and racial politics in general. And by noting the particularity of Sonia's politeness, the narrative is highlighting choice and agency. Sonia agrees to try the lipstick and even agrees to pay the saleswoman five dollars upfront. This sale improves the saleswoman's disposition and she relaxes from the cautious deference that being a salesperson required and seems to lapse into familiarity:

> Miss Ingram brightened. The deal was closed. She pushed back a puff of straw-colored hair that had slipped from under her Persian lamb cap and fallen over the faint rose of her cheek.
>
> "I'm mighty glad," she confided, "that the cold weather is in. I love the cold. It was awful, walking the streets in that nasty old August weather. And even September was rather close this year, didn't you think?"
>
> Sonia agreed. "Sure was."
>
> "People," confided Miss Ingram, "think this is a snap job. It ain't. I work like a nigger to make a few pennies. A few lousy pennies." (138–139)

The narrative has prepared the setting for this moment, such that the reader is inclined to juxtapose Sonia's generosity against the saleswoman's racist attempt at class solidarity. The next sentence, after this moment, is not about Sonia or the saleswoman; it is about Maud Martha: "Maud Martha's head shot up" (139). Disturbed from her thinking and not-thinking, Maud Martha looks at Sonia, who has a "sympathetic smile" that she holds on to, even as her "eyes turned, as if magnetized, toward Maud Martha." Nothing is said and the strangeness of it all allows Maud Martha to think about what just happened in an internal dialogue that the novel frames by quotation marks. First she thinks that the saleswoman could not have said the racial epithet, since "Mrs. Johnson wouldn't let her get away with it. In her own shop" (139). Then Maud Martha mulls over what she would have done had she been Sonia Johnson, and had the woman really said that word:

> I wouldn't curse. I wouldn't holler. I'll bet Mrs. Johnson would do both those things. And I could understand her wanting to, all right. I would be gentle in a cold way. I would give her, not a return insult—directly, at any rate!—but information. I would get it across to her that—" Maud Martha stretched. "But I wouldn't insult her." Maud Martha began to take the hairpins out of her hair. "I'm glad, though, that she didn't say it. She's pretty and pleasant. If she had said it, I would feel all strained and tied up inside, and I would feel that it was my duty to help Mrs. Johnson get it settled, to help clear it up in some way. I'm too relaxed to fight today. Sometimes fighting is interesting. Today, it would have been just plain old ugly duty. (139–140)

Maud Martha's interior dialogue is fanciful and interactive, as she even pauses in its midst to remove her hairpins and to stretch; she tries to imagine what her social and political obligation would be to this external moment, if it had occurred.

Of course, the woman did say the word and after she leaves, Sonia Johnson gives a short explanation of why she did not confront the saleswoman—that she, Sonia, is a Negro, not a nigger, that the meaning of the word is relative, that black people have to stop being so sensitive. As Sonia speaks, Maud Martha "stared steadily into [her] irises. She said nothing. She kept on staring into Sonia Johnson's irises" (142). The chapter ends there, strikingly and without resolution; the specificity of this incident, or of Maud Martha's opinion on it, is never recalled in the rest of the novel. In fact, it is not at all immediately clear how the title relates to all that has just happened. And yet the quiet and intent staring at the end of the chapter might suggest that Maud Martha is trying to make sense of it all: her own anger and responsibility, what she thinks of Sonia's supposed abdication of responsibility, what is means to bear the burden of being black—that "duty" mentioned in her interior dialogue.

It is remarkable that this highly racialized scene goes unresolved and remains inconsequential to the rest of the story. Furthermore, it is astonishing that the chapter privileges Maud Martha's deliberation as action, such that rather than respond to the incident, she thinks about what it means to be responsible and what race means to her. In her self-solace, Maud Martha is not left with a clear sense of what she might have said, or what was right; she does not have a clear sense of how she should have behaved. What is highlighted is her thinking on it, the feeling it, the wondering where the balance of power was. It is important not to mistake the interiority here as synonymous with passivity or to infer that either Brooks's novel or the reading of this scene is a disavowal of the intensity and intention of racist violence. For sure, everything about the novel's focus on everyday scenes suggests that racism, sexism, and poverty matter and have an impact. And still what is given weight here is a consciousness of quiet, the idea that the relationship Maud Martha has to the world is not determined entirely by her gendered or racialized identity. Maud Martha's quiet is neither immune to nor consumed by racism's or sexism's unrelenting meaningfulness. In many ways, the internal dialogue Maud Martha carries on with herself is a surrender to the humanity of her interior. This is part of her "doing quietly," her trying to live through the self she inhabits in face of the possibilities the world presents to her.

In an earlier moment in the novel, Maud Martha refuses to kill a mouse caught in a trap. This act of leniency causes her to feel a "new cleanness," since "a life had blundered its way into her power and it had been hers to preserve or destroy. She had not destroyed" (70–71). In this instance, the novel makes clear its awareness of the ubiquity of power and violence, as well as Maud Martha's capacity to enact or be subjected to both. It is with such awareness that the chapter concludes with this assessment of agency:

> In the center of that simple restraint was—creation. She had created a piece of life. It was wonderful.
>
> "Why," she thought, as her height doubled, "why, I'm good! I am *good*."
>
> She ironed her aprons. Her back was straight. Her eyes were mild, and soft with godlike loving-kindness. (71)

The allusion to God and the reference to Maud Martha's doubled height insinuates the agency of the moment. Further, the repetition of the word "good," which is an echo of the language used in her manifesto earlier—to donate to the world a good Maud Martha—reminds the reader that Maud Martha is a human being in the process of becoming her self and developing an awareness of (her) power. And still, this scene with the mouse is different from another where Maud Martha has to kill and prepare a chicken for dinner. In this regard, Maud Martha assures herself that the chicken will be tasty and proceeds with the killing without hesitation. It is not, then, simply the case that Maud Martha is against using power; it is more that the use of power is part of what she considers in her everyday life. This is the context for reading her response to the salesperson in the hair salon: that she is trying to understand what power means, who has it and when, how it is used. Indeed, part of Maud Martha's work of paying attention is to experience herself as a source of power. Quiet requires the consideration of power as an aspect of human life, especially since discourses of identity sometimes put forth understandings of power that, if taken wholesale, forgo the complexity of living.

What is also being questioned in these moments from *Maud Martha* is what it means to act, what it means to do something on one's behalf. Sometimes, Maud Martha acts explicitly in regard to threats against her being (when she quits her job, when she refuses to buy a hat from a racist shopkeeper). But sometimes the novel describes her doing less than one might expect.[9] In the penultimate chapter, the beautifully titled "tree leaves leaving trees," a white Santa Claus ignores Paulette, Maud Martha's daughter. Paulette senses that Santa does not like her ("He didn't look at me, he didn't shake *my* hand" [174]) and Maud Martha tries to assure her otherwise, even as she, Maud Martha, notices the slight and is enraged by it. "Listen, child," she says to Paulette, "People don't have to kiss you to show they like you . . . Santa Claus loves every child . . . You watch and see. Christmas'll be here in a few days. You'll wake up Christmas morning and find [the toys] and you'll know Santa Claus loved *you too*" (175). In the next few paragraphs, Maud Martha thinks about how different people might have responded to Santa's slight:

> Helen, she thought, would not have twitched back there. Would not have yearned to jerk trimming scissors from purse and jab jab jab that evading eye. Would have gathered her fires, patted them, rolled them out, and blown on them. Because it really would not have made much difference to Helen. Paul would have twitched, twitched awfully, might have cursed, but after the first tough cough-up of rage would forget, or put off studious perusal indefinitely.
>
> She could neither resolve nor dismiss. There were these scraps of baffled hate in her, hate with no eyes, no smile and—this she especially regretted, called her hungriest lack—not much voice. (175–176)

Notably, Maud Martha neither wants to explode in rage (though she does have rage) nor to ignore the insult. There is no resolution for her, and she rues the lack of a voice that might articulate the anger and protect her daughter. There is, as always, this challenge: The world is inclined to mistreat people who are black and female, to either ignore them or stereotype their humanity. In the midst of such mistreatment, these people feel like Paulette—they are aware that the world thinks they are nothing and might even begin to wonder if in fact the assessment is true. The novel is astute to the mistreatment as well as the danger of being focused only on the mistreatment, and though Maud Martha has no answer (save for her quick and harsh response to Paulette), the chapter ends with this prayer she conjures up for Paulette:

> Keep her that land of blue!
>
> Keep her those fairies, with witches always killed at the end, and Santa every winter's lord, kind, sheer being who never perspires, who never does or says a foolish or ineffective thing, who never looks grotesque, who never has occasion to pull the chain and flush the toilet. (176)

Maud Martha hopes that Paulette can do as she has done—to find agency through her interior consciousness. This is the most human protection that she can imagine.

What is compelling about Maud Martha is that she does not internalize what happens in the world outside her. She engages it for sure, considers it, even sometimes responds to it directly. She meditates on it, but she does not merely internalize it. Her deep attention to her interior is a stay against the social world, a way of keeping the happenings of the world as much at arms' length as they are within arms' reach. She doesn't live her life as a perform-ance in response to race, gender, or class; nor is she naïve about the conse-quences of identity and injustice. For her, black humanity is not achieved solely or primarily in protest. As James Baldwin notes, "our humanity is our burden, our life; we need not battle for it; we need only to do what is infinitely more difficult—that is, accept it" (23). Ideologically, this captures the inclination of the dear Maud Martha.[10]

Part of the challenge of reading Maud Martha's racial discourse is that the book seems to demand that we see its title character as a human being, even as she is black and female and her life is affected by those social dimen-sions. This is a conundrum of identity politics, such that a marginalized subject becomes representative of her difference and therefore cannot be seen as the universal ideal. (It is in this regard that we use the generic term "man" in common parlance to talk about people who are male and female, though the reverse does not work.)[11] So Maud Martha is trying to uphold its title character as a human subject, nothing more or less. Brooks is masterful in using shifts in narrative voice to conflate Maud Martha's thoughts with general meditations about the human condition. This is especially evident in the chapter "at the Burns-Coopers'," which describes Maud Martha's first attempt to work outside the home as a domestic helper for a middle-class family. The first day of work is filled with lots of moments where Mrs. Burns-Cooper, her husband, and mother-in-law treat Maud Martha as the help, not another human being. By the end of the day, Maud Martha has resolved to quit:

I'll never come back, Maud Martha assured herself, when she hung up her apron at eight in the evening. She knew Mrs. Burns-Cooper would be puzzled. The wages were very good. Indeed, what could be said in explanation? Perhaps that the hours were long. I couldn't explain *my* explanation, she thought.

One walked out from that almost perfect wall, spitting at the firing squad. What difference did it make whether the firing squad understood or did not understand the manner of one's retaliation or why one had to retaliate?

Why, one was a human being. One wore clean nightgowns. One loved one's baby. One drank cocoa by the fire—or the gas range—come the evening, in the wintertime. (163)

The chapter ends on this note of agency. Interestingly, Maud Martha does not argue with Mrs. Burns-Cooper or demonstrate in any other way, and she realizes that she could not explain her reasons for quitting, not only because Mrs. Burns-Cooper might not be able to understand them but also because her reasons for quitting are simple and beyond clear explanation: She is a human being. There is a sense of interiority in the way that Maud Martha acknowledges the full range of thoughts, including those which are not expressible.

But interiority is also in the way that the passage moves from Maud Martha's thoughts to a poetic meditation on humanity: "One walked out from that almost perfect wall, spitting at the firing squad." Of course, this image is Maud Martha's creative rendering of what her quiet action feels like—the hanging up of the apron as a moment of battle. But the narrative shift is also challenging the reader to see Maud Martha's humanity through the subjectivity of the "one." She is not leaving as part of a battle over class differences; she is leaving because she is a human being and she knows how a human being should feel doing the everyday work of their lives. A reader might be inclined to suggest that Maud Martha is being passive, or that her action is ignorant of the social dynamics that are at play. But it is clear that Maud Martha is aware of, and responding to, those social dynamics: In the last sentence, the narrative notes that cocoa can be drunk by the fire or the gas range; this distinction is clearly about class since not everyone has a fireplace. What is striking about this scene is not only how Maud Martha responds to classism but also how her response is attuned to her interior. Here, the dilemma of quitting is not merely a reaction but a meditation, a scene in the play of her inner life—which is why she does not try to explain.

And Maud Martha refuses to be "either victim or hopelessly exceptional," and instead is just an individual in the midst of her life—nothing more or less than that.[12]

In her influential study *Black Feminist Criticism*, the late Barbara Christian gives an excellent exposition on the aesthetic impulse of *Maud Martha*:

> Gwendolyn Brooks claims that her intention in writing *Maud Martha* was to paint a portrait of an ordinary black woman, first as a daughter, then as a mother, and to show what she makes of her "little life." What Brooks emphasizes in the novel is Maud Martha's *awareness* that she is seen as common (and therefore as unimportant), and that there is so much more in her than her "little life" will allow her to be. Yet, because Maud Martha constructs her own standards, she manages to transform that "little life" into so much more despite the limits set on her by her family, her husband, her race, her class, whites, and American society. Maud Martha emerges neither crushed nor triumphant. She manages, though barely, to be her own creator. Her sense of her own integrity is rooted mostly in her own imagination—in her internal language as metaphors derived from women's experience, metaphors that society usually trivializes but which Brooks presents as the vehicles of insight. Though Maud Martha certainly does not articulate a language (or life) of overt resistance, she does prepare the way for such a language in that she sees the contradiction between her real value as a black woman and how she is valued by those around her. (176)

What Christian captures so perfectly is the novel's commitment to the interior, the way that Maud Martha's consciousness moves toward sovereignty, and how unusual it is to see a black character represented in this way. In this way, Brooks's *Maud Martha* is a study of quiet.

———

In this chapter and the previous one, the discussion of the inner life has highlighted the role of desire. In Marita Bonner's essay, desire was noted in the urge to "dash three or four ways" like a kitten in a field full of plump mice; for *Maud Martha*, desire is announced in the first chapter's catalog of what she liked and would have liked, that random effervescent list of affections. Literary scholar Claudia Tate notices how important desire is to a characterization of black consciousness, especially a consciousness that is free from the limits of racism. In her book *Psychoanalysis and Black Novels: Desire and the Protocols of Race*, Tate categorizes desire as an interiority that reflects something meaningful about one's selfhood. She argues that desire should "not simply mean sexual longings but all kinds of wanting, wishing, yearning, longing and striving—conscious and particularly unconscious" (10). Desire is constitutive of the subject in that it is a measure of the self.[13]

Though it is of and from the interior, desire is neither a place of origin nor exclusive of what is exterior. In fact, desire is not pure and can be triggered externally, and the pursuit of desire often requires engagement with that which is beyond the interior. This consideration of desire as being more than solipsism is important for African-American culture, where, as Tate notes, the imperative of the political often precludes a consideration of desire, as if desire itself has no political or social relevance. And when black cultural critics have engaged desire, they "have been much more invested in defining desire as—indeed, confining desire to—the consolidated aspiration for black civil rights than appreciating desire as the performance of existential freedom" (10). Tate calls this "desire as political prerogative" and bemoans the way it undermines considerations of desire that are less about collective civil rights and more about the quirkiness of human subjectivity.[14] What Tate is addressing is the impact that publicness has on how we think of black subjectivity.

Conceptually, desire is essential to Audre Lorde's notion of the erotic, as described in her classic essay "Uses of the Erotic: The Erotic as Power." Lorde characterizes the erotic as a resource "rooted in the power of our unexpressed or unrecognized feeling" (53), going beyond the sexual connotation of the term to describe an agency that is interior and largely inexpressible. Though Lorde suggests that this resource is "deeply female" and addresses her essay to women, her idiom is not limited only to women; here and elsewhere, she reminds us that the feminine exists in every human being.[15] The erotic, she says, "is a measure between the beginnings of our sense of self and the chaos of our strongest feelings. It is an internal sense of satisfaction to which . . . we know we can aspire" (54). For Lorde, the erotic is one's capacity to feel great power and to engage it meaningfully; in this way, the erotic might be described as the only worthwhile measurement for one's humanity.

Like Tate, Lorde is aware of the danger that public expectations pose to the willfulness of the erotic:

> When we live outside ourselves, and by that I mean on external directives only rather than from our internal knowledge and needs, when we live away from those erotic guides from within ourselves, then our lives are limited by external and alien forms, and we conform to the needs of a structure that is not based on human need, let alone the individual's. But when we begin to live from within outward, and allowing that power to inform and illuminate our actions upon the world around us, then we begin to recognize our deepest feelings. (58)

Lorde emphasizes the erotic as an interiority as a way to guard against the imposition of "external directives," those social and political discourses which give us our racial and gendered names, and which are also mobilized in civil rights efforts. Her argument does not dismiss the need to be engaged with the exterior world, but instead privileges what the interior can offer to our living.

What is at stake with desire is the freedom to surrender to what you feel, the human right to live through pleasure. For sure, everyone feels, but often feeling is surpassed in favor of what has to be thought, done, resisted. Yet pleasure can characterize a certain sovereignty of subjectivity. In her best-selling book *Wild Mind: Living the Writer's Life*, Natalie Goldberg narrates an anecdote that exemplifies this idea effectively:

> A writer I know who is now in her sixties told me that in her late twenties, she had a nervous breakdown because she didn't know who she was. She moved to New York City from the rural South, and she was estranged from her family. She wandered down thirty-fourth street, completely lost. She said she found a therapist who slowly, over three years, saved her life. In the very first session of her therapy, the therapist asked her to find one thing that she liked, just for herself, not because her mother said it was good or the South said it was good or because she wanted to impress a New Yorker. Finally, by the end of the hour, she came up with one thing. She knew, irretrievable, just for herself, that she honestly liked the taste of chocolate. From that one pleasure, she and the therapist began the construction of an authentic life. (159)

This is a powerful example of the role of pleasure in constructing a subjectivity that is of one's interior. Notably, the therapist encourages the writer to avoid pleasures that are inspired by familial or social relationships or identity. She, the writer, identifies chocolate. And even if her affinity for chocolate is, unconsciously, a learned appreciation, that she can claim it as her own is what makes it possible that this single pleasure can anchor this woman's life practice. To identify a pleasure is to ask an unanswerable but necessary series of questions—What do I love? What brings me joy? What and how do I feel or want to feel? Subsumed in those questions is a recognition of self, as if to engage each of those questions is to first admit that there must be a "me" there, something undeniable and complicated, something other than the world might know. The possibility that these questions might have definite answers is not what makes them potent; indeed the agency is in the asking, in the pursuit.[16]

Pleasure can be externalized but it can also be another means by which one can express sensibilities of one's inner life. Hence, a novel about a dark-skinned black girl who is less attractive than her more graceful sister opens: "What she liked was candy buttons, and books, and painted music (deep blue, or delicate silver) and the west sky, so altering, viewed from the steps of the back porch; and dandelions."[17] This sentence captures the inclinations of Brooks's novel, since the world Maud Martha lives in is not only that which is outside her but the one she imagines and, through imagination, experiences. In the very last chapter, Maud Martha notices the sun's radiant beauty, a thing which "made her whisper, What, what, am I to do with all this life?" (178). This is exactly her imperative all along—to not squander life to the violence of the world, and to hold on to the power of one's imagination. What am I to do with all this life? The question might sound frivolous and apolitical, but Maud Martha is astute to the realities of the world and the willfulness required to go outside: "And exactly what was one to do with it all? At a moment like this one was ready for anything, was not afraid of anything" (178).

With that much life in her, Maud Martha and Paulette head outdoors, amid the battered bodies of men back from war, their drinking and despair, "the stories of the latest of the Georgia and Mississippi lynchings" (179). The text is, as always, aware of the harshness of life, especially of the threats against people who are black and female, people like Maud Martha. Still the battle is not divined only to the exterior world and the last few paragraphs of the novel balance this ethic so beautifully that they deserve to be quoted in full:

> But the sun was shining, and some of the people in the world had been left alive, and it was doubtful whether the ridiculousness of man would ever completely succeed in destroying the world—or, in fact, the basic equanimity of the least and commonest flower: for would its kind not come up again in spring? come up, if necessary, among, between, or out of—beastly inconvenient!—the smashed corpses lying in strict compo-sure, in that hush infallible and sincere.
>
> And was not this something to be thankful for?
>
> And, in the meantime, while people did live they would be grand, would be glorious and brave, would have nimble hearts that would beat and beat. They would even get up nonsense, through wars, through divorce, through evictions and jilting and taxes.
>
> And, in the meantime, she was going to have another baby.
>
> The weather was bidding her bon voyage. (179–180)

At the end, the dandelion returns with its undeniable simplicity and tenac-ity. What the passage asserts is that even in the face death, taxes, and heart-break, people still can be glorious and brave. There is nothing in these final words that makes light of racism or sexism or wanton violence—in fact, these are mentioned explicitly. But all is not the world outside; the inside too is a life, one that is capable of feeling and knowing and pleasure. And the human heart, powered by the agency of one's inner life, is agile enough to negotiate the world.

For all its agency, part of pleasure is the sheer indulgence of its surrender, the pleasure in being nothing to no one. After all, a large part of the concept of pleasure is deeply individual and it runs against the expectations of the social world. This delight of being nothing is represented in "Daystar," one of the poems from Rita Dove's prize-winning collection, *Thomas and Beulah*:

> She wanted a little room for thinking:
> but she saw diapers steaming on the line,
> a doll slumped behind the door.

So she lugged a chair behind the garage
to sit out the children's naps.

Sometimes there were things to watch—
the pinched armor of a vanished cricket,
a floating maple leaf. Other days
she stared until she was assured
when she closed her eyes
she'd see only her own vivid blood.

She had an hour, at best, before Liza appeared
pouting from the top of the stairs.
And just *what* was mother doing
out back with the field mice? Why,

building a palace. Later
that night when Thomas rolled over and
lurched into her, she would open her eyes
and think of the place that was hers
for an hour—where
she was nothing,
pure nothing, in the middle of the day. (61)

Thomas and Beulah tells an invented story of Dove's maternal grandparents
in two sections, with the Thomas poems focused on his haunting memory
of the death of his childhood friend, Lem, and the Beulah ones shaped
around her insatiable imagination. In "Daystar," Beulah's aptitude for fan-
tasy is captured in easy narrative form, ushered along by a progressive series
of "s" sounds that one hears especially in reading the poem aloud. But it is
how Beulah finds comfort and solace in the ordinary—the dead cricket, the
tree leaf—that is notable here, especially that her observances are part of a
practice of aliveness: they are how Beulah relieves some of the pressure of
being mother and wife, and perhaps even of having been a daughter in an
abusive childhood home. As confirmed in other poems, Beulah's affection
for the ordinary is magical; she imagines palaces and sees towers of lights in
the midst of the everyday. This is her aliveness, a practice where she can give
up her social identities and be truly nothing, pure and obligated only to her
imagination; indeed it is a space of being that she can revisit in the dark of
night when the intimacy of lovemaking only feels like obligation.

Beulah's nothingness constitutes an identity that is not tethered to her more public or social identities but instead is a precious, selfish, secret identity formed in pleasure.[18]

In many ways, pleasure is contradictory to the assumed collectivity of black racial identity; that is, pleasure often seems too individual and self-indulgent to be useful to collectivity. Still, it is also possible that the self-regard of pleasure can inspire awareness of others. Think back to the end of *Maud Martha* cited earlier, when the protagonist surrenders to the spectacular feel of the beautiful weather. Her sense of wonder starts with herself as she whispers "What, what am I to do with all this life," a perfectly self-indulgent question. Then, the question is rephrased, the pronoun "I" being replaced with "one." This shift sets up Maud Martha's broad assessment of the resilience of humanity. For her, the sun is shining and the feeling it inspires is a sign that the "the ridiculousness of man would ever completely succeed in destroying the world." As Maud Martha experiences the abundant wonder of the weather, she thinks of "people in the world [who] had been left alive." Her sense of self is neither exclusive nor is it built on the disadvantage of others; her agency does not leave her as a woman alone against and away from the world. Her agency is based on the human capacity to feel and crave. It is her right but it is neither exclusive to her nor does it leave her any less capable of being aware (of herself or others).[19]

The right to be nothing to anyone but self—this is the right that black people, and black women specifically, don't get to inhabit. And yet, this notion of being for self is essential to experiencing and living through one's humanity. If the quiet subject is a subject of the interior, then selfishness is necessary. She, the quiet subject, is not immune or allergic to interaction with others; it is simply that interaction with others does not overdetermine the quiet self. This is the existentialist notion of being a part of and apart from the world, and it is represented successfully in the novel when Maud Martha, believing that she is dying from a cancerous tumor, takes an assessment of her life as "decent childhood, happy Christmases; some shreds of romance, a marriage, pregnancy and giving birth, her growing child, her experiments in sewing, her books, her conversations with friends and enemies" (144). What is notable here is how the list situates marriage next to her books and her sewing, as well as the evenness of the phrase "conversations with friends and enemies." It is remarkable how quiet this is, how much it suggests that her life has been shaped by her interior. After this assessment, Maud Martha concludes that her life had been "interesting, it had been rather good, and it was still rather good. But really, she was ready [to die]. Paulette would miss her for a long time, Paul for less, but really, their sorrow was their business, not hers. Her business was to descend into the deep cool, the salving dark, to be alike indifferent to the good and the not-good" (144). This is the perfect description of Maud Martha's quiet—to imagine that one's business in the world is to be "indifferent to the good and the not-good," to engage life as it comes, to move and be moved. Her statement speaks of a vibrant, self-aware relationship to the world. In the course of Maud Martha's life, profound things happen, but she is not dramatic. She is not audacious, though she is alive. Her business is not to privilege race or gender or class or the social relationships they foster—as in white people are awful, so is poverty, men are oppressive—though these realities impact her. Nor is her business to be consumed with social expectations. No, her business is to understand and explore her desire, to be alive until such is no longer possible. The ethic here is as Brooks states in a poem from *In the Mecca*: "Conduct your blooming in the noise and whip of the whirlwind" (54).[20] Surely there is a certain self-centeredness in this agency of the interior, but this self-centeredness is neither isolating nor isolationist. Instead this agency "circulates like a gift; an empty gift which anybody can lay claim to by filling it to taste, yet can never truly possess. A gift built on multiplicity. *One that stays inexhaustible within its own limits.* Its departures and arrivals. Its quietness. Its quietness" (Trinh T. Minh-ha, *Woman. Native. Other*, 2).

———

Maud Martha is not an ambassador for her race or her gender, but an embassy for her own difficult selfhood. It would be an overstatement to say that *Maud Martha* is a rejection of the public world—the book is too quiet to do that. But what is striking is the way that it maintains a fidelity to the wild inner life of a black female character who often does or says very little, and yet whose agency is broad and deliberate. This fidelity is *Maud Martha*'s quiet, its study of power and how to do quietly. It is as if Brooks's novel acknowledges that life consists of a series of indignities, some small, some motivated by social identities, some lethal and institutional, but indignities nonetheless—acts of mistreatment or moments of inadequacy or inferiority that rub against one's sense of self and agency. Sometimes, the source of the indignity is clear—the saleswoman in the beauty salon, for example, or the Santa Claus who ignores Paulette—but sometimes the source is more amorphous or cumulative. Whatever the case, throughout the novel, Maud Martha has not been poised to respond to these indignities, but to live through and with them; that is, her surrender to her interior means that her life is not organized by the experience of or her response to these indignities—her life includes but is far more than these.

The examples in the novel are a redefinition of what standing up for one's self means: standing up for one's self doesn't have to be triumphant, but can be, simply, the work of reveling in flowers or blue sky—the daily practice of understanding what you love and why. That is enough. In this regard, *Maud Martha* is not a novel of triumph, just an everyday story that has no real beginning and no end. And it is through this aesthetic that the novel can present the life and struggle of a black woman without falling into a discourse of resistance. Though Maud Martha may be displaced in the world, she does not react as if she is displaced or as if displacement is her subjectivity. Because it is not.[21]

———

Quiet helps us to understand the activism involved in being aware, in paying attention, in considering. So much of how we make sense of the world is through social identities, as well as through a discourse of cause and effect: this happens because of that, this produces that. Sometimes these firm logics undermine the opportunity to be in wonder at what is happening to you as well as to be aware that you "happen" to the world. As writer Loni Jones notes, "The most profoundly human act we can commit is to feel" ("Making Holy," xiii). Quiet revels in the action that is feeling.

Quiet is the habitat of the inner life, a selfhood not based on race or gender but on the rages of the interior, a subjectivity sobered and armed by possibility.

CHAPTER 4

Quiet, Vulnerability, and Nationalism

So far the discussion of quiet has focused on examples of individuality, on the ways that one person negotiates her inner life, racialization, and her sense of humanity. This has been the case with Marita Bonner's essay and Gwendolyn Brooks's novel, and it has been useful for introducing the notion of quiet. But it is inevitable to ask this: Does the concept of quiet have the capacity to speak to black collectivity? What could quiet mean to how we think about and represent blackness as a communal identity? Part of what makes these questions necessary is the vital role that community has played in black culture and history. As discussed earlier, the notion of blackness itself is collective, a designation of characteristics about a group; however much an individual person might experience racialization uniquely, the social meaningfulness of race is dependent on it being collective. It is for this reason that black people's engagement of and fight against racism is communal. So if quiet is to be a useful aesthetic in how we think about black culture, the question of community is unavoidable. That is, how does a concept of quiet reflect or influence notions of communal blackness?

This latter question is one about the relevance of quiet to black nationalism. Generally, nationalism is any concept that advocates for the rights of a people, especially in terms of self-definition and self-determination; this characterization is true of black nationalism. In *The Golden Age of Black Nationalism, 1850–1925*, William Jeremiah Moses argues that slavery is "the cause of black nationalism . . . [since] it endowed [black people] with a sense of common experience and identity" (16). Moses realizes that black nationalism is different from most other nationalisms "in that its adherents are united neither by a common geography nor by a common language, but by the nebulous concept of racial unity," the commonality of experience that slavery and racial oppression provides (17). Though scholars differ on the defining figures or birthdates of black nationalism, it is Martin Delany, an abolitionist, writer, and physician prominent in the mid-1800s, who is considered its forefather. And yet black nationalism can be seen prior to Delany, in organized slave rebellions, as well as in the efforts of religious leaders (for example Richard Allen, founder of the AME Church in 1816) and free black societies in the northern United States. These early examples of black nationalism foster others in the late nineteenth century and beyond, including the civil rights and black power movements in the 1950s and 1960s.

Central to nationalism is a sense of collective identity, what Jeffrey Stout has called "blackness as an emblem" (242). This identity is imaginary as well as material, geographic as well as historical, embodied/corporeal as well as psychic; politically, it can be pluralistic, integrationist, and/or separatist. The multiplicities of these characterizations are reflective of the fact that black nationalism is an expansive concept, despite the narrow ways in which it is sometimes represented. And yet the capaciousness of nationalism does not hinder its capacity to inspire collectivity and has not undermined its singular role in motivating social change through three centuries of black freedom movements.[1]

There are many ways that nationalism seems antithetical to quiet, perhaps most notably in the matter of publicness: Nationalism is definitively public in its use of social arenas to assert black self-determination. Part of its publicness is the advocacy of resistance to dominant, racist ideologies and the celebration of a singular emblematic identity. Some would argue that black cultural nationalisms reflect, even embrace, heterogeneity, but this argument underplays the reductiveness that is a part of any call to unity. Moreover, nationalist ideologies help to reinforce the equivalence between blackness and resistance.[2]

This claim is exemplified in the prevailing representations and interpretations of the civil rights movement, especially the images and moments that are iconic of the era: Dr. King and Malcolm X. Bull Connor. Freedom Riders. Marches and bus boycotts. Emmett Till and the four little girls killed in that church bombing in Birmingham. Dogs and fire hoses and batons. "We Shall Overcome." Black power slogans and songs of the movement. Washington in August 1963. These are some of the icons we use to try to summarize this incredible period in American history. In truth, there is or can be no language that captures it all, no representative symbol that speaks to the history or to the lives of the people who lived those years; any one signal moment or image or incident we select runs the risk of flattening out human complexity and obscuring more than it reveals. And yet, as with most historical periods, the civil rights movement is readily codified into a series of idioms that communicate a familiar notion of public expressiveness. This characterization is not wrong in itself—certainly there were marches and singing, the awful physicality of dogs and crowds being dispersed by local police forces, lots of vile and violent action as well as the heroic behavior that matched and even surpassed it. These are part of the truth of the story. And still, as it is with another set of icons from the era, Tommie Smith and John Carlos, the stories we tell about civil rights tend to privilege what is exterior while giving limited if any attention to what could be called quiet. In this way, the notions of resistance, and of triumph over victimization and violence, that are so prevalent in the narrativization of civil rights are contrary to the interiority of an aesthetic of quiet.[3]

The discussion here is not about the relevance or significance of civil rights history, but about our depictions of that history and what is emphasized as the stories are told and retold. This question about the pitfalls of representation has been central to civil rights scholarship, including concerns about the tendency to misrepresent and lionize Dr. King and Malcolm X, the superficial presentation of Rosa Parks and of the Montgomery bus boycott, the disregard for the significant contributions of women, or the inclination to think only of national leaders and organizations. Recently, there has been much emphasis on telling the story of the movement through the lives of ordinary people, or at least on giving more attention to those folks whose names are not in historical boldface. Renee Romano and Leigh Raiford, in the edited collection *The Civil Rights Movement in American Memory*, note that such interrogation of the narratives of civil rights is necessary to avoid "the facile, easily consumable narrative of living heroes, bygone villains, canonized martyrs, and steadfast success" (135).[4] This comment is an excellent summary of the anxiety of representation, though the question about quiet is a bit finer: Is it possible to portray the civil rights movement in a way that celebrates the inner life, in a way that uses the notion of interiority as a template for thinking about black collectivity?

Part of the challenge of thinking about quiet and civil rights is the concept of vulnerability. In general, any nationalism aims to make its people more secure and less subject to violence—to reduce victimization. An aspect of nationalist thinking about victimization is the creation of a collective narrative about injury. Debra King, in her elegant book *African Americans and the Culture of Pain*, describes this dynamic astutely. King notes that race as a concept, and the racism it produces, create a context where James Byrd's mutilated body is not individual but "a victim: a symbolic scapegoat for interracial healing, a haunting image of racially motivated hate, and an icon for activism's call. In other words, he is not a man but a discourse expressing the need and hope for racial equality" (2). King here is writing about Byrd's horrific death in 1998 at the hands of three white men in Jasper, Texas who tied him to a truck and dragged his body for two miles, though her point is relevant to the 1960s, too. She goes on to argue that "the black body is always a memorial to African and African American historical pain" (3), an equivalence that is the legacy of white racist violence and the discourses of black response to that violence. One of the exquisite insights of King's study is its awareness of the way that black pain is important to white racism (which both inflicts and disavows it) and black nationalism (which wants to prevent and memorialize it).

The collective reality of injury is not only a central aspect of nationalism but also shapes what vulnerability can mean to black culture. Conceptually, victimization and vulnerability are nearly synonymous, hence both are judged to be antithetical to the nationalist cause. That is, in face of systemic violence against black people, as well as more individual acts of maiming and meanness, the notion of vulnerability is neutered; rather than being seen as a quality of an inner life and a necessary human capacity, vulnerability becomes defined as a liability to black survival. In this example, it seems that the terms of nationalism are too rigid to be able to advocate for the fragility that is a part of being alive; its ambition cannot permit what looks like frailty. Nationalism is pride and boldness, clarity of self and defin-itive resistance, and the pursuit—if not achievement—of triumph over victimization. Vulnerability is not consonant with much of this.[5]

And still, if vulnerability is essential to being human, then it must be present in those moments that we use to illustrate nationalism, even if it is not given much attention. Such is the case in images of Smith and Carlos, but there are other examples too: think about the interiority that is indi-cated in the freedom songs. Based largely on revised spirituals, the iconic songs of the movement were not fighting songs, but reflective and hymn-like melodies with sentiments of interiority (such as "We Shall Overcome"). Furthermore, as T. V. Reed argues in *The Art of Protest*, "singing could be a plain old source of pleasure and recreation. Movement work was often unimaginably arduous. In such a context ... there needs to be time for pleasure and relaxation ... There was music around just for fun" (36). In this reading, singing and the pleasure it brings are exemplary of an inner life.

With this notion of interiority in mind, we can look again at some of the images in Steven Kasher's *The Civil Rights Movement: A Photographic History, 1954–1968*, many of which are faces we know well or of situations whose social significance is apparent. There is the UPI photograph of two young black men sitting at a lunch counter, reading (78). In one way, they are at a stand-off with the two white waitresses who watchfully ignore them; these boys have no plates of food in front of them, and no one seems to be moving to offer them service. In another moment, they might be assaulted with condiment bottles or verbal epithets. This assessment takes account of the social history of the image, especially the evidence it offers of the perva-siveness of both racism and black resilience. But there is something else implied in looking at this image of these young men, something that sug-gests an inner life: they are not (only) in a stand-off but they are also *reading*; their minds are likely wandering over many things, including the words on the page. There is something self-focused about their act of reading, a process that stirs the imagination and strengthens the self—a consummate kind of agency, perhaps. One cannot ignore the social context of this pic-ture, but one should not disregard the intimacy of their posture that is so crucial to the power of this image. They are two young black men, reading, in a moment of grace, their minds aflame with things ordinary and extraor-dinary. We know the story of resistance here but what is also essential to

Figure 2. Lunch counter protest in North Carolina, 1960. Courtesy of Corbis Images.

understanding the breath of humanity is noticing the specific loveliness of these two young men. Indeed it contributes mightily to appreciating the full grandness of our civil rights history.

Many of the photographs from the lunch counter sit-ins offer glimpses of black humanity in this way, as if to remind us that this is a necessary complement to the publicness of the moment. (This sensibility also corresponds with the fact that some of these young people prepared for sit-ins by practicing meditation, by going inside.) A similar quality is evident in another image, Danny Lyon's *SNCC Workers Visiting a Supporter, Near Albany, Georgia, 1963* (99). Here, without the caption, the political significance is not as legible as is the everydayness of these people being together. In fact, it is the everydayness of their gathering that makes this image important to our archive of civil rights, since it could make us think of the exchange of jokes or gossip or recipes that surely happened alongside more serious initiatives, exchanges that are random bits of life being lived but that are often lost to history's big arc. Such characterizations of quiet are readable in many memoirs of the era—the reflective interiority near the end of Malcolm X's *Autobiography*, the titles and some of the anecdotes of Septima Clark's *Ready from Within* and James Farmer's *Lay Bare My Heart.*

Figure 3. Danny Lyons, *SNCC Workers Visiting a Supporter, Near Albany, Georgia, 1963*. Courtesy of the artist and Magnum Photos.

Eric Sundquist, in *King's Dream*, reminds us that Dr. King himself not only called for social change but also believed deeply in the power of the self as an agent and location of change; speaking in 1967, King proclaimed that the black person "will only be truly free when he reaches down to the inner depths of his own being and signs with the pen and ink of assertive selfhood his own emancipation proclamation" (226). It is striking to notice this language of interiority in the midst of an assertion for black civil rights.[6]

Because quiet does not readily fit the needs of nationalism, what goes missing or unacknowledged in depictions of black collectivity is the interior, especially the sense that collectivity can be represented in a way that is conversant with vulnerability. None of this is to belittle the importance of nationalism and its vocabulary; indeed, how could one not love nationalism and its determination to protect us, to convince us of our human significance? The point, instead, is that the ability of nationalism to argue for black humanity is hamstrung without a concept of interiority.

———

If the question is how to portray black collectivity through the idioms of quiet, then it is to James Baldwin's *The Fire Next Time*, published in 1963, that we must turn. In two first-person essays, Baldwin uses vulnerability as a metaphor for the threat and endangerment that racism produces. Here, the political volatility of the sixties is construed through interiority, and black experience is described entirely through a vocabulary of intimacy. In the pages of *Fire*, there are no grand statements of nationalism, even though Baldwin is clear in his indictment of racism; instead, the narrator's trembling, quirky humanity stands as the example of what it meant to be black in America during the freedom movement, of what it means to be self-determined.

By the time *Fire* became a best-seller, Baldwin was already a writer of great reputation—his first novel, *Go Tell It on the Mountain*, arrived to acclaim in 1953 and was followed by four other works, including *Notes of a Native Son*, *Giovanni's Room*, and *Another Country*. And yet *Fire* propelled him to national prominence, including a cover story in *Time* magazine. In the first decade of his career as a writer, Baldwin had devoted significant attention to the essay (the two pieces in *Fire* were first published in *The Progressive* and *The New Yorker*) and was also a noted civil rights activist. All this suggests that Baldwin was a public intellectual, one of the era's definitive race men of letters, despite speculation that he was gay.[7] Other black male activists, people like Amiri Baraka, Eldridge Cleaver, and Hoyt Fuller, were writing aesthetic calls to arms and were quick to deride any black writer who did not follow suit—which only makes the quiet posture of Baldwin's collection more remarkable. Like Brooks's *Maud Martha*, *Fire* celebrates the agency that is found in the inner life even in the midst of the imposition of the world outside. One could say that the collection is about American racism, but it is more accurate to say that *The Fire Next Time* is Baldwin's meditation on his own vulnerability.

The negotiation of intimacy is evident in the first essay, "My Dungeon Shook: Letter to My Nephew on the One Hundredth Anniversary of the Emancipation," whose title mixes the public racial narrative (emancipation, but also the phrase "my dungeon shook," which is from a spiritual) with the privacy implied by a letter addressed to a relative. As discussed earlier, the letter genre is a cozy, often feminine, means of communication, and its urgency to be read is contextualized by closeness. Therefore Baldwin's choice to write this as a letter indicates a different kind of conversation about race, specifically an intent to encompass the public discourse of the failings of American freedom within the vagaries of a correspondence between a nephew and an uncle.[8]

In keeping with this aesthetic of intimacy, the essay begins thus: "Dear James: I have begun this letter five times and torn it up five times. I keep seeing your face, which is also the face of your father and my brother. Like him, you are tough, dark, vulnerable, moody—with a very definite tendency to sound truculent because you want no one to think you are soft" (3–4). Baldwin's narrator starts with familial affection and narrative tenderness. Furthermore, the essay reinforces its intimacy by making clever use of the fact that Baldwin and his nephew share the same first name; in that regard, the salutation "Dear James" reads like a journal entry or a letter to the self. This is a remarkable opening to an essay about race at the height of the civil rights movement and by a writer of Baldwin's prominence. (That Baldwin also starts by acknowledging his futility in writing the letter—having started over five times—is another example of tenderness and vulnerability.)

Representations of domesticity are also important to Baldwin's deployment of closeness. For example, soon after the narrator mentions that his own father "is dead . . . had a terrible life [because] he was defeated long before he died because, at the bottom of his heart, he really believed what white people said about him," he turns to the domestic: "I have known [you and your father] all your lives, have carried your Daddy in my arms and on my shoulders, kissed and spanked him and watched him learn to walk" (4). Domesticity here is a human virtue, illustrative of the imperative and capacity to nurture, and the narrator continues this characterization in one especially lovely passage:

> I don't know if you've known anybody from that far back; if you've loved anybody that long, first as an infant, then as a child, then as a man, you gain a strange perspective on time and human pain and effort. Other people cannot see what I see whenever I look into your father's face, for behind your father's face as it is today are all those other faces which were his. Let him laugh and I see a cellar your father does not remember and a house he does not remember and I hear in his present laughter his laughter as a child. Let him curse and I remember him falling down the cellar steps. (4–5)

This is an emphatic depiction of Baldwin as a person whose intellectual and moral subjectivity has been formed in acts of nurturing. That is, he knows what it is to care for someone, to see and want to soothe their pain, which means that he is fully capable of criticizing the country's legacy of racist violence. He says as much in the sentence that closes this early part of the letter: "I know what the world has done to my brother and how narrowly he has survived it . . . This is the crime of which I accuse my country and my countrymen, and for which neither I nor time nor history will ever forgive them, that they have destroyed and are destroying hundreds of thousands of lives and do not know it and do not want to know it" (5).[9]

The narrator's domestic authority reflects the overall balance in the letter between the tenderness of his instructions to his nephew, and the pointed language that describes the harshness of racism: "Please try to remember that what they believe, as well as what they do and cause you to endure, does not testify to your inferiority but to their inhumanity and fear. Please try to be clear, dear James, through the storm which rages about your youthful head today, about the reality which lies behind the words *acceptance* and *integration*" (8, emphasis in original). These two sentences move from the private mentoring exchange between two men who are related, to a philosophical comment about the limits that racism threatens to impose on one's humanity. In this balance is Baldwin's refusal to relinquish the examination of racism to the meager imagination of publicness. He is determined to hold on to what is intimate and precious between him and his nephew, and he focuses on the meaningfulness of race as it affects their inner lives. Race is their distinct idiom, and the essay proceeds as a love letter between two men, one that embraces affection and vulnerability. In his attention to interiority, what motivates Baldwin's letter writing is not only racism as a public discourse but the real impact racism can have on his nephew's heart, as it seems to have had on his brother's and his father's. The crisis he is writing about is as much to ensure that a child's tears after falling down a flight of stairs can be heard, as it is to expose the structures of poverty and hatred. His is a particularly intimate take on the injuries of racism.

Part of this interior conversation about race is a negotiation of audience. Even though Baldwin's use of the letter implies that his nephew is his only audience, it is clear that he is also speaking to black people on one hand, and white people on another. Since, in the logic of race, black people are part of his larger family, his address to them runs throughout the essay; it is insinuated especially in his caution about becoming hardened in the face of enduring racism. But he engages white readers much more directly and chasteningly as "they," a third-person eavesdropper whom he acknowledges as a secondary audience. His references to this auditor are often parenthetical and display an ambivalence of inclusion—clearly "they" are not part of the direct address but they are also to be included in the intimacy, since they too are a part of the world of people.

Baldwin is both playful and expert in managing this aspect of the essay:

> Now, my dear namesake, these innocent and well-meaning people, your countrymen, have caused you to be born under conditions not very far removed from those described for us by Charles Dickens in the London of more than a hundred years ago. (I hear the chorus of the innocents screaming, "No! This is not true! How *bitter* you are!"—but I am writing this letter to *you*, to try to tell you something about how to handle *them*, for most of them do not yet really know that you exist. I *know* the conditions under which you were born, for I was there. Your countrymen were not there, and haven't made it yet . . .). (6, emphases in original)

Notice how he balances his tenderness to his nephew ("my dear namesake") with an even-handedness toward these people he calls "your countrymen." It is interesting that he uses this phrase, since it signals a kind of kinship, as if ideally, everyone could be part of the same national family. It is unclear if the use of "your" is sarcastic, since earlier he refers to them as "my countrymen," but it is clear that it is a term of ambivalent endearment. That is, Baldwin is arguing in *Fire*, as he has elsewhere, that the fruits and failings of America belong to black and white people alike, differences notwithstanding. And though he takes up this public aspect of the race question, he remains committed to the intimacy that drives the essay: "I am writing this letter to you," he notes, without having to say the other half of the phrase— "not to them." This is an explicit rejection of the public dimensions of the conversation since Baldwin refuses either to be enraged at white people or to plead for their understanding.[10]

The managed inclusion of the white reader and the clever incorporation of the collective black voice are important to the essay's balancing of the interior and exterior. Indeed, given how much race is a communal identity shaped by publicness, it might be impossible to have a discussion of racism that is completely interior. But the very aesthetic of Baldwin's essay—as a letter that highlights domesticity—keeps intimacy at the center. More impressive is the way that Baldwin uses the legacy of racial injury to teach his nephew about the importance of vulnerability. For Baldwin vulnerability is not to be disavowed in favor of righteousness; instead, vulnerability is a part of righteousness and is essential to the human interior that he so values.

The excellence of Baldwin's intelligence is characterized by what he knows about being human. The writer Hilton Als, in an exquisite essay entitled "Family Secrets," makes this assessment of Baldwin's body of work: "As I read Baldwin in my present incarnation, I realized that he did not have a great formal mind. He did not have an expansive command of American history or politics. He wrote out of a sense of presumed intimacy with the reader." One might hear Als's comment as an indictment, but it is instead a perfect and affectionate appraisal of what is quiet about his essays in *The Fire Next Time*—that Baldwin's study was intimacy. He did not write to tell us of history in either broad strokes or stunning detail; he did not write to capture the ambition and anxiety of black or white people. He wrote to explore vulnerability, loss, rage, possibility, fear; he wrote from and through his interior, and as a result his meditation on racism in this letter to his nephew is an example of what quiet could mean to the representation of black collective identity.

Baldwin's use of intimacy is even more evident in the second essay in *The Fire Next Time*, "Down at the Cross," where his address turns from his nephew to himself. Subtitled "A Letter from a Region in My Mind," this essay uses Baldwin's religious coming-of-age as a vehicle for thinking about the growing role of the Nation of Islam in the black freedom struggle. The context for the essay is intriguing—Baldwin, as a Christian civil rights activist, is assigned by *The New Yorker* to interview Elijah Muhammad, leader of the Nation of Islam. At this point, Baldwin had already expressed some skepticism about the Nation and its leaders, so in many ways the assignment to interview Muhammad is overdetermined by publicness. In this context, it would be hard to imagine how intimacy could figure in the resulting essay, but Baldwin is up to the task, beginning thus: "I underwent, during the summer that I became fourteen, a prolonged religious crisis" (15). With this invocation, the narrator is cast as a young person at the height of adolescence and ensconced in vulnerability; he is not James

Baldwin, the accomplished adult, ready to take on another debate on racism in the United States. The essay concentrates its attention on this idea of an adolescent subjectivity, the mood of doubt and confusion and passion that characterizes this age. Remarkably, for the first third of the essay Baldwin explores adolescence as a time of terror, without even hinting at the conversation with Muhammad to come.

One can see the idiom of adolescence in his discussion of the relationship between religion and safety, for example:

> The word "safety" brings us to the real meaning of the word "religious" as we use it. Therefore, to state it in another, more accurate way, I became, during my fourteenth year, for the first time in my life, afraid—afraid of the evil within me and afraid of the evil without. What I saw around me that summer in Harlem was what I had always seen; nothing had changed. But now, without any warning, the whore and pimps and racketeers on the Avenue had become a personal menace. It had not before occurred to me that I could become one of them, but now I realized that we had been produced by the same circumstances. (16)

This description of the vulnerability that pushed him into the assumed safety of Christianity recognizes threats that are both personal and social. For the narrator, puberty is a profound terror of the body as well as the psyche, especially for a young person who is black in a racist culture and homosexual in a homophobic one; this terror is magnified as sexuality merges with poverty to produce "whores and pimps and racketeers." And a terror it truly is: Baldwin's language is luscious as he describes the girls, who "only slightly older than I was, who sang in the choir or taught Sunday school, the children of holy parents, underwent, before my eyes, their incredible metamorphosis, of which the most bewildering aspect was not their budding breasts or their rounding behinds but something deeper and more subtle, in their eyes, their heat, their odor, and the inflection in their voices" (16–17). The rhetorical set-up here is perfect as Baldwin introduces the girls with plentiful markers of innocence, and then explains this transformation that seems like something of an assault to them. They become monstrous "in the twinkling of an eye."[11] The onslaught of adolescence is not limited to the girls, as Baldwin characterizes his own awkwardness: "I had no idea what my voice or my mind or my body was likely to do next" (17).

The corporeal assault of puberty, the body coursing with hormones and in flux; the interplay of sexuality, sensuality, and youthful desire; the wish for safety and the thrill of adulthood just-within-reach; the loneliness and dread and awe: these are the ideas Baldwin uses to frame his discussion of religion, race, and civil rights. This vocabulary is suggestive of the inner life, and yet Baldwin finds it to be up to the task of illustrating the social tensions of the sixties. For him, the trembling tumultuous adolescent body is a well-suited coordinate for the national body politic. This focus on an intimate portrayal does not belie the deep threats of racism, a point that is especially clear when he describes being frisked as a ten-year-old (!) by two policemen "making comic (and terrifying) speculations concerning my ancestry and probable sexual prowess" (20). But what the focus does is to establish vulnerability as a meaningful framework for thinking about black collective identity. Rather than present himself as an expert or public intellectual, he returns to being a fourteen-year-old boy, confused and yet determined to survive. It is from this narrative subjectivity, this limbo of the interior, that he studies black humanity. No matter how acute his insights are about the evils of white people, he refuses the "pulpit or soapbox" (48) of a nationalist rhetoric. He instead chooses to consider vulnerability.[12]

By the time we get to his meeting with Elijah Muhammad, the aesthetic of intimacy is entrenched. Indeed, his description of the interview starts with a sense of trembling that the reader can appreciate as more than an acknowledgment of the social scope of the moment. Of standing at Muhammad's front door, Baldwin writes,

> I was frightened, because I had, in effect, been summoned into a royal presence. I was frightened for another reason, too. I knew the tension in me between love and power, between pain and rage, and the curious, grinding way I remained extended between those poles—perpetually attempting to choose the better rather than the worse. But this choice was a choice in terms of a personal, a private better (I was, after all, a writer): what was its relevance in terms of a social worse? (60–61)

This moment of fright recalls the young Baldwin described earlier, though the narrator here is explicitly aware of the potential conflict between the private and the political. More important, this self-consciousness confirms that Baldwin's narrator has no interest in a public fight with Elijah

Muhammad; his interest is in exploring the terror he feels and sees. In this regard, the rest of the essay spends more time characterizing the thoughts running through the narrator's head than rendering the exchange with Muhammad. One characteristic passage shows Baldwin's attempt to answer the question about his identity as a Christian. Having said that he left the church twenty years prior, Muhammad asks "And what are you now?" Baldwin writes:

> I was in something of a bind, for I really could not say—could not allow myself to be stampeded into saying—that I was a Christian. "I? Now? Nothing." This was not enough. "I'm a writer. I like doing things alone." I heard myself saying this. Elijah smiled at me. "I don't, anyway," I said, finally, "think about it a great deal."
>
> Elijah said, to his right, "I think he ought to think about it *all* the deal," and with this the table agreed. But there was nothing malicious or condemnatory in it. I had the stifling feeling that *they* knew I belonged to them but knew that I did not know it yet, that I remained unready, and that they were simply waiting, patiently, and with assurance, for me to discover the truth for myself. For where else, after all, could I go? I was black, and therefore, a part of Islam, and would be saved from the holocaust awaiting the white world whether I would or no. My weak, deluded scruples could avail nothing against the iron word of the prophet.
>
> I felt that I was back in my father's house—as, indeed, in a way, I was—and I told Elijah that *I* did not care if white and black people married, and that I had many white friends. I would have no choice, if it came to it, but to perish with them, for (I said to myself, but not to Elijah), "I love a few people and they love me and some of them are white and isn't love more important than color?" (70–71)

Here Baldwin seems to return to the conflicted consciousness of adolescence in that he is determined to assert his position forcefully but is also unsure of his rightness. His authority in the passage is figured on self-questioning and vulnerability.

The description of the meeting continues in this fashion, with long passages where Baldwin retreats to his interior (for example, wondering about the viability of the creation of a black nation in the southern part of the country, or struggling to balance his commitment to love with the enduring evidence of human incapacity to truly love). And what is remarkable is how much Baldwin tells us about his thoughts, and how little we get not only of Elijah Muhammad but of the larger argument about race and religion. The essay reads as a profile of Baldwin and of his subjectivity in formation.

In their use of intimacy, Baldwin's essays in *The Fire Next Time* liberate the discussion of racism from the limited attributes of nationalism: the ideas are not just righteous and assured, and they do not deploy doubleness, masking, or even outright rage; instead they surrender to the full beautiful ambivalence of the inner life. Said another way, Baldwin's consideration of racism refuses to let racism define the nature of his humanity and struggle. His argument doesn't assume a posture of resistance because it is located so intimately and because its idiom is vulnerability. The result is a discussion of black identity that speaks to the volatility of the sixties and the ravages of racism through an aesthetic of interiority. This is the quiet of Baldwin's nationalism, that his investigation exhibits vulnerability, multiplicity, confusion, and intimacy, and generates from the inner life.

Some might consider Baldwin's essays too personal to be representative of collectivity, though it is also true that the intimacy allows Baldwin's narrator to connect his experience with that of others. His use of adolescence, for example, shapes his concern for his peers, who also experienced wild changes in their bodies. Furthermore, it is a sense of closeness that authorizes his tender caution about internalized racism to his nephew and, implicitly, to black readers. In these essays, intimacy is not solipsism but instead is the capacity to feel and to connect.[13]

———

Nationalism is, after all, a search for a name, for an identity that asserts security, something that can be complete and authentic and singularly restorative. The problem is that no name is ever these things, that names always fall short, always feel imprecise or constraining or downright foreign. This is true of individual names, the ones we are given or inherit or choose, and is even more so of names that are collective and social.

The act of naming, in its attempt to mark identity, is an inherently public gesture; in this way, having a name is almost contrary to the notion of interiority. And yet names are part of the reality of the modern world, even more so for black people, whose racial identity is a name that clings to the social body and that represents for its subject. It is this process of naming and representation that nationalism aims to manage, such that the collective racial identity can stand for certain things. So, in the context of thinking about quiet, is it possible for nationalism to give up its desire for a name that is complete, singular, and coherent; is it possible for nationalism to endure a name that is more reflective of the inner life, one that disarrays more than coalesces, one that turns away from the troubles and limits of publicness?[14]

These questions about identity are engaged in Marlon Riggs's documentary *Black Is . . . Black Ain't*. Produced in 1994, the film is a whimsical documentary that explores the vagary of black identity on at least two levels—it is at once a film about Riggs's particular thoughts about his own relationship to race, as well as an exhibit of the impossible, instrinsic contradictions of racial identity. In this way, the film is a search for black identity that sanctions process over product. Essentially, *Black Is . . . Black Ain't* is a nationalist call to arms that is full of urgency and self-determination on one hand, and is centered in the aesthetics of interiority at the same time.[15]

The best example of the film's approach to collectivity is summarized in its preface, the opening two minutes composed of three quick scenes and an introductory comment from Riggs. The first of these three scenes is the image of a naked black figure walking through the woods. The image is out of focus and it is hard to tell, accurately, if the body is young or old, even male or female; what is clear is that the person is dark-skinned and slight of build. Then the figure comes into focus and Riggs's face is visible as he pushes branches out of his path; the only sound we hear is that of his feet crushing leaves, his arms breaking branches. This visual moment transitions to another—this time Riggs is clothed and is standing before a small group of young black people (seven or eight of them). They are in a parking lot of a gas station in what looks like a rural community, since the gas station is really two pumps near a field. The camera circles as he asks if they were told why they are gathered, and then proceeds to say that he is making a documentary for public television. As quick as with the first, this scene gives way to the third, which is harder to describe precisely: the camera moves randomly and jarringly through a hospital, showing the tiled floor, a doctor at a desk, a nurse with Styrofoam cup in hand, the moving wheels of a gurney, the nurses' station, various machines; these images are intercut with images of a clapperboard, a microphone, and a film technician. There are faint sounds from the hospital in the background—a telephone, the echo of a staff person's voice, the din of a page on the PA system—but these are backdrop to Riggs's voice, layered on top of itself, as he alternates talking about the film and his failing health. He states that production on the film has finally begun, that his T-cell count has fallen, as has his weight; he mentions being worried but that he keeps this to himself. He notes that his weight and T-cell count are the same, and at this instance numbers float on screen. He asks "What's happening to my body?" The layering of his voice is something like a chorus, and it mimics the pastiche quality of the images, which are superimposed on each other, translucent and ghostly, articulate and at the same time multiple, even a bit unclear. These images and their wall of whispered sound disorient the viewer.

What's happening to my body? After this question, Riggs's voice comes into single focus, even as his image—shot from chest up, seated—is imposed against the floating of images from the hospital: "AIDS forces you—because of the likelihood that you could die at this moment—AIDS forces you to deal with that and to look around and say, hey, I'm wasting my time if I'm not devoting every moment to thinking about how I can communicate to black people so that we start to look at each other—we start to see each other." During this statement, Riggs's image eventually becomes clear, and then the screen fades to black. A choral chant—"black is, black ain't," repeated in alternating double time—bleeds in, first as background and then, after Riggs is done, in the foreground. On the black screen, as Riggs finishes his aesthetic statement, words appear that claim that Riggs challenged homophobia and racism during his life, and that he died during the production of the film, which was completed in his honor.

This opening preface is a nationalist declaration as Riggs sets out to initiate a conversation with black people about themselves and their experiences—even the urgency made by his poor health is characteristically nationalist. What is amazing, then, about his nationalism is that it is built on the ailing body and artistic will of a gay black man. Riggs, as the narrator and protagonist, becomes the leading and directing voice of the discussion. The film is subtitled "a personal journey through black identity," which is appropriate, since it is Riggs's exposed body that stands in for black collectivity. When he asks what is happening to his body, the question vibrates beyond him to the community of people he is speaking of, to, and with; it becomes an articulation of collective concern. The case being made is that a conversation about blackness can be told this intimately.[16]

That Riggs's body serves as the "document" of black community—that it is his body which carries this documentary, or at least serves as a jumping-off point for a consideration of blackness—is part of the aesthetic of intimacy here. And in true documentary fashion, Riggs the director weaves together excerpts from iconic cultural artifacts, interviews with leading scholars, scenes of dance and recitation of poetry, with the opinions of everyday black people, young and old, all responding to the questions and themes about black identity and culture. He imagines the dialogue broadly, but more impressive is that he is willing to let it wander, that he is able to give up wanting to control this discussion of what constitutes blackness. The very aesthetic of the film, from the opening preface onward, reflects this sense of irresolute complexity. Things are overlaid on each other, opinions are competing and contradictory, few if any answers are given. For sure, Riggs's vision of blackness is feminist and progressive, but beyond this, the film remains open, right down to the title that at once avows and denies blackness. Riggs celebrates the evidence of the ambiguity of blackness, as if this were the defining strength of black people—that we are many, that we are different. And as robust as his presence is as narrator and protagonist, he does not comment on or evaluate the many opinions on the film; the multiplicity stands on its own.

This multiplicity is related to a more profound aspect of Riggs's approach to cultural nationalism—that he centers black vulnerability. Indeed, Riggs seems to take the aesthetic of interiority represented in Baldwin's *Fire* one step further by showcasing his own human frailty, first and most obviously through his illness and his fear as he realizes that he is closer and closer to death. But the vulnerability is more substantial than this—there is Riggs's discussing his struggles with skin color as a child; Barbara Smith and others talking about sexism and homophobia in the black community; a section on the limits of black masculinity and the silence it imposes on black men; and especially the brief exchange with the young boys who yearn for a better life than that of gang violence. Ideologically, the vulnerability is there as Riggs showcases fissures in the black community, as he allows dissonance to exist. This practice goes against the nationalist inclination to represent a unity anchored in pride. Surely there is a sentiment of pride in *Black Is . . . Black Ain't*, but that pride does not come at the expense of showing the range of other sentiments in and about black collectivity.[17] Perhaps the most astute representation of vulnerability is in the attention Riggs gives to his dying body, as if to argue that frailty is relevant to the nationalist project of self-definition and self-determination. Indeed, in centering the conversation about black identity on the body of a gay black man living with and dying from AIDS, Riggs disabuses us of the idea that pride and power are only to be found in familiar idioms of strength.

Riggs's film, then, is a reimagining of nationalism, and his very visible and ailing body reforms the idea of what strength is, or can be, in a collective narrative of black identity. Remember that in the early 1990s when the film was made, the shame around HIV and even homosexuality was still prevalent enough that Riggs could have been co-opted by silence. But not here: Riggs's body is presented without cover, as if to inaugurate a new sense of how to think about black pride.[18]

Black Is . . . Black Ain't is less about offering us a name that will soothe and protect, and more about the unnameable complexity of our lives. For all its power, the film is committed to our capacity to face and embrace what will not hold. This is its quiet, punctuated at the end by a return to the scene of Riggs walking in the woods, a descent into a botanical interior, his naked body still out of focus, profoundly intimate.

To resist shame, to be triumphant, to have a clear and unsullied name: these impulses are a part of the functioning of any nationalism. As such, nationalisms often try to assert a single, definitive identity—this is who we are and what we believe, this is the story of our trial and success, this is our name. But names, to be sure, are often more frail than they pretend.

Riggs's film reflects a trend in contemporary black culture toward expanding the boundaries of blackness and nationalism, a shift most noticeable after the 1960s. No segment of black cultural studies has contributed more to this project than black feminism. One of the more distinctive redefinitions of nationalism is evident in the concept of intersectionality, the idea of social identities as overlapping and multiple forces, rather than discrete and/or hierarchical ones. This claim is exemplified in the Combahee River Collective's "A Black Feminist Statement" (1977),

where intersectionality is used not only to argue that oppressions are inter-
locking but also to suggest that collectivity necessarily implies difference.
The women of the Collective write transparently about their disagreements
with black men and nationalism, white women and feminism, the progressive left and with each other: "we experienced several months of comparative inactivity and internal disagreements which were first conceptualized as
a Lesbian-straight split but which were also the result of class and political
differences" (17). This is the "reality of their politics" and it reflects a sense
that collectivity is impossible under one all-embracing name. This reality
doesn't disarm their activism, but instead energizes it; and what makes
"A Black Feminist Statement" so remarkable as a manifesto is its implicit
argument that a singular conceptualization of race is insufficient to support
a meaningful collectivity.[19]

One of the intellectual legacies of intersectionality—and of black women's
insistence on thinking about gender, class, sexuality, and so on—is that it
has loosened the exclusive grip of race on how one thinks about the subjectivities and experiences of people who are black. Intersectionality has made
it possible, at least metaphorically, for blackness to stand for something
more than or different from its name.[20] The idea here is not to suggest that
there are no meaningful social categories or identities; that is both imprac-
tical and unrealistic. Indeed, as Judith Butler argues in *Undoing Gender*,
"a life for which no categories of recognition exist is not a livable life" (8).
Instead the intent is to find a way to make the name of blackness capacious
enough so that its articulation can hold a wide variety of habits of being.

A superlative example is to be had in Alice Walker's definition of womanism, a bold example of an explicit attempt to define a group identity, in
this case, black feminism. Published as a prefatory note to her 1983 collection *In Search of Our Mothers' Gardens*, the piece entitled "Womanist" has
become iconic in black women's cultural studies. Presented in four parts,
it reads:

WOMANIST

1. From *womanish*. (Opp. of "girlish," i.e. frivolous, irresponsible, not
   serious.) A black feminist or feminist of color. From the black folk
   expression of mothers to female children, "you acting womanish," i.e.,
   like a woman. Usually referring to outrageous, audacious, courageous

or *willful* behavior. Wanting to know more and in greater depth than is considered "good" for one. Interested in grown up doings. Acting grown up. Being grown up. Interchangeable with another black folk expression: "You trying to be grown." Responsible. In charge. *Serious.*

2. *Also:* A woman who loves other women, sexually and/or nonsexually. Appreciates and prefers women's culture, women's emotional flexibility (values tears as natural counterbalance of laughter), and women's strength. Sometimes loves individual men, sexually and/or nonsexually. Committed to survival and wholeness of entire people, male *and* female. Not a separatist, except periodically, for health. Traditionally a universalist, as in: "Mama, why are we brown, pink, and yellow, and our cousins are white, beige and black?" Ans: "Well, you know the colored race is just like a flower garden, with every color flower represented." Traditionally capable, as in: "Mama, I'm walking to Canada and I'm taking you and a bunch of other slaves with me." Reply: "It wouldn't be the first time."

3. Loves music. Loves dance. Loves the moon. *Loves* the Spirit. Loves love and food and roundness. Loves struggle. *Loves* the Folk. Loves herself. *Regardless.*

4. Womanist is to feminist as purple is to lavender. (xi–xii)

What is notable is the way the piece (is it a poem?) mimics the form of a dictionary entry, giving the etymology of the term and examples of usage; it even presents the more standard entry before the more colloquial ones. But the term's multiple entries also work as a kind of devolution that undermines the idea of defining, even as it is trying to articulate what constitutes the habits of being of a womanist. Walker's definition is an anti-definition, at once giving name while trying to forgo the limitations of the processes of naming.[21]

In the first entry, the term is located as clearly and as historically as possible; this is the most definitive of the four. The definitiveness here is in the assertion that a womanist is "a black feminist or feminist of color." This is often the way "womanist" is used, as if this single sentence were the full extent of the idea. But the fact that Walker offers three other entries suggests that the term has layers of complexity, and the definitiveness of the first—with the term and its opposites neatly catalogued—is upended by the second entry, which begins, signally, with the word "also." What is striking about the second entry is the hesitancy of nearly all of the statements, how they remain open and suggest possibility: "A woman who loves other women, sexually *and/or* nonsexually . . . *Sometimes* loves individual men, sexually and/or nonsexually" (emphases added). The repeated use of "and/or" or conditional adverbs like "sometimes" makes the definition fluid, as if being a womanist can be many things, even things that seem contradictory. There is complexity here, and Walker sustains it by proclaiming that a womanist is "committed to the survival and wholeness of entire people, male *and* female," a point of expansiveness that is reinforced as well as complicated by the very next: "Not a separatist, except periodically, for health." The last two statements of the second entry are introduced with the word "traditionally" as if to imply that there is nothing essential about a womanist's ways of being, though some of her commitments have a long history. Again, this is remarkable openness for a definition that is, in effect, a statement of cultural nationalism.

The third entry is the most stunning as the form of the definition gives way to a recitation of affection, of the things the womanist loves. This catalog is a list of desire, a rehearsal of the interior of the womanist that cannot be captured by any definition or statement of collective identity: "Loves music. Loves dance. Loves the moon. *Loves* the Spirit. Loves love and food and roundness. Loves struggle. *Loves* the Folk. Loves herself. *Regardless.*" Reminiscent of Brooks's *Maud Martha* ("What she liked was candy buttons"), these words are a remove from the exterior of what a womanist does or how she acts and thinks, and surrender instead to the meaningfulness of what she loves. And though some of the loves can be read as terms of racial or cultural affiliations (for example, folk and Spirit), this entry is largely about human affections. The womanist is no longer specifically a woman or a black person; she is, instead, a lover of certain human beauties.[22] It is important that the abundant openness of this definition be read in relationship to the previous two, so as to maintain fidelity to a practice of black femaleness that is at the core of Walker's definition. That is, one would not want to isolate the third definition as a way of disregarding race and gender. And still, the fact that this third one abandons the traces of a social identity supports the larger inclination of the definition—to name in a way that motivates and inspires rather than limits. There is something freeing and alive in this rapturous catalog, as if the womanist person is recalling to her-self "Oh yes, these things I love, these things I love."

The last entry, an analogy, seems clear at first—"womanist is to feminist as purple is to lavender"—but is less so the more one thinks about it. Is it race and color that is being invoked, or class? Is womanism a more vibrant shade of feminism, or is womanism the origin of feminism (as purple is to lavender)? Is it a difference of degree—and degree of what? As neat as the analogy seems, it ends up being inconclusive.

Walker's definition is a sublime example of a quiet subjectivity, since it refuses to try to name with precision even as it embraces the agency to be had in articulating one's habit of being. "Womanist" reflects a balance between the cultural nationalist need to define the group, and the quiet subject's will to be quiet. In this regard, womanist is not a name, not in the traditional sense. And yet, the expressiveness of womanist inspires reverie and dreaming, as a name—a free and interior one—can do.

Racial names, be they restorative or pejorative, work as shorthand for the specificity of black humanity. It is this that Riggs and Walker seem to challenge, suggesting instead that there ought to be—that there are—many points of self within nationalism. Not race as a single name, especially one that is figured on publicness, but something more attuned to the whimsy of the interior, fleeting but no less meaningful to one's agency—a name that is quiet.[23] This idea is not unfamiliar to black culture, though it often gets subsumed by the seductiveness of resistance. The final words here should belong to Nikki Giovanni, whose poem "Revolutionary Dreams" is flawless in noticing the radical capacity of the inner life:

> i used to dream militant dreams
> of taking over america
> to show these white folks how it should be done
> i used to dream radical dreams
> of blowing everyone away
> with my perceptive powers of correct analysis
> i even used to think
> id be the one to stop the riot and negotiate the peace
> then i awoke and dug
> that if i dreamed natural dreams

of being a natural woman
doing what a woman does
when shes natural
i would have a revolution (20)

———

The expectations of resistance have shaped how we think of black people,
especially representations of collectivity. This is a part of the limitations of
a discourse of public expressiveness, and it was evident at the inauguration
of Barack Obama as the forty-fourth president of the United States in
January 2009. At the event, Elizabeth Alexander read a slim, occasional
poem titled "Praise Song for the Day," a piece inspired by W. H. Auden and
Gwendolyn Brooks. The poem is masterful on the page but seemed less so
in this moment; indeed, many people felt underwhelmed by her reading,
largely because Alexander is a poet who reads with measured emphasis
rather than dramatic performativity. Perhaps she did not match this
moment when the whole watching audience wanted an expressiveness that
would speak to their excitement, to the historic election of the country's
first black president, to the hope brimming around the corner and the
desperations lingering in the air. Perhaps she did not—or even could
not—match the public expectations of the moment.

But perhaps what happened was that her poem was quiet. The poem
begins with articulations of the everyday, actions unmarked by political
significance—just everyday things: "Someone is stitching a hem,"
"Someone is trying to make music somewhere," "A woman and her
son wait for the bus." The narrator, a keen observer, detects every
interaction or the lack thereof ("Each day we go about our business,/walk-
ing past each other, catching each other's/eyes or not"), and also notices
"each/one of our ancestors on our tongues"—that there is heft and history
in these everyday moments. After these unadorned accounts of the
everyday, the poem moves into three stanzas where the action is more
metaphorical:

We encounter each other in words, words
spiny or smooth, whispered or declaimed,
words to consider, reconsider.

We cross dirt roads and highways that mark
the will of someone and then others, who said
I need to see what's on the other side.

I know there's something better down the road.
We need to find a place where we are safe.
We walk into that which we cannot yet see.

Unlike the straightforwardness of the previous stanzas, these are spoken through a mostly collective voice and describe in broad, metaphorical language—not a mother and child trying to catch a bus, but a people looking for a place to be safe. Which people, and what is the place they seek? Are the musician and the mother and the farmer—all catalogued earlier in the poem—are they the "we" in search of safety? Is this what constitutes their everyday actions?

The next stanza is the volta, a point of shift in the poem, and it was largely unheard on the day of the inauguration—"Say it plain: that many have died for this day./Sing the names of the dead who brought us here,/who laid the train tracks, raised the bridges, // picked the cotton and the lettuce." In a poem that is already written in plain language, the moment of the narrator's self-admonition is striking—say it plain, as if the narrator were chiding herself for not being clearer about the violent human history that is written in the everyday catching of a bus, the making of music, the teaching of young people. This admonition reflects a balance that the narrator is trying to strike between our national history in its expansive, deadly, racist sweep, and the humanity of everyday lives that is linked to this history. Alexander's poem is a praise song to the quiet of living, a praise song that takes account of what is public, but that doesn't equate humanity only to that accounting. At the poem's end, the narrator proclaims that we need a new word to capture the possibility that this historic moment represents, and settles on a simple one: love. Why love? Because love, as a framework for our habits of being, might be capable of encompassing our grievance and our joy, our violence and our human triumph. Love is a conceit that is political *and* intimate. In the midst of love, "anything can be made, any sentence begun," a reference which recalls the teacher earlier in the poem. And what is not noticeable in listening to the poem is clearer in reading it: that the last line, "praise song for walking forward in that light," is widowed, a single-line stanza whereas all the other stanzas were tight tercets. It is as if the other two closing lines that would complete the final tercet have not yet been written. The poem ends in possibility, in honor of the agency of the very people it has been observing.

"Praise Song for the Day" is a consummate quiet achievement, especially in the way it moves from public to intimate, the way its political acuity does not overshadow the breath of the people making signs, watching the sky, sewing—people doing their everyday work of living. And yet the lukewarm response it received suggests that perhaps what listeners wanted from the poem written by a black American poet to commemorate the inauguration of the first black U.S. president was a more dramatic poem, one with more colorful references that reflect the complicated history of black (and non-black) life in this country. These things are, of course, in the poem, tucked underneath its delicate narrating of the everyday. For example, when the narrator starts to "say it plain," she is expressing anger and outrage, naming the legacies of oppression. But perhaps we missed this not only because it is hard to understand a poem in one reading, in one listening, but also because the poem didn't merely engage a discourse of resistance or of public expressiveness—a discourse that would have been more readily embraced because it is so pervasive, so expected. Instead Alexander's praise song honored the interior; it was quiet. The poem was true to its name, praise song, not just a song of shouting and glory, but a song telling the story of many.

Alexander's inaugural reading makes clear how complicated it is to represent collectivity; in fact, her cause was more challenging because she was engaging the collectivity of Americanness as it is shaped by a history and legacy of racism. And the reading stands as an example of why we need a discourse of quiet to contribute to how we see and engage each other, to exist alongside all of the other cultural terms we use to make sense of each other. It is in considering quiet that we realize the power of Alexander's poem, the way it showcases human beings whose everyday acts are not countenanced exclusively by resistance, and how it notices human beings whose living is sovereign.[24]

Being able to see humanity amid the discourses of the social world is where beauty lies. This is certainly the case with the image of Smith and Carlos, which becomes more compelling as we imagine their inner lives. At the end of Gwendolyn Brooks's *Maud Martha*, when the narrator throws her hands up to the shining sun and wonders "What am I to do with all of this life?," the question is animated by the belief that there is something beautiful and worthwhile about life, that despite the war and divorces and other ravages of the world, the narrator is—or is becoming—a being of grace. There is a striking parallel between this sensibility and a passage from Baldwin's *Fire*:

> When I was very young, and was dealing with my buddies in those wine- and urine-stained hallways, something in me wondered, *What will hap- pen to all that beauty?* For black people, though I am aware that some of us, black and white, do not know it yet, are very beautiful. And when I sat at Elijah's table and watched the baby, the women, and the men, and we talked about God's—or Allah's—vengeance, I wondered, when that vengeance was achieved, *What will happen to all that beauty then?* (104–105, italics in original).

Baldwin's meditation is explicit in arguing that the beauty of humanity is threatened by the social and political terms by which we live our lives. And the threat is not just to the beauty but also to the very awareness people have that such beauty is theirs for the taking.

Baldwin's question is ultimately about the limits of the freedom that nationalism imagines; it is as if he wonders—so what happens when we win, or lose? His question tries to expand how we think of freedom, moving it beyond the idea that freedom is to be achieved through a public fight. What about the freedom within? By now it should be clear that the intent here is not to discredit the importance of social struggle, but instead to undo the stranglehold that idioms of resistance have on how we think about black humanity.[25]

To ask about the freedom within is to reimagine the collective such that the inclination to stand up for yourself is no longer limited to responding to the actions of others; instead, standing up for yourself means understand- ing your heart, your ambition, your vulnerabilities—it means engaging and living by these. Standing up for yourself is not oppositional, but abundant. The poet Afaa M. Weaver, in "Masters and Master Works: On Black Male Poetics," suggests as much:

> The choice now for black male poets is to embrace this space where they can ask themselves this question of what constitutes beauty and ask it in

terms of their own lives, and not those lives weighed by the suppositions of group identity. Time has moved on, and if black male poetics is to assume a more manifest place, even as poetry itself is marginalized in exponential leaps in every waking second, then black male poets must explore the beauty of the quality of being human. Assume that humanity and not the task of proving the same. Black male poetics must upend and suspend the idea of race.

There is now no more greatness for a black male poet to assume other than a commitment to reality and the investigation of that reality arising from a deeper self-awareness. Racism is not dead, but we are now in a vortex of confluences, where the black male poet can opt to free himself from freeing the race. The first person he can save is himself, perhaps the only person. Another set of literary choices waits for black poets as a prize, not a predator in the grass, if they can see the current vortex or junction in time as an invitation to be free to be poets and to have a greater freedom as human beings.

The loveliness of Weaver's sentiment is in his attention to the "quality of being human"—which he names as a beauty—as well as his assumption that blackness is already human. As such, he commits to a different relationship with the imperative of freedom, and his argument suggests that the pursuit of this beauty might well be a new kind of nationalist project.

———

It is not clear that quiet can work for what we call nationalism, though it is clear that quiet can be collective—it inspires connection. So perhaps the way to think of it is through the notion of love, that "mightiest word," as Elizabeth Alexander termed it. Baldwin himself describes love as a force of humanity in an extended meditation in the last twenty pages of *Fire*: "Love takes off the masks that we fear we cannot live without and know we cannot live within. I use the word 'love' here not merely in the personal sense but as a state of being, or a state of grace . . . in the tough and universal sense of quest and daring and growth" (95). Not merely personal, love for Baldwin is relevant to our social lives and is an idiom of "quest and daring and growth." This specificity recalls the terms of interiority that have populated both of the essays in *Fire*—fear and terror and vulnerability, what is sensual and embodied, the willingness and capacity to grow, the universality of trembling.

Love is an ethic, a responsibility to and of the self. And in its self-centeredness, it is not apolitical but neither is it driven by the terms set by political or social discourse. There is no responsibility greater than this self-righteousness, this pursuit of right that is motivated by knowing that one does not know, that one is frail and is subject to harm or to being wrong . . . this pursuit that is animated by the terror and beauty of human life. Love demands a descent into the interior, leaves us filled with vulnerability and ambition and rage that rivals anything the social world can produce; it fosters connection without forgoing the particularity of the inner life. Love is the practice and the prize.[26]

CHAPTER 5

The Capacities of Waiting,
the Expressiveness of Prayer

If we go back to the image of Smith and Carlos on the podium in 1968, it is evident that quiet is a call to rethink expressiveness. That is, rather than imagine expressiveness as public and dramatic, the argument for quiet asks about expressiveness that is shaped by the vagaries of the inner life. Such expressiveness is not necessarily articulate—it isn't always publicly legible, and can be random and multiple in ways that makes it hard to codify singularly. And yet reconsidering expressiveness is important, given the high premium that publicness carries in black culture. So, what can a notion of quiet do for how we understand expressiveness? Specifically, what are the qualities that characterize quiet expressiveness?

These questions are related to larger discussions about the nature of language. Modern linguists have argued varyingly about how language works, but it is the study of poetry that most exposes the tension between the literal and figurative aspects of language. The concept of figurative language "has always involved a contrast with the 'proper' meaning of a word, its supposed rightful meaning, the idea which comes directly to mind when the word is used," literary theorist Thomas McLaughlin asserts ("Figurative Language," 81). What McLaughlin is trying to make clear is the balance between the expectation of language as a vehicle for expressing shared notions and the almost inherent multiplicity in the meaning of words. Figurative language is language as an inexact medium, abundant at the same time that it approximates precision; it is language that resembles the wild copiousness of the interior.[1]

These ideas about language are relevant to thinking about expressiveness and black culture. For one, McLaughlin's distinction between proper and figurative meaning makes reference to the fact that communication presupposes a listener, invoking the issue of audience negotiation that is readily apparent in black expressiveness. Furthermore, the acknowledgment of language's figurative capacities is heightened by the particular role that language has played as a tool of black oppression and liberation. As Keith Byerman notes, "language . . . has always been a source of power in black life, and its ramifications continue to be explored in black literature. A recurrent theme is the conflict between those who use words to constrict, objectify, and dehumanize, and those who insist on the ambiguous, ironic, liberating aspects of language" (*Fingering the Jagged Grain*, 6). This historical reality inflects any discussion of what black expressiveness can mean.[2]

It is poetry as a genre that best exploits these conundrums of expressiveness, the gaps and insinuation and juxtaposition that make meaning tenuous and rich. As Aimé Césaire argues, poetic language respects the "knowledge born in the great silence of scientific knowledge" ("Poetry and Knowledge," 134). Césaire is distinguishing between the exactness of scientific thinking, and the truths that poetry can reveal about human life. For him, what is transcendent about poetry is its reliance on a kind of inexpressible expressiveness, its pursuit and celebration of that which cannot fully be revealed (146). Césaire is not alone in this line of argument; the poet Carl Phillips notes that poetry speaks not as "documentation—which is part of the business of prose—but as confirmation—echo—of something essential to being human, flawed, mortal" (*Coin of the Realm*, 161). Phillips is referring to the way that poetry often abandons the sequential logic of prose and surrenders to what is random and excellent. In fact, because poetry does not depend on characters to tell its story, it does not have a reliance on identity as fiction does; poetry can be about a sensation, a moment, a something that is impressive and coherent—or not. In this regard, the aesthetic of poetry is almost intrinsically quiet.

The point here is not to privilege poetry as a genre, but instead to use what we know about the capacities of poetic language as a frame for rethinking expressiveness. One could argue that all language use is figurative in the ways described above, functioning on gaps, elision, accidents, coincidence; the truth of its expression is always partial, though no less significant for its partiality. There is a humanness to the partiality, in fact, a sense that what is true is beyond the limits of our social rules, so the best we can get is a glimpse. This is a notion of language as the domain not of meaning but the stuff of dreams, abundance, and inexactness.[3]

Essential to poetry's expressiveness is form, the particular shape of a poem. Indeed, it is the form of a poem that contributes mightily to its figurative qualities: whereas content can be easy to comprehend—what happens, where it happens and to whom, what is being described—form is often more implicit, and its contributions to meaning are not always clear or definitive. One can see this in thinking about how a line break or an example of alliteration inflects what is being said, or how the overall shape of the poem (is it in predictable stanzas?) influences what we perceive. Even aspects of form that are explicit, for example particular genres such as a sestina or a sonnet, do not contribute to meaning in conclusive or predictable ways. It might seem counterintuitive to suggest that form creates spaciousness since, on the surface, form implies structure; after all, a sonnet is fourteen lines and a sestina ends each line with one of six repeated words. But in reading a poem, structure itself becomes another variable of the process of deciphering.

In black cultural studies, considerations of form are often secondary to those of content. That is, the critical emphasis tends to be on what a work says or means, more than on the impact of its structure or genre or literary features. This prevalence of content is not exclusive to black culture; instead it is a common disposition of everyday readers that results from the fact that asking and understanding "what" is easier than thinking about "how" (the latter requires technical knowledge and language). And still the emphasis on content in black culture is particular to the issue of publicness: Racist discourses expect black art to tell the true story of black life unvarnished by craft, which is also an expectation of nationalism. This reinforces the social imperative of black art and it encourages us to read black cultural works as social documents or as texts of resistance. What is lost here is not only an appreciation of artistic value but also a sense of how form can disturb the assumed precision of content and support a reconsideration of expressiveness.[4]

The impact of form is hard to talk about in the abstract, so let's look at Natasha Trethewey's "Incident," a poem from her Pulitzer prize–winning collection *Native Guard*. "Incident" is a pantoum and therefore it is composed of quatrains that rely on overlapping repetition: the second and fourth lines of a stanza become the first and third of the next, and the final line of the poem repeats the very first. Trethewey's poem reads:

> We tell the story every year—
> how we peered from the windows, shades drawn—
> though nothing really happened,
> the charred grass now green again.
>
> We peered from the windows, shades drawn,
> at the cross trussed like a Christmas tree,
> the charred grass still green. Then
> we darkened our rooms, lit the hurricane lamps,
>
> At the cross trussed like a Christmas tree,
> a few men gathered, white as angels in their gowns.
> We darkened our rooms and lit hurricane lamps.
> the wicks trembling in their fonts of oil.
>
> It seemed the angels had gathered, white men in their gowns.
> When they were done, they left quietly. No one came.
> The wicks trembled all night in their fonts of oil;
> by morning the flames had all dimmed.
>
> When they were done, the men left quietly. No one came.
> Nothing really happened.
> By morning all the flames had dimmed.
> We tell the story every year. (41)

The content of the poem is fairly easy to summarize—it is about the violence of a cross-burning by Klansmen in a family's front yard in the American South—but what is the impact of Trethewey's rendering of this iconic narrative in such a tight form? For one, the story seems to unfurl and has more dimensions and points of understanding than an anecdote about a cross burning might otherwise have. For example, the meaning of the repeated phrase "nothing really happened" is broadened to suggest at least four things: nothing but the cross burning happened, though the family was bracing for much more; or no one—no neighbors or law officials—intervened, that night or in the days after; or, the men were disappointed that family did not agitate in a way that would authorize violence greater than the burning; or that the term "nothing" is an understated assessment made in the safety of being at some relative distance from this moment. It is the repetition and juxtaposition inherent to the pantoum that amplifies the simple idiom "nothing really happened," and which helps to give rounded-ness to a story that could be told with less dimension. Another example of the poem's expansiveness is the way that the men become white via repetition—at first, the whiteness is not clearly identified as their racial identity ("a few men gathered, white as angels in their gowns") but instead is part of the narrator's reading of the symbols of the incident. It is only in the next iteration that the men are white, and the harshness of that name—"white men"—is so much more threatening and definitive than the earlier line. Again, repetition provides greater texture.[5]

Like many poetic forms that rely on strict rules of repetition, the pantoum is highly structured, even awkwardly so; still the form is key to the multiplicity and ambivalence of the story that the poem tells. This is quite an achievement, since cross burnings are so quintessentially fraught with meaning that they can efficiently sum up whole chapters of the public discourse of race in the United States. And yet Trethewey's poem offers a nuanced portrait that has varying levels of horror and concern, as well as a sense of everydayness (it is casually titled "incident"). There is more than one story here, even as the narrator says that "we tell the story every year," and as the poem unfolds, one can imagine the competing stories in the annual telling—some filled with fear and resentment, some with humor, some with bravado and invented bravery, and so on. The humanness of the people who experienced this incident and the fact that it must have involved a range of emotions, not only in the moment it was happening but especially in the recollection from year to year—this humanness is sustained via the form of the poem, the way none of the emotions is expressed definitively or singularly. The poem and the story it tells are haunted, packed full of what is unsettled and unresolved, complicated and multiple. Violence happened for sure, but amid that violence were the ones who experienced it; their experience was and is still, in each telling, magnificent, and it cannot be narrated completely, and hence the poem repeats lines of the story as if to create a narrative that respects the flexibility of expression. This is the achievement of the poem—to use form to tell a story quietly, which is to tell it with the expressive complexity of the inner life.[6]

The language of Trethewey's poem is spare and simple, even as the anecdote extends beyond the boundaries of realism. This is a crucial point, since realism is the de facto aesthetic expectation of black art. Whether from within or outside of black culture, realism is attractive because it emphasizes the real and promises to represent an object or experience in a straightforward and concrete manner. This promise is compatible with the political dimensions of blackness, especially the argument that art has the obligation to challenge racist characterizations. Because of its easy fit with nationalism, realism has accrued a kind of authority in black culture. And though one is hard pressed to argue against the important role that realist depictions have played in documenting black humanity and experience— and the benefit of those depictions to civil rights achievements—the prevalence of realism also reinforces the troubling idea that blackness is singular. Besides, rather than reinforce facile notions of blackness, realism, as an aesthetic concept, should remind us of the constructedness of the real, the fact that a thing is being represented.[7]

The limitations of realism might explain the popularity of surrealism amongst some black artists: Surrealism moves away from a commitment to realistic representation and focuses instead on the unconscious, the marvelous, and the fantastic. The surrealist aesthetic is interested in the magic of unexpected intersections—not a characterization of the social notion of time, for example, but time as it is felt in lived experience, morphing and irregular and sometimes mundane. Surrealism is a language of possibility, a dream language that honors the inexpressible. This language is poetic in its approximation of abundance, feeling, excellence, intensity.[8]

Such an expressiveness is legible in the work of Lorna Simpson. One of the most celebrated contemporary visual artists, Simpson first gained wide attention for her black-and-white photographic series in the late 1980s and early 1990s. These pieces mostly feature black female subjects whose bodies are cropped and whose faces are hidden from the viewer; they highlight repetition as each piece showcases two or more figures in similar postures, dressed in stark, simple clothing (suits or white shifts). Simpson's striking visuals are sometimes accompanied by phrases or sentences, and their overall composition have a documentary quality, as if each subject is being catalogued for study, as if her hair and body and temperament are being diagnosed. In this way, the work evokes a sense of realism and speaks to the larger social narratives about black women (facelessness as marginalization, for example). Yet this realism is complemented, even disturbed, by the surreal ghostliness of the repetition: Each duplicated figure exhibits subtle differences in posture or the fall of her dress, as if the careful viewer is seeing shades of one person's complexity. The subject becomes a body of multiplicity, a being of nuance whose humanity is illegible if one only reads through a social lens. These are magical women who seem timeless and mysterious. Simpson's work doesn't offer an objective truth about black women but instead indulges in whimsy. Indeed, in her odd and beautiful juxtapositions Simpson offers a visual language that unravels our racialized and gendered expectations. As Holland Cotter writes in a review of Simpson's work, "Most of the figures in her pictures . . . [are] . . . generic presences, adaptable to any narrative. The implication is that there are many narratives of race available, all of them conditional and subjective, created by the pressures of personal experience, interpretation and memory." There is no single integrity here—not of body or politic or agency; just the vagary that is more reflective of the wildness of life as it is lived.[9]

One of Simpson's achievements as an artist is the ability of her work to take on matters of gender, race, and violence without disavowing complexity in her visual language. This is evident in looking closely at one of her more iconic works, *Waterbearer.* The composition here is consonant with Simpson's aesthetic—a black woman figure, dressed simply in a shift, whose face is out of view and who is framed by a text that is foreboding and vague—though the piece is different from the others because of its single subject. The expansive capacity of Simpson's language is noticeable in the dissonance between the text and the image, for while the figure evokes strength and vulnerability and dancerly grace, the caption seems to deny this very humanity. Here we have a black woman, holding two water vessels (one plastic, one pewter). Her water-pouring could be an act of labor and subjection, something spiritual and cleansing, something more mundane. Her pose is rife with motion, not just in the tilt of her head or the creases in her dress or the cascade of the water, but also in the engagedness of her

SHE SAW HIM DISAPPEAR BY THE RIVER,
THEY ASKED HER TO TELL WHAT HAPPENED,
ONLY TO DISCOUNT HER MEMORY.

Figure 4. Lorna Simpson, *Waterbearer*, 1986. Gelatin silver print, vinyl lettering. Photograph 45 × 77 (framed), 55 × 77 inches overall. Courtesy of the artist and Salon 94, New York, N.Y.

action, as if we are watching her move. The posture also calls to mind Themis, the Greek titan of justice, or even the emblem of crucifixion. And yet, in all this, this black woman is mysterious to us. We have to ponder who she is, what she is doing and thinking; we are struck by the competing litheness and firmness of her bearing of water, and she seems to float in a timeless nowhere. All of this ambiguity is in contrast to the caption, which speaks to racial and gendered violence in an iconic way: a man missing, a "they" who are questioning, a woman who bears witness and who is discounted. The astute viewer knows this narrative and might be inclined to use it to frame the figure. But even the caption itself is ambivalent, not in terms of the threats it describes, but in the exactness of what it says— Is the man who disappeared black? Is he killed or on the run? What is his relationship to the woman, and who are the inquisitors? Is the woman in the image the same as the woman announced in the text?

There are more questions in the caption than there is clarity, and the questions multiply when you consider the accompanying image; as a result, the overall expressiveness of Simpson's piece work is figurative: It doesn't say any one thing, though it is powerful and articulate. Moreover, it pulls the viewer into imagining the inner life of the subject, for though we are called to notice the racialized and gendered body in a political context, we are also compelled to pay attention to the very human simplicity of the body posed as elegantly as it is. We don't, in fact, know very much about this woman who is turned from us and engaged in pouring water; it is as if Simpson is showcasing her inner world by reminding us of our lack of access to that world. This is an important achievement in the piece because some of its compositional aspects are so dramatic that it could easily be more shrill or categorical. And in this regard, Simpson's *Waterbearer* seems to marvel in an expressiveness that is quiet.[10]

Simpson's use of juxtaposition and sparseness to explode expressiveness is reminiscent of the qualities of Whitfield Lovell's *KIN VII (Scent of Magnolia)*, the frontisiece of this book. As discussed in the introduction, Lovell's piece seems to invite the viewer to imagine a broad inner life for his figure. What sustains this invitation is the spare quality of the composition, and the relationship of the image to the artifact—each placed just so, just next to each other without excessiveness. Lovell's work is pure visual poetry, his drawing enjambed and aligned above the wreath, and meaning left open: Who is that man? What was he thinking then, and what was the taste he liked the most? Was he a poet, a lover of words, or did he prefer the lilt of a soft piano? What to make of these flowers that are part of his profile? These questions are only askable if we forgo a lens of public expressiveness, and instead allow the possibility that he has an interior life that is largely inaccessible to us. Commentators have noted a certain haunting quality in both Simpson's *Waterbearer* and Lovell's work overall, an assessment that makes sense given how their subjects seem so exposed and vulnerable, not just to violence but to life itself. In this regard, they are ghostly in the way that Avery Gordon uses the term—that ghosts are bodies of wild agency that are not fully comprehensible to our social and political language.

The expressiveness of poetic language works on a level beyond what is social or political. One might even say that it is a language that tries to approximate sensation rather than ideology. It can be definitive or dramatic, this language, but it is reflective of the interior and so its sureness is fleeting or at least multiple. This point is hard to describe clearly, though there is an example in Gwendolyn Brooks's *Maud Martha*: part of it is the way the novel approximates a short story whose economy requires that most of the action is left unarticulated. The chapters are anecdote-sized and are catalogs of sensation rather than the full-fledged declaration of belief. The breadth of Maud Martha's interiority happens off the page and is not fully legible to the reader. In this regard, *Maud Martha*'s expressiveness is respectful of a certain ineffability, of the idea that language cannot suffi-ciently represent the interior; in fact, the novel seems to be built on that principle.

There is yet another example at the end of Marita Bonner's "On Being Young, a Woman, and Colored," where the narrator launches into a flour-ish, proclaiming that she and her protagonist are "ready to go wherever God motions." This final section is written more poetically than the rest of the essay—sentences that are short and full of allusions, ellipses, and incomplete thoughts. To make sense of the end of the essay is to engage these juxtapositions, the pieces of thoughts that form a composite rather than a strong declarative statement. Indeed, what is clear at the end of the essay is not so much the specificity of Bonner's arguments, but a strong feeling—the wealth of anxiety and excitement and willfulness of the narra-tor's ambition. This palpable feeling is a proxy for what is not fully said or fully sayable in words; it is the sublime of quiet, an awesome quality of experience that is hard to express clearly. As the narrator gives up clarity and instead surrenders to these wild feelings, it is the surrender that is expressive.[11]

———

Another idiom for thinking about quiet expressiveness is prayer. Concep-tually, prayer is an expression of one's contemplation and dreaming. And yet this expressiveness cannot be articulated completely or precisely; it is figurative and poetic. In this sense, prayer is a type of exceptional commu-nication that is "much richer than speech alone. It is a particular kind of speech that acts, and a peculiar kind of action that speaks to the depths and heights of being" (Zaleski and Zaleski, *Prayer*, 5). The language of prayer is fashioned from a deep level of human understanding that exists beneath or beyond what is conscious. And the very magic of prayer, its will and ability to make something happen, is consonant with ineffability.[12]

Inherent in prayer is the idea of self as audience; that is, the praying subject speaks to a listener who is manifest in his or her imagination. Even in many orthodox or evangelical contexts, the closeness one has to God in a moment of prayer is related to the strength of one's faith. The emphasis in prayer is not so much on the deity who is listening as it is on the subject who is praying and his or her capacity and faithfulness. In this way, prayer reflects the most perfect communication—to speak to one who is and is not one's self. This excellent conversation exposes the praying self as both needy and capable.[13]

An essential aspect to the idiom of prayer is waiting: the praying subject waits with agency, where waiting is not the result of having been acted upon (as in being made to wait), but is itself action. In waiting, there is no clear language or determined outcome; there is simply the practice of contemplation and discernment. This is a challenge to the way we commonly think of waiting, which is passive; it is also a disruption of the calculus of cause and effect which shapes so much of how we understand the social world. Conceptually, prayer makes space, and in this space the praying subject explores the inner life, encounters and tries to give name to desires and vulnerabilities. One waits, waits to see one's own self revealed, to feel the range of sentiments that manifest when one sits and . . . waits. This waiting is tingly and it can momentarily liberate the self from the strictures of its social identity. "Waiting is something full-bodied" and voluptuous, and it is in waiting that the self becomes more capable of its own human bigness.[14]

Waiting has no audience or cause. We often think of waiting as a term in need of a preposition—waiting *for* someone or something, waiting *to* embark or retreat. There are many examples of this in classical literature where seafaring or war-making men, or even just men of adventure, head off and leave behind women, children, and the old to wait for their return. But waiting is not the opposite of adventure and discovery, as Zora Neale Hurston shows in various moments in her novel *Their Eyes Were Watching God*. In a scene discussed earlier, after Jody slaps her for burning dinner, Janie, the novel's protagonist, "stood where he left her for unmeasured time and thought. She stood there until something fell off the shelf inside her. Then she went inside there to see what it was" (67). This is a terrific characterization of waiting as a place of stillness that is also filled with change. In her waiting, Janie finds "that she has a host of thoughts she had never expressed to him, and numerous emotions she had never let Jody know about" (68). Waiting here is active, even renegade; it is surrender. It can be wild and energetic, but it is not urgent; waiting is its own thing, self-indulgent, like falling into water. As it is for Marita Bonner's narrator ("So being a woman you can wait"), there is no waiting "for," no result expected; the act itself is the result, the encounter with one's interior is the achievement.[15]

There is a sublime agency to be found in waiting, a point that is demonstrated in Dionne Brand's poem, "Blues Spiritual for Mammy Prater." Brand's poem is the standout her 1990 collection *No Language Is Neutral*, which was shortlisted for Canada's Governor General Award, and which explores the politics of language through the experiences of various Caribbean women subjects. "Blues Spiritual" is a fifty-one-line description of its title subject, a woman who was born into slavery. No specific date or place is given though we are told, in an epigraph, that Prater was 115 years old when she sat for a photograph. It is this image and gesture that serves as inspiration for Brand's narrator.*

Like Trethewey's "Incident," Brand's "Blues Spiritual" relies on repetition; it consists of three stanzas of almost equal length, each describing the same few details in unadorned language with minimal punctuation and no capitalization. The story the poem tells is not of Prater, but of her waiting to take the photograph. The narrator describes, over and again, Prater's waiting—waiting until technology was capable, waiting through a century of labor and struggle, waiting with what looks like silent patience but which is really something more difficult to pin down precisely. This reiteration of Prater's capacity to wait is complemented by the few details the poem offers about her age, her pose, her marked legs, her black dress, her expressive eyes. Because the details are so few, much of the poem studies her waiting and theorizes what it means.

Brand's piece is a straightforward narrative poem and it reads without effort, but if you could see it, you might notice the way its simplicity belies the dynamism of the narrator—that it is the narrator's meditation on the photograph that is being described in the poem, more than it is anything essential about Mammy Prater. The narrator is determined to read Prater's

*The poem was not available for quotation. The reader may be able to find it online.

life and agency through the image, and to find the story that she, the narrator, needs to hear. To the narrator, the photograph is evidence of Mammy Prater's agency, waiting as an act of willfulness and defiance. The narrator is looking for a forbearer, for inspiration, and Prater's waiting is the perfect legacy to claim. In this way, the photograph is a story of triumph in the narrator's rendering.

And yet, the poem, in its repetitive stanzas, seems incapable of telling us much about Mammy Prater other than the few stark details. Indeed, Prater's life seems to evade capture and what we get is a glimpse of her—a snapshot—while the fullness of her humanity is left inexpressible. This is the genius of Brand's poem—that the narrator gets to use Mammy Prater for her self-indulgent needs, even as the poem itself avoids caricaturing its title subject. The poem cannot tell us what Mammy Prater was thinking on the day of the photograph. Did the act of sitting remind her of anything? Was she tired? Was she hearing her heartbeat? Were there birds overhead, or was the day cloudy—and how did this affect her mood? As the narrator repeatedly engages the few details in the photograph, and muses on the meaning of Prater's waiting, she also confirms what we ought to know already: that it is not possible to sum up 115 years of living—of any kind of living, never mind the kind that Prater was sure to have had—in a poem or novel or in any language. And even when we need definitive stories to inspire us, that need should not override the reality that human life is beyond neat description. What is most important about Mammy Prater cannot be known, and the poem respects the sovereignty of the inner life.

In its wishfulness the poem is the narrator's prayer, full of her desire and vulnerability, her expression of faith and neediness; it is an expression of the narrator's longing.

Brand's poem illustrates at least two different examples of waiting: the first is what the narrator imagines for Prater, that she waited for the right moment to take this photograph. In the narrator's mind, this waiting is robust—it has anger and impatience, is intentional and not, is a mark of strength and despair. But there is a second quality of waiting exhibited by the form of the poem—the way that the repetition of the few details of the poem slowly produces a distinct but incomplete image of Mammy Prater. That is, in reading and re-reading the three stanzas and noticing how they revisit the same scant details, the image of Prater unfolds in slow motion, arriving in pieces and never in full clarity. The poem sets us up to wait for Mammy Prater, to wait for her to reveal herself (or to be revealed). And the waiting is rewarded, though not with a picture of a representative black woman, but instead with the realization that the incompleteness is as it should be; the reward is noticing how beautiful Mammy Prater is because she is left unknowable. There is a respect for what cannot be expressed, even in a poem of such capable expressiveness.

Prayer is dreaming and self-assessment, wild motion rapt with possibility and ache, a self-conversation that is driven by the abundance of imagination. And yet this self-indulgence does not correlate with solitude. In fact, the connective intimacy of prayer is evident in the narrator's effort to study Mammy Prater: "Who were you," she seems to ask, "and how did you live? What can I learn from your living?" And though her questions go unanswered in one sense, the connection she has with Mammy Prater is vibrant, an exchange between the praying subject and her imagined, perfect listener.[16]

This idea that prayer can articulate beyond its own self-indulgence is important to thinking about the bowed heads of Tommie Smith and John Carlos; that is, to read their protest as quiet expressiveness does not disavow their capacity to inspire. In fact, nothing speaks more to their humanity—and against the violence of racism—than the glimpse of their inner lives. The challenge, though, is to understand how their quiet works as a public gesture, without disregarding its interiority. This is always a conundrum because of the ease with which the terms of publicness overdetermine how we read human behavior, though the novelist Colm Toibin provides an instructive example in an essay, "A Gesture Life," on Pope John Paul II. Remembering his experience of a papal mass, Toibin writes:

> The ceremony lasted for hours. He did not once lose the full rapt attention of the crowd. He did nothing dramatic, said nothing new. Before he spoke—and every word he said was translated into many languages on our radios—he remained still. There must have been music. But it was the lights that I remember and the sense that he had no script for this, that it was natural and improvised and also highly theatrical and professional. More than anything, it was unpredictable.

And in that first hour, or maybe half-hour, he did something genuinely astonishing. With a million of us watching, he lifted his hands and cupped them over his face. It was nothing like a gesture of despair; he did not put his head in his hands out of unhappiness. He held his head high and proud so that it could be seen, and he left his hands in place covering it. The crowd watched him, presuming this would last a few moments as he sought some undistracted purity for his prayer or his contemplation. We waited for him to lower his hands, but he did not. He stayed still, the world gazing up at him. *What he did ceased to be a public gesture, but became instead intensely private.* It was like watching somebody sleeping. I do not know how long it lasted. Maybe twenty minutes; maybe half an hour. He was offering the young who had come here in the infant years of Eastern European democracy not a lesson in doctrine or faith or morals but some mysterious example of what a spiritual life might look like. Somehow he managed to put a sort of majesty into it. Even those among us, like myself, who had no faith anymore and a serious argument with the church had to watch him in awe. *He was showing us his own inner life as beautifully simple as well as strange and complex.*

Toibin captures what is sublime in the pope's display, how this gesture that is done in public also retains all of the vulnerability and unpredictability of the interior. There is inspiration in this gesture which serves both the pope (his moment of contemplation, as if seeking a clear inner space from which to pray) and those in attendance, especially Toibin. This is prayer as self-indulgence and connection, and it is also true of Smith and Carlos's expression of protest—not so much the fists and the gloves, but the bowing of the heads. However planned that bowing was, it is also such a human act that it manifests as a sign of their inner lives; it makes the whole thing transcendent in a way that is beyond words. And their capacity to speak to collectivity is not hindered by the interiority of their gesture; in fact, the inspiration of their public display is in seeing its deep human privacy.

This is the expressiveness of quiet.

Conclusion

TO BE ONE

Quiet is the subjectivity of the "one."

The concept of oneness is often used to characterize human essence, the energy of the inner life that constitutes a person's being. This idea is distinct from the notion of the individual, which is a modern classification based on the ideals of liberal humanism—for example democracy, mobility within the public sphere, access to property and human rights; as a term "individual" describes a person in relationship to political and social institutions. And oneness is also different from the idiom "the self," which often reflects subjectivity shaped by the awareness of another. Though all three words can be used synonymously, the concept of oneness is the name given to a person's spirit, that quality of existence which is not constrained by the limits of the social world. Oneness is the human being as a life force.[1]

There is an understandable skepticism in writing about oneness, not only because it is difficult to explain precisely but also because evidence of it is hard to come by. Perhaps the best way to be clear is to emphasize its spiritual quality: oneness signifies the human as a creature of appetites and intensity. In this regard, oneness is the human soul, the abundance of will, hunger, fear that propels each person through the world.

Quiet is the subjectivity of the "one."

Literary theorist Hortense Spillers proclaims that "What is missing in African-American cultural analysis is a concept of the 'one'" (*Black, White, and in Color*, 394). Spillers is right, since the concept of oneness is too messy to fit with our common thinking about blackness. Oneness asserts the right of a human being to be just that—a human being—and this assertion privileges the inner life. And yet the interiority of oneness does not correlate with being immune to or isolated from the social world. In fact, in insisting on the right to be a human being, oneness infers that a person is a citizen of humanity and has license to be of the whole world. This is humanity as abundance and ambivalence.[2]

Oneness, then, constitutes a sense of being capable of and related to everything. This quality of copiousness is evident in Maud Martha's exclamations in Brooks's novel—the way that Maud Martha's desires (candy buttons, books, painted music) are disparate and varied, unrelated to gender or class or race, even as these desires inflect her relationship to those social identities. At the end of the novel, when Maud Martha wonders what to do with all this life, the question is an exemplary expression of abundance: her humanity is everything, and therefore she is, or can be, everything. The abundance of oneness authorizes a kind of radical freedom, as if one's existence is no longer defined by membership in a community or group. One is everything and, in a way, also nothing. This existentialist pairing of abundance and nothingness is characterized by Maud Martha's wondering about the consequence of her life. It is there, too, in Rita Dove's "Daystar," where Beulah covets that moment where she was "nothing,/ pure nothing, in the middle of the day."

This idea of not mattering is of particular relevance, given the deep history of literal and figurative erasure of black people. Mattering, socially and politically, is a grand concern; indeed, the centrality of expressiveness and demonstrativity in black culture is directly related to the seeming inconsequence of black life. It is hard to ignore or diminish this threat—the realities of black history corroborate it too well. But there is also something to be said for rethinking what nothingness can mean to how we think about black identity. An instructive example shows up in Toni Morrison's novel *Sula,* which, though a story primarily about the friendship between two women, opens with an extended scene involving Shadrack, a veteran of the First World War who is battling trauma. In the scene, Shadrack loses consciousness after being caught in enemy fire that leaves many of his fellow soldiers dead; he even watches the spectacle of a decapitated body running despite its headlessness. Regaining consciousness in the infirmary, Shadrack experiences his body—especially his arms—as being beyond his control; he is afraid of the monstrosity of his arms and the independent movements they make. Though still traumatized, Shadrack is released to make room for patients with greater physical injuries and soon gets caught in another moment of panic, which leads to his arrest for "vagrancy and intoxication." In prison, pained by a severe headache and staring blankly at the wall, he is struck by a desire, one that he had earlier when his hands first became monstrous: to see his own face. His hope is that this would help him to remember who he is, though he also wonders if his face would mimic the monstrosity and unreliability of his hands, if in fact his whole body has gone rogue:

> He looked for a mirror; there was none. Finally, keeping his hands carefully behind his back he made his way to the toilet bowl and peeped in. The water was unevenly lit by the sun so he could make nothing out. Returning to his cot he took the blanket and covered his head, rendering the water dark enough to see his reflection. There in the toilet water he saw a grave black face. A black so definite, so unequivocal, it astonished him. He had been harboring a skittish apprehension that he was not real—that he didn't exist at all. But when the blackness greeted him with its indisputable presence, he wanted nothing more. In his joy he took the risk of letting one edge of the blanket drop and glanced at his hands. They were still. Courteously still. (13)

It is stunning that Shadrack finds his reflection in the most modest of reflections—in toilet water. His pursuit of his reflection is a meditation on racial identity: the blackness he sees is "definite" and "unequivocal" and lets him know that despite encounters with the social world that seem to suggest otherwise, he, Shadrack, exists. But Morrison's characterization is notable in the way it proclaims that in the midst of this indisputable blackness, Shadrack wanted "nothing more." The use of the word "nothing" could be read to infer that Shadrack's identity is nothing, as in he wanted more of the nothing that he saw. This nothing is the categorical excellence that calms him, and Morrison's diction nicely conflates abundance with nothingness such that what Shadrack did not see before he used the blanket was the same as what he saw afterward. This claim is supported by the sentence "The water was unevenly lit by the sun so he could make nothing out" if one reads the word "nothing" as a proper noun—that what he saw was named "nothing." The point here is that this pivotal scene is figured on the racial anxiety of not mattering. And as much as Morrison's language permits Shadrack to see his indisputable presence—and isn't indisputable blackness the ambition of cultural nationalism?—it also suggests that this presence is as ephemeral and fleeting and immaterial as the nothing it is supposed to vanquish. This is an astonishing realization of the boundlessness of his humanity, and it helps Shadrack to inhabit a liberated relationship to fear, especially to that one fear all human beings have—the fear of death. Shadrack becomes an emblem of what is means to live an abundant life, and it is from his example that Sula takes her most radical cues.

Nothingness and abundance are relatives, if not synonyms: nothing is, literally and always, something, and in a state of abundance where everything is plentiful, no one thing is ever supremely significant. This congruence is part of the spirituality of oneness.[3] And in the embrace of nothingness there is also a celebration of vulnerability, the unsettling realization of the inconsequence of any one human being in the vastness that is the world. This vulnerability is an essential human doubt, and it fosters agency just as well as does being clear, sure, and indisputable.

Oneness, then, is important to understanding black cultural identity beyond the limits of public expressiveness or a discourse of resistance. Within the concept of oneness, vulnerability is a human condition, not merely a particular form of black violation; vulnerability is ordinary, necessary, not exceptional. Every human being has to encounter humility, has to be able to feel and countenance fear—an inner life depends on having an awareness of what it is to feel small and wreckable and desperate (as well as what it is to feel brave, strong, and capable). Oneness returns the mystery of being human to the black subject, who often seems to be known even before he or she arrives. And it allows a black person to claim frailty as a meaningful part of life. Whatever its fault lines, the idea of oneness is important for considering the inner life, to be able to say, as Michael Harper does, that one's life exists in a "fresh space with no reference other than to its internal oneness" (quoted in Alexander's *Black Interior* 63–64). It may seem fanciful to wish away the exterior world, but what Harper is implying is something else: to return the complexity of the inner life to its rightful place in how we understand black cultural identity. His claim is not against the exterior so much as it is in favor of the interior.

And yet if the idea of oneness is to be meaningful to thinking about black culture, it must be capable of balancing the social and political realities of blackness. It is not possible to dismiss the ways in which the collective experiences of racial blackness, not only as threat or violence but also as joy and creativity, inform the inner life of any person who is black. This balance is expertly handled in Morrison's *Sula*, where the title character's sense of her racial and gender identities feeds rather than hinders her humanity. That is, Sula's capacity to encounter fear and humility as well as to live via the compass of her inner self, is motivated by her understanding of the limits that blackness and femaleness are supposed to represent. Describing the early friendship between Sula and Nel, the narrator notes that because each girl "had discovered years before that they were neither white nor male, and that all freedom and triumph was forbidden to them, they had set about creating something else to be" (52). Both girls invent themselves as the human beings the world will not allow them to be—adventuresome and imaginative, endangered and wild.

Of course, Nel grows up to suppress her wildness in favor of becoming a wife, mother, and regarded member of the black community; Sula, on the other hand, nurtures her heedlessness, leaving and returning to the community at will since she is of it and it of her, though she does not belong to it singularly or exclusively. What animates Sula's abandon is her belief that being black and female is no different from being any other kind of human, and just before she dies, she makes this clear in her last conversation with Nel. The exchange is really an extended argument in which Nel is hoping to extract an apology from Sula for her indiscretion with Nel's husband Jude. Nel is trying to understand Sula through the lens by which she, Nel, has lived her life—she worries, for example, about Sula being alone in the house and dying without the steady company of another. "You need to be with somebody grown," Nel blurts out, which starts a terrific back-and-forth exchange:

"I'd rather be here, Nellie."
"You know you don't have to be proud with me."

"Proud?" Sula's laughter broke through the phlegm. "What you talking about? I like my own dirt, Nellie. I'm not proud. You sure have forgotten me."

"Maybe. Maybe not. But you a woman and you alone." (142)

This is Nel's line of argument—that being a woman, Sula is supposed to be limited by the vulnerabilities and opportunities that women are supposed to have. A few moments later, in her exasperation, she asserts "You can't have it all, Sula," to which Sula replies:

"Why? I can do it all, why can't I have it all?"

"You *can't* do it all. You a woman and a colored woman at that. You can't act like a man. You can't be walking around all independent-like, doing whatever you like, talking what you want, leaving what you don't."

"You repeating yourself."

"How repeating myself?"

"You say I'm a woman and colored. Ain't that the same as being a man?" (142)

Morrison uses the crispness of black vernacular to encapsulate Sula's argument—that being a black woman is, or should be, the same as being a man: it is to be human, and the whole world of possibility and disappointment should be one's right. It is notable that Sula is not merely arrogant in her dying moment—she is also humble and aware of her frailness ("I like my own dirt, Nellie. I'm not proud"), a point which she makes explicit later when she concedes that her manner of living has produced loneliness: "Yes. But my lonely is mine. Now your lonely is somebody else's. Made by somebody else and handed to you" (143). This biting comment is Sula's assessment that she is capable of loneliness and indignity, and it reminds us that she appreciates the ambivalence of living, be it harsh and difficult or wondrous and embracing. She, Sula, is a human being: simply, boldly, humbly that.

This is Sula's oneness, and Morrison's novel does a spectacular job of describing one black woman's struggle to live by the spirit of her inner life, even in a world where social identities mark out careful boundaries and expectations. *Sula* is a novel of interiority, and though the title character's spirituality is often unnoticed in favor of celebrating her audacity and expressiveness, it is a quiet spirituality that makes her so compelling. She is a meditation, a study of humanity; Sula is quiet. It is in this way that she appears as a timeless figure in the novel: Though she dies twenty years before the end of the story, she is always around, a part of the atmosphere. In the moving conclusion of the novel, Nel realizes that what she was mourning was not the lost relationship with her long-gone husband, but the freedom and humanity licensed by her friendship with Sula. Walking past the cemetery on her way home,

> Suddenly Nel stopped. Her eye twitched and burned a little.
> "Sula?" she whispered, gazing at the tops of trees. "Sula?"
> Leaves stirred; mud shifted; there was the smell of overripe green things. A soft ball of fur broke and scattered like dandelion spores in the breeze.
> "All that time, all that time, I thought I was missing Jude." And the loss pressed down on her chest and came up into her throat. "We was girls together," she said as though explaining something. "O Lord, Sula," she cried, "girl, girl, girlgirlgirl."
> It was a fine cry—loud and long—but it had no bottom and it had no top, just circles and circles of sorrow. (174)

Sula is in the air, her presence described as the stirring of leaves and shifting of mud. The language here is omniscient, as if the leaves are moving by the grace of something divine. This organic quality speaks to Sula's oneness, the way that her agency is shaped by the spirituality of being human. In her oneness, Sula is sound and color and the elements, everything and nothing all at once.

———

Oneness is the interior as a place capable of discovery, of wandering, the risk and freedom to be had in being lost in one's self. Recent scholarship has emphasized the importance of migration and movement as a way to expand what racial identities mean. Concepts like postcolonial, diaspora, transnational, and cosmopolitanism have highlighted how movement across national boundaries produces identities that are more fluid and complicated than commonly thought.[4] Still, discussions of these ideas privilege literal movement, the crossing of state borders or some other engagement of social or political institutions; what is often missing is a consideration of the mobility that is part of interiority, the inevitable human capacity to wander without ever taking a step.

Such movement is apparent in Dionne Brand's poem discussed in the previous chapter: In "Blues Spiritual," motion is in the form of the poem, the way the lines unfurl, each offering up another aspect of Mammy Prater. The poem itself is a moving text, as if the narrator's sight is roaming around the photograph from detail to detail, revisiting Prater's age and dress and hands and eyes each time, discerning something new each time. Each stanza is one long sentence, barely punctuated and without capitalization as the words roll into each other until they stop at the stanza's end. Brand's use of enjambment emphasizes this coursing quality as the phrases dangle at the end of a line, disconnected from and yearning for the words around the corner on the next line. But there is also motion in the interior that the narrator imagines for Mammy Prater, whose cool pose represents more than a century of experience and observation. What looks like stillness in the photograph is, in the narrator's contemplation, a whole world of agitation. The poem is alive with movement as the narrator searches inside her imagination to construct the inner life of her photographic subject. And it is the sparseness of Brand's lines that facilitates this movement, as if each detail, revisited over and again, is a bead on a rosary, as if the poem is an incantation. The poem wanders over Mammy Prater, giving up clarity in exchange for the freedom of journeying.

Perhaps wandering is the only movement that the interior permits?

It is a principle of wandering that shapes Ruth Ellen Kocher's 2002 book *When the Moon Knows You're Wandering*. A collection of twenty-eight poems that interrogate the search for home, the book is an inquiry of the haunt and thrill of being lost. Kocher is not yet a major poet in African-American letters, but her consideration of identity is a brilliant exploration of migration and movement. Her poems are full of ships and windows and even Houdini, as well as expert use of line breaks and slant rhymes. *When the Moon Knows You're Wandering* is an investigation of paths that are lost and then found and then lost again, and what it might mean to "abandon the paths of one's past." And what is striking in the collection is how much this journey is interior and spiritual. In the title poem, the speaker seems to catch sight of herself outside late at night. The movement is not that of a person walking, but what she thinks about, the interior wandering inspired by the moon's particular light:

> The shadow slant of your own body
> somehow takes the ground in,
> desperately wanting the surface of grass,
> rock of the familiar in the moon's eye:
> light that blues your midnight form.
> How many years have you been gone?
> And who drove you away—not a man or a stone
> seeming to mark some path you run towards,
> but a wind that rose in the pink depth of your lung
> like first breath, the exaltation of knowing
>
> you are lost. Say your own name backwards to prove
> you exist, an ancient tongue that steels the simple evening air on which
> you rely like Pharoh building the tomb for years.
>
> Know your old age already in youth as if you began
> wrinkled and bent to the earth with old sorrows, cold hands.
> You are not the field of wars that turn the earth over
> and over like a thin coin, the girl suffering
> ebola near a tree while her brother, coughing,
> digs her grave. Go where you will.
> The sun rises there. The water flows.
> Women wake in the middle of the night
> trying to remember their names, their faces.
> The names of their fathers.
> Keep this blue light near your heart,
> the dull thunder of your want
> tracing each step, each pace that seems like direction.
> The moon knows you're wandering,
> even though the road thinks you're home. (37)

The poem opens with hesitation in the way that the word "shadow" delays "slant," and how the adverbs "somehow" and "desperately" seem to procrastinate the thought. There is cautiousness, maybe even fear, as the narrator—speaking via direct address—sees herself. And why not fear when one considers all the terrible histories that are supposed to give the speaker her name? These demurrals change course with the question, "How many years have you been gone?" which brings forth the speaker's realization of her choice—the "first breath" that made being lost more seductive than being familiar and at home. Being lost—and studying this lostness—is who the speaker is, a point that is dramatized by the excellent enjambment that closes the first stanza and opens the second: "the exaltation in knowing // you are lost." The stanza break turns the phrase into a statement, rather than only being the end of sentence: lost is the speaker's clear and perpetual name. The narrator reminds herself that she is not merely the devastation brought by war, colonialism, and patriarchy, but that she has "the dull thunder" of her heart and the blue light of the moon as guideposts. "Go where you will," she urges, knowing that even with this map of confusion, she is wandering; the road might think she is on her way home, but the moon knows better. The poem's action is completely interior, a journey that unfolds as the speaker thinks about who she is, how she got here, and where might she be headed. What contributes further to the movement is the way the narrator speaks to herself in the second person, as if her whispers are a journey from self to self. "Go where you will"; "you are lost," indeed.

It is not that home has no appeal for the speaker in Kocher's poem, but that wandering is a more possible practice. Home, that place of origin which shapes a person's identity, is an essential human condition, but it is also confinement and limitation. This is the dilemma that the speaker is figuring out as she ponders the moon's counsel: not home as a static somewhere but home as a search. In her essay "The Site of Memory," Toni Morrison writes that "all water has a perfect memory and is forever trying to get back to where it was" (77). Morrison's characterization of water is useful to thinking about home and wandering: Here water is a wandering body, and the excellence of its memory is qualified by the word "trying." Water belongs to no one, seems to come from and travel to everywhere; whatever origin water has, it carries with it— rocks and dirt and things that mark where it has been. Water is always in movement, even when it looks still, though its aim is not about progress or destination, just movement, the rush of energy, the exertion of force. Water wanders.

The interiority of quiet is like the wander of water, the freedom in being lost or compassed by vagary. It is almost an exilic condition, this quiet that is the inner life of every human being.[5]

———

It has become comfortable to think of black culture as bold expressiveness that reflects resistance. In this context, blackness serves as an idiom of rebellion and hipness, representing what is cool and edgy, even radical and vulgar. These qualities don't really represent identity but instead are metaphors for larger social ideas about race; they are repositories for our cultural anxieties. Nathan Huggins, in his book, *Harlem Renaissance*, notes exactly this role that blackness plays in American culture: "So essential has been the Negro personality to the white American psyche that black theatrical masks had become, by the twentieth century, a standard way for whites to explore dimensions of themselves that seemed impossible through their own *personae*" (11). Constructions of blackness-as-resistance, then, serve the needs and fantasies of the dominant culture. And yet it is difficult to dismiss resistance entirely, since it is a legitimate framework for understanding some aspects of black experience and has been readily embraced by black people. No, the problem is not resistance or the notion of public expressiveness per se, but the way in which these notions have become the dominant perspectives for thinking about blackness. In fact, the dominance is so commonplace and singular that it is almost unconscious.[6]

Hence this argument for quiet: The quiet subject experiences identity as oneness. He or she is not resistant but is simply one. For the quiet subject, identity is humanity and vice versa: being human is one's first identity, the default for understanding what joy and humility and vulnerability mean. The quiet subject finds agency in the capacity to surrender to his or her inner life. If there is a fearlessness in this surrender it is because of the freedom of falling into what cannot be known entirely, as well as falling into all that one is. This is the idea of oneness as everything and nothing, an excellence that cannot be known completely. Quiet, then, is a call to give up the need to be sure, to give up the willfulness of being a resistant public subject, and to embrace surrender. Such surrender is both conscious and beyond consciousness, and it must be chosen—it is an active state.

The oneness of an inner life does not mean that a person is without connection; indeed intimacy, the exchange and tension and conflict that is
human contact, is part of living an interior life. Contact is essential to the
humanity of oneness: in Marita Bonner's essay, the narrator connects with
her protagonist; in *Maud Martha*, the title character is engaged with her
daughter and husband as well as with many random people; Sula's oneness
links her to Nel and Shadrack, whose own oneness provokes Sula and others in the community. One cannot live without intimacy, without the success and failure of connection—those experiences animate the inner life.
There is no promise that intimacy will work or be sustained, but human
beings need it anyway. In this regard oneness, despite its name, is not a concept of individualism but instead is the spirituality of quiet as an essence of
what it means to be human. And being human ultimately means being
capable of engaging, even needing, others who are human.[7]

Quiet and interiority are not exclusive to black women's culture, though
many of the examples in this book come from work by black women. It is
the case that black women, and women of color in general, have thought
through the challenges of identity politics and have articulated ideas (like
intersectionality) that reflect how complicated it is to codify human experience in social terms. Moreover, historically, the concept of interiority
has been constructed as the domain of women, and as a result, it is often
women's culture that has labored to make the terms of inner life (domesticity, privacy, vulnerability) meaningful rather than pejorative. This is true
for black women artists who have exhibited a deep value for interiority,
even as they were often excluded from the discourses of white femininity
that inform many notions of the interior.[8]

None of this is to suggest that interiority, and by extension, quiet, is a
black female idiom. That is, though it is important to honor the ways that
ideas from black women's culture inform this concept of quiet, the meaningfulness of quiet is not exclusive. There are, in fact, many other examples
and dimensions of quiet that are not explored in this book but that warrant
brief and incomplete mention here.[9]

- Randall Kenan's beautiful collection *Let the Dead Bury Their Dead*,
  which uses the short story form to imbue his subject with pauses and

gaps—sly, soft, tense moments; brief pregnant exchanges. These affect
the characterization of blackness in the novel, blackness which is
essential and present and thriving and threatened, and yet which
is not preordained or uncomplicated.

- Much of Jay Wright's poetry, which covers such interesting black
  interiors. In fact, Wright begins most of his readings with this phrase,
  "Now I speak with reluctance," which seems like an acknowledgment
  of the dangers of publicness.
- Cornelius Eady's *You Never Miss Your Water*, a heartbreaking collection
  of twenty-one poems about the death of his father. This book is
  exceptional for the way the narrator's observation is so interior, for the
  management of the prose line and characterization of a voice that
  roams and wanders and aches. (This work could be a relative of
  Brooks's *Maud Martha*.)
- The film *Monster's Ball*, which ends with two characters—one white
  and male, one black and female—sitting, silent, in thought, the bigness
  of race and gender their private territory to encounter. Many critics
  have concerns with the film, especially the portrayal of Halle Berry's
  character, but the film could also be read as a meditation on the interior
  dimensions of race and racism.

The examples are not limited to particular artifacts.

- Recipes, as cultural narratives, are arguably quiet. Literally, a recipe is a
  set of instructions for making something. It tells a culinary history of a
  people and, for marginalized populations, a recipe can be an essential
  cultural practice. Yet recipes are flexible enough to endure change. In
  fact, all recipes, even ones that are proclaimed to be authentic, are
  subject to the whim and desire of the person doing the making. In this
  way, the essence of recipes is not only their capacity to regulate
  authenticity but also their variation, the richness of difference they
  inspire.[10]
- The example of music, especially jazz, is mentioned earlier but bears
  repeating: Music is a quiet expressiveness in the way that its meaning
  depends on making sense of the notes that are played and the gaps in
  between.

And then there are other examples by black women artists.

- The film *Daughters of the Dust*, which director Julie Dash considered producing as a silent film as a way to deal with the challenges of representation.
- Pat Parker's poem "For the White Person Who Wants to Know How to Be My Friend," which celebrates the broad humanity of blackness with humor and irony, cataloging some popular stereotypes but refusing them as a shorthand for understanding any particular black person. The poem asserts that black humanity is variable, and that in the work of coming to know any black person, it is as insufficient to consider only racial identity as it is to ignore that identity.
- Jamaica Kincaid's *A Small Place*, a stunning essay about colonialism and tourism. Like James Baldwin in *The Fire Next Time*, Kincaid's narrator uses vulnerability as a trope of investigation. Rather than polemic, the rage here is interior and beautiful, and what Kincaid is able to notice about the dynamics of humanity is all the greater for it.
- Meshell Ndegéocello's album *Bitter*, an exemplary study of the ravages and agency of vulnerability.
- Nikky Finney's *Head Off & Split*, which takes its cue from the title act of beheading and gutting a fish, the inside parts discarded. In these twenty-seven poems, Finney's speaker ventures to keep all the parts, including the nasty belly of the thing, so as to be able to consider what is foul and inconvenient and spiny alongside what is juicy and delicious. These poems explore the experience of being ravishing and being ravished, consumed in the fire of life's awe—and the exploration is a remarkable marriage of the political and the intimate.
- That magnificent work, *Thomas and Beulah*. What Rita Dove manages to do is tell a story of the black twentieth century through the lives of one black man and one black woman, without forgoing their humanity in favor of the needs of the larger story. Indeed, Dove's expertise gives both Thomas and Beulah their own fullness, not the expected sentimental story of two black people whose love for each other bolsters them against the violence of their era, but two human beings who marry but whose interiors are wildly their own.
- And then there is Toni Morrison's *Beloved*, perhaps the most epic novel of black American life, which is conceptually interior, focusing "on an

astonishing act of violence committed not *upon* but *by* a slave woman" (Rody, "Toni Morrison's *Beloved*," 93). Of course the novel addresses the horrors done to Sethe and other enslaved peoples, but its greatest attention is to Sethe's interior—and her humanity. It is in this way that Morrison's work is a revelation.

And there are many other works that can be read using the framework of quiet, and that in their reading can help expand our understanding of what quiet can mean to how we think about black culture.

———

There is not much else that can be said about blackness as a public discourse. Indeed, nearly all of what has been written about blackness assumes that black culture is, or should be, identified by a resistant expressiveness—a response to racial oppression, a speaking back to the dominant ideology, a correction of the willful errors of racist history. What else, then, can be said of race as a public discourse? Perhaps nothing; perhaps what is left is to explore other ways of thinking about black culture, not ones that ignore racism or aim to supplant the importance of a discourse of resistance, but ones that help expand how we read what black culture means. The representation of black subjectivity as resistant has become a convenient simplification of what is surely more complicated; it is an easy template that does not encourage deeper, closer interrogation of cultural texts and moments. Our understanding of black culture becomes flat, and our sense of what characterizes black representation appears as a list of familiar terms—expressiveness, resistance, colorful, loud, dramatic, doubled. What would it mean to consider black cultural identity through some other perspective, like quiet, like interiority? Indeed what makes a concept of quiet so important to thinking about black culture is that by and large, quiet is antithetical to how black culture is engaged.

Quiet: conceptually, quiet is the capacity and quality of the interior, of the inner life. In this regard, quiet is inevitable, it is essential to humanity. Quiet is not tethered to what it is public; it is not the performance of a social identity. It is a manner of being that is deep within us, a being that is not always exactly quiet—it can be raging and wild, is a place of desire and anxiety; it holds all that is. Quiet is hard to write about, as the inner life is hard to describe, but it exists and it is a meaningful idiom for understanding other qualities of black culture.

Quiet is the subjectivity that permits the vagary of humanity and that pushes against social identity and its narrow corners. Quiet is desire, and vulnerability; it is disarray, the willingness to give up the seduction of saying your name clearly and singularly, as a stay against the world. Quiet is related to the names you call yourself, the ones that cannot be spelled or fully pronounced.

Quiet is uncertain and it is sure; trembling and arrogant. Quiet is faith in that it can embrace what there is little evidence of. Quiet can exist without horizon, and it has no consecutive. Quiet is like the moon, rarely showing its full wondrous sphere and instead offering slivers of its potent, tide-shifting self.

Quiet is to feel deeply and to feel what is deep. It is the space of interrogation, of being able to ask and ponder beyond what might be appropriate. A practice of knowing that is incomplete.

Quiet is the expressiveness of another language, is sublime. Unspeakable but still expressive. Even attempts throughout this book to describe quiet likely fall short, and yet quiet exists: it is there in Maud Martha's abundance of loves, the things she notices; it is in Nel's cry at the end of *Sula*: "Oh Lord, Sula . . . girl, girl, girlgirlgirl." What else is that but the interior, an experience so exquisite that it is beyond our social idioms. "Oh Lord, Sula . . . girl, girl, girlgirlgirl." Sublime.

Quiet is voluntary—it has to be chosen, it is a surrender. It is unconscious too, but it has to be chosen. It can be terror, and joy.

Quiet is Tommie Smith and John Carlos, whose stance on a podium in Mexico City in 1968 is not just an emblem of protest but is also humanity. It is not only the performativity of their act that should be moving, but the inner life—the gorgeous vulnerability—that we can glimpse. Their presence is not perfect, but it is excellent because it hints at the miracle of being alive. Oh my goodness, such beauty.

The human heart does not only resist; its beat is insistent, lurching, pulsing, but its agency is not only resistance.

———

Quiet is the syntax of possibility, the capacity of the inner life. It is the unappreciated grace of every person who is black. Quiet is inevitable, one's fullorbed life.[11] Quiet is.

Acknowledgments

This book is inspired by and dedicated to the many black women and black feminist scholars and artists, especially from the 1980s and 1990s, whose thinking has changed my own. Many of them are named in the preceding pages, and I'd like to add one more: Monique Savage.

I thank Whitfield Lovell and Lorna Simpson for their work and generosity, and Elizabeth Alexander for her very early encouragement. I am grateful to the many lovely colleagues and friends who have read and nurtured the ideas here, including Paula Giddings, Vicky Spelman, Dennis Miehls, Liz Pryor, Claudia Nogueira, Jim Hicks, Sarah Leslie, L. H. Stallings, Don Wilson, and Ann Ferguson. That gratitude also extends to colleagues I met years ago in Sarajevo, especially Ksenija Kondali, Sanja Sostaric, and Mehmet Can. I also thank Nikky Finney and Rita Dove for the gift of their attention.

The Provost's Office and the Committee on Faculty Compensation and Development at Smith College have provided me with extraordinary research support for the writing of this book. I am also thankful to my colleagues in the department of Afro-American Studies and the program for the Study of Women and Gender. I have been fortunate to have the research assistance of a stellar group of students—Kathleen Daly, Hillary Knight, Caroline Rex-Waller, Geraldine Richards, and Chelseá Williams—as well as the keen attention of students in my classes.

I am thankful to Katie Keeran, the editor for this work, for her wisdom but also her patience; that thanks extends to all the other good folks at Rutgers University Press and the two anonymous readers. Margaret Case's astute reading nudged the writing to greater clarity and helped me avoid some awful errors. Parts of the introduction and chapter one have been published previously in two different forms: "The Trouble with Publicness: Toward a Theory of Black Quiet," in *African American Review* 42, nos. 2–3 (Summer/Fall 2009): 329–343, and "More Than You Know: The Quiet Art of Whitfield Lovell," in *The Massachusetts Review* 52, no. 1 (2011): 57–63. I am grateful to the editors in each case for permission to reprint here.

I thank my parents, three sisters and their families. And I thank my "friends in the spirit," including Adrianne Andrews, Peter Sapira, David Osepowicz, Dawn Fulton, Suzanne Gottschang, Alan Dayno, Gerold Ebner, Liz Hanssen, Jayne Mercier, Gary Lehring, Daphne Lamothe, Darcy Buerkle, Benita Barnes, Jennifer Randall, Paul Amador, and Rene Heavlow.

Always, I think of my mother's mother, Esther Pemberton, whose hand is all over my every shape. And finally, my heart thanks Peter Riedel, who is and who lets me be quiet.

Permissions

STRANGE FRUIT, words and music by Lewis Allan. Used by permission of Edward B. Marks Music Company. Copyright © 1939 (Renewed) by Music Sales Corporation (ASCAP). All Rights for the United States controlled by Music Sales Corporation (ASCAP). International Copyright secured. All rights reserved. Reprinted by permission.

"Womanist" from *In Search of Our Mothers' Gardens: Womanist Prose*, copyright ©1983, reprinted by permission of Houghton Mifflin Harcourt Publishing Company. Reprinted by permission of The Wendy Weil Agency, Inc. ©1983 by Alice Walker.

Elizabeth Alexander, excerpt from "Praise Song for the Day" from *Crave Radiance: New and Selected Poems 1990–2010*. Copyright © 2009 by Elizabeth Alexander. Reprinted with the permission of The Permissions Company, Inc. on behalf of Graywolf Press, Minneapolis, Minnesota, www.graywolfpress.org.

"Daystar" from *Thomas and Beulah: Poems*, Carnegie Mellon University Press, Pittsburgh, PA © 1986 by Rita Dove. Reprinted by permission of the author.

"Revolutionary Dreams" from *Re:creation* © Nikki Giovanni 1968. Reprinted by permission of the author. From *The Collected Poetry of Nikki Giovanni: 1968–1998* by Nikki Giovanni. Copyright compilation © 2003 by Nikki Giovanni. Chronology and notes copyright © by Virginia C. Fowler. Reprinted by permission of HarperCollins Publishers.

"The Second Sermon on the Warpland" from *In the Mecca* by Gwendolyn Brooks. Reprinted by consent of Brooks Permissions.

Notes

INTRODUCTION

1. The bowed heads were probably in part an attempt to look away from the American flag, similar to Vera Caslavska's own silent gesture of turning her head slightly to the right and slightly down during two medal ceremonies, in protest of the Soviet Union's invasion of her country, Czechoslovakia.

2. The image is engaged most commonly as a piece of "social movement photography," in the way that Leigh Raiford uses the term; see especially pages 225–226 of "Restaging Revolution." For an excellent discussion of Smith and Carlos, see Amy Bass's *Not the Triumph but the Struggle: The 1968 Olympics and the Making of the Black Athlete.* Notably, in Smith's autobiography, *Silent Gesture,* he briefly talks about a range of thoughts while in the blocks at the start of the race (22); he also repeatedly describes himself as a quiet person, especially in regard to Carlos's more exuberant personality.

3. In this regard, Walter Johnson's thoughtful essay "On Agency" is instructive in the way it cautions social historians against the pitfalls of the concept of resistance. I thank Elizabeth Pryor for alerting me to Johnson's work.

4. There is such a rich body of work here that it is almost impossible to cite completely. Some recent useful references in terms of studies of the limits of blackness include Reid-Pharr's *Once You Go Black,* Gilroy's *Against Race,* Holt's *The Problem of Race in the Twenty-first Century,* Wright's *Becoming Black,* the introduction of Jarrett's *African American Literature beyond Race,* Warren's survey of the historical discussion of activism and black intellectualism in "The End(s) of African American Studies," Brown's *Writing the Black Revolutionary Diva,* Carby's *Race Men,* Ellis's "The New Black Aesthetic," and Golden's notion of post-black in *Freestyle.* The point about the specific contributions of black women studies is addressed in chapters 2, 4, and 6, though one could call up the names of Susan Willis, Hortense Spillers, Kimberlé Crenshaw, Cheryl Wall, bell hooks, Trinh T. Minh-ha, Barbara Smith, Ann DuCille, Farah Jasmine Griffin, Mary Helen Washington, Barbara Christian, Patricia Hill Collins, Mae Henderson, Nellie McKay, Claudia Tate, and

Gloria Hull as a start. The list of black artists would be even longer, though it is important to notice Ralph Ellison's excellent and still relevant "The World and the Jug" (which makes the interesting claim that the black novel is always "a public gesture, though not necessarily a political one") and James Baldwin's "Everybody's Protest Novel" (where he describes black culture as being imagined as a "counter-thrust" to the "thrust" of dominant culture); particular references to other artists can be found in the body and notes of the pages ahead. Finally, there have also been works by more conservative writers, like John McWorther. What makes his arguments distinct from the one above is that McWorther implies that racism and a discourse of resistance is no longer relevant; the argument in quiet is to ask what other capacities, besides resistance, inform black culture—a very different question.

CHAPTER 1 — PUBLICNESS, SILENCE, AND
THE SOVEREIGNTY OF THE INTERIOR

1. This claim about the relationship between publicness and black culture is based on reading publicness through Jürgen Habermas's notion of the public sphere, articulated in his classic *The Structural Transformation of the Public Sphere*, as well as Michael Warner's and Nancy Fraser's engagement of Habermas in Craig Calhoun's edited volume, *Habermas and the Public Sphere*. For a fuller explication of this claim, see my essay "The Trouble with Publicness: Toward a Theory of Black Quiet." Also see Houston Baker's essay "Critical Memory and the Black Public Sphere," which argues that black culture is "drawn to the possibilities of structurally and affectively transforming the founding notion of the bourgeois public sphere into an expressive and empowering self-fashioning" (13). Baker goes on to suggest that black culture situates its "unique forms of expressive publicity in . . . relationship . . . to the sense of publicity itself as authority" (13–14).

2. Du Bois's use of double consciousness is cited often, but it is Ernest Allen, Jr.'s "Du Boisian Double Consciousness: The Unsustainable Argument" that takes a broad historical look at the term. In this work, Allen makes an excellent and well-researched argument that the term is not crucial to Du Bois's ideas; indeed, Allen argues convincingly that the specific notion of a black double consciousness was generated from critical misinterpretation of Du Bois's first chapter of *Souls*. As good as Allen's argument is, it misses the ways that a notion of double consciousness is engaged in the opening passages of the chapter—how those opening passages expound on Du Bois's definition of the term. Further, that so many scholars have found the term to be useful in describing black experience is reflective of the general power of doubleness as a characteristic of racial blackness; it matters less if they extrapolate more from Du Bois's chapter than he himself might have intended. For examples of the lasting significance of the idiom of doubleness in Du Boisan scholarship, see Dolan Hubbard's introduction to *The Souls of Black Folk: One Hundred Years Later* (especially pages 5–7 and 12–13) as well as essays in that collection by Keith Byerman, Amy Kirschke, Shanette Harris, Carolyn Calloway-Thomas, and Thurmon Garner. Also see work by Paul Mocombe (*The Soul-less Souls of Black Folk*) and especially Dickson Bruce, Jr. ("W.E.B. Du Bois and the Idea of Double

Consciousness") and Bernard Bell ("Genealogical Shifts in Du Bois' Discourse on Double Consciousness") that trace the evolution of the concept in Du Bois's work. For a more general engagement, see Gerald Early's *Lure and Loathing*. Finally, for an extended and excellent consideration of the limits of Du Boisian double consciousness in relationship to works by black women, see Kimberly Nichele Brown's *Writing the Black Revolutionary Diva*, especially chapter 1.

3. It is important to keep in mind that *The Souls of Black Folk* is one of the early examples of black public intellectualism, perhaps along with Booker T. Washington's *Up from Slavery* and Anna Julia Cooper's *A Voice from the South*. Unlike Washington's immensely popular work, Du Bois's collection, though often narrated in the first person, abandons the aesthetic of memoir in favor of an interdisciplinary mix of history, sociology, and literature. This approach, similar to Cooper's, is not accidental: for one thing, it mirrors his Atlanta University Studies from a few years earlier. More important, it works against the expectation that the story of black people be told through autobiography. *Souls* is a decidedly scholarly version of the story of black experience. As Henry Louis Gates, Jr., and Terri Oliver suggest in the introduction to the Norton edition of *Souls*, the book emerges as a result of the battle for public visibility between Du Bois and Washington. This argument is given full life in Hazel Carby's excellent chapter "The Souls of Black Men" in *Race Men*, and is corroborated by Dolan Hubbard in the introduction to *The Souls of Black Folk: One Hundred Years Later*. For further consideration of the public dimensions of Du Bois's book, see Robert Stepto's *From Behind the Veil*, which characterizes the composition of *Souls* as Du Bois's attempt to gain "greater authorial control of what is, in effect, not simply a single volume but a major portion of his canon up to that time" (53). Stepto also describes *Souls* as a quest narrative of racial self authentication, as Du Bois writing a "generic narrative" that positively represents the race's doubled self-conscience (pages 53–54, 61–66). Also see Nellie McKay's "The Souls of Black Women Folk in the Writings of W.E.B. Du Bois," which addresses the binary of public-private.

4. In addition to Hine's "Rape and the Inner Lives of Black Women in the Middle West," see Evelyn Higginbotham's notion of a "politics of respectability" in *Righteous Discontent*. Also see Tricia Rose's *Longing to Tell* and Evelynn Hammonds's "Black (W)holes and the Geometry of Black Female Sexuality"; both address the way a discourse of Victorian femininity mixes with racism to produce a code for black female behavior.

5. Hine notes a similar irony in her essay; see page 916. There is a long intellectual history that explores the implications of disguise, ruse, and doubleness in black culture, or marginalized cultures in general. The most thorough consideration is in James C. Scott's argument for a hidden transcript and for the idea of infrapolitics in *Domination and the Arts of Resistance: Hidden Transcripts*. Scott does well to give attention to the potent "discourse that takes place 'offstage,' beyond direct observation of power holdings" (4), exploring the articulate ways in which ruse and disguise can affect the public, official realm. This interest in the role of doubleness in black culture is also at the center of works as varied as Henry Louis Gates's *The Signifying Monkey*, Houston Baker's *Blues, Ideology and Afro-American Literature*,

John L. Gwaltney's *Drylongso*, and Robin Kelley's *Yo Mama's Disfunktional*. Although each of these texts acknowledges ideas that seem similar to quiet (Scott even has a section on quiescence), their arguments ultimately emphasize and privilege what is public.

6. These concerns about the mask could also be raised of the notion of invisibility; see Todd Lieber's "Ralph Ellison and the Metaphor of Invisibility in Black Literary Tradition," which links the two idioms. For a general discussion of masks, see Adam Lively's *Masks: Blackness, Race and the Imagination*. Though he does not cite Dunbar's poem, Lively explores the mask as a way to understand how race functions, including how it serves as a meaningful concept of white engagement of racial blackness. In relationship to black culture, Lively argues that the mask is a trope for "attacking and subverting white values. In the face of white surveillance, blacks' principal weapon in this cultural war was humour, and the indirection allowed by disguise or mask" (5). He goes on to say that "for a whole series of twentieth-century writers, blackness has been expressive of the sense that one must wear a mask before the world" (283). For a specific engagement of the mask in Dunbar's work, see John Keeling's "Paul Dunbar and the Mask of Dialect" and Daniel P. Black's "Literary Subterfuge: Early African American Writing and the Trope of the Mask." Also see Rafia Zafar's *We Wear the Mask: African Americans Write American Literature, 1760–1870*, where the concept is linked to issues of mimicry and invisibility for the early black writer, though not specifically to Dunbar's poem.

There is a larger conversation here about performance and publicness. For further study, see Michael Warner's argument about the performative expectation that is a part of engaging the public sphere in "The Mass Public and the Mass Subject"; Nancy Fraser, who writes in "Rethinking the Public Sphere" that "participation [in the public sphere] means being able to speak in one's own voice, and thereby simultaneously to construct and express one's cultural identity through idiom and style" (126); Houston Baker, who argues in "Critical Memory and the Black Public Sphere" that blackness is often negotiated through the performative; and Monica Miller's discussion of performance, publicness, and black representation in *Slaves to Fashion: Black Dandyism and the Styling of Black Diasporic Identity*.

7. Signifying is largely studied as a verbal practice, even though its rhetorical implications extend to literary examples. For a consideration of signifying, see Geneva Smitherman's *Talkin That Talk: Language, Culture and Education in African America*, especially pages 26, 138, 220, and 255. Smitherman repeatedly explains that signifying is based on indirection and subtlety as much as it is on public expressiveness (indeed, she makes a distinction between the performativity of the verbal sparring of "the dozens" and the more general indirection of signifying). Also see Robin Kelley's discussion of the public dimensions of signifying in "Looking for the Real Nigga" in *Yo Mama's Disfunktional*.

8. The secondary scholarship on this novel is prolific, especially on the topic of silence and voice. Specifically, many scholars have noted the use of free indirect discourse in relation to interiority; see, for example, Barbara Johnson's classic "Metaphor, Metonymy and Voice in *Their Eyes Were Watching God*," her essay with Henry Louis Gates, Jr., entitled "A Black and Idiomatic Free Indirect Discourse," and Carla Kaplan's

The Erotics of Talk. Of particular note is Maria Racine's "Voice and Interiority in Zora Neale Hurston's *Their Eyes Were Watching God*," which reads Janie's coming to voice as a process that includes this public moment with Jody. Racine's essay is notable because it does not overprivilege the publicity of this scene.

9. The case could be made that black expressiveness, rather than being a function of the public sphere, is an African cultural retention. But even these examples of expressiveness, as discussed in work by John Michael Vlach and Robert Farris Thompson, for example, read expressiveness for its public capacities, for its resistance to white cultural dominance and as a tonic against obscurity (Vlach, *By the Work of Their Hands*, 19). The case that public expressiveness is a feature of black culture has been made in various studies, including Geneva Gay and Willie Baber's *Expressively Black*, Shane White and Graham White's *Stylin'*, Monique Guillory and Richard Green's *Soul*, even Gina Dent's *Black Popular Culture*, and is also evident in the many declarations of black aesthetics from the Harlem Renaissance or from the black arts/black aesthetic movements.

10. The use of "quiet" here is not intended to resonate with the term "quietism" as used in philosophy or in theology.

11. The "interior" is a complicated term because it is used varyingly by different disciplines (for example, philosophy, psychology, psychoanalysis). Most relevant might be the uses of interiority as a term of Victorian notions of domesticity and the private sphere. Here, the interior is gendered female and is private, which also means it is politically irrelevant, whereas the exterior is male, public, and politically relevant. For example, Tamar Katz, in *Impressionist Subjects*, argues that femininity and domesticity are the ideological twins of interiority (see especially pages 4–7, though the entire book is an excellent consideration of the gender politics of the public sphere and the idioms of domesticity). But this easy conflation of the interior with a binary of public/private or male/female is dangerous, because it elides some of the complicated realities of Victorian domesticity. Nancy Armstrong, in *Desire and Domestic Fiction*, rightly suggests that interiority figures as both masculine and feminine; that is, as the idea of subjectivity becomes a valued idiom in modernity, the characteristics of interiority and domesticity—introspection, thoughtfulness, emotional competence—become applicable to men also. And yet Armstrong is clear to note that, despite this elasticity, the politics of gender leave women's interiority as a less political trait—confined to the domestic or private sphere. It is this collapsing of the interior with the private that makes interiority a disfavored concept, at least politically. See especially Lauren Berlant's *The Queen of America Goes to Washington City* on the dangers of privacy; Seyla Benhabib's "Models of Public Space," which asserts that "whereas questions of justice were from the beginning restricted to the public sphere ... the private sphere was considered outside the realm of justice" (92); and Angela Davis's "The Legacy of Slavery: Standards for a New Womanhood" for a discussion of this binary in regard to black female identity.

The use of interiority in this book is intended to reflect a mode of subjectivity that is not synonymous with the idea of an intimate or domestic or private sphere; in this regard, this use of the interior earns from Elizabeth Grosz's *Volatile*

Bodies and "Refiguring Lesbian Desire," as well as Galen Johnson's "Inside and Outside: Ontological Considerations" and Dorothea Olkowski's "The Continuum of Interiority and Exteriority in the Thought of Merleau-Ponty" (especially page 2). Johnson's essay is especially useful not only because it argues against the "philosophical privilege" of the exterior, but for this passage defining the interior: "There is an inner life. It is the life of thought, the life of the heart, the life of dream and memory. These are interiors that encounter lines of exterior force that shape, fold, or break them . . . It is philosophically difficult to speak of interiority in light of the weight of the outside" (26).

For further consideration of interiority, see the preface and introduction of *The Black Interior*, where Elizabeth Alexander describes the interior as an "inner space in which black artists have found selves that go far, far beyond the limited expectations and definitions of what black is, isn't, or should be" (5). Also see Hortense Spillers's definition of interior intersubjectivity, a common psychoanalytic term; Spillers quotably proclaims that the subjectivity of the interior "is not an arrival but a departure, not a goal but a process, and it conduces to neither an answer nor a 'cure,' because it is not engendered in formulae and prescriptions. Moreover, its operations are torque-like" (*Black, White, and in Color*, 383).

The term "selffullness" is described in my book *Black Women, Identity, and Cultural Theory: (Un)Becoming the Subject*.

12. Much work has been done to explore the politics/aesthetics of noise as well as to deconstruct silence—see, for example, Jacques Attali (*Noise*), Fred Moten (*In the Break*), and John Cage (*Silence*). Also much has been written about the role and nature of silence in black or minority cultures; see Trinh T. Minh-ha, *Woman. Native. Other*; Evelynn Hammonds, "Black (W)holes and the Geometry of Black Female Sexuality"; Marlene Nourbese Philip, *She Tries Her Tongue, Her Silence Softly Breaks*; bell hooks, *Talking Back*; and especially King-Kok Cheung, *Articulate Silences*, and Patricia Hill Collins, *Black Feminist Thought*. As these works notice, silence can be expressive and nuanced, so although this book prefers "quiet" as a term for clarity's sake, the distinction between the two is not always necessary or possible. A further discussion of silence occurs in note 7 of chapter 2.

13. It is helpful to remember the case already made about resistance in the introduction, especially note 4.

14. The term "irreverent" echoes Alexander's argument about the urgency of rescuing blackness from the limits of publicness and the expectations of nationalism; see her discussion of the burden of authenticity on pages 5–8 of *Black Interior*. Of the many black writers who have argued for a black interior, it is Zora Neale Hurston who makes the case most plainly and directly in "What White Publishers Won't Print." This is in keeping with Hurston's characteristic anxiety about the expectations and limits of racial identity.

15. See Leigh Raiford's brief but astute discussion of the power of lynching photographs in "The Consumption of Lynching Images," especially page 272. Also see David Marriott's important chapter on photography and lynching in *On Black Men*. Thanks to Nikky Finney for a conversation that helped make this point clearer.

16. The same is true of much of the civil rights movement, which is remembered for its publicity, though it also has quiet and reflectiveness at its heart; see chapter 4 for a further discussion of this point.

17. For a consideration of existentialism in black culture, see Lewis Gordon's *Existentia Africana*, especially chapter 1. The larger point here is that blackness exists as a concept and as such, it is explored, argued, engaged, rejected, and theorized, especially by people who seem to embody its identity. This contemplative dynamic is evident in much of the work by black writers and artists, from Fanon and Du Bois and Anna Julia Cooper, to Langston Hughes and Kara Walker and Toni Morrison. (This is part of the self-reflexiveness of race as Lively discusses it.) Existentialism is explored further in chapter 3.

18. For a broad discussion of the nature of photography, see chapter 1 of Liz Wells's *Photography: A Critical Introduction*, 2nd edition. This sense of photography's ambivalence and multiplicity is argued in Susan Sontag's *On Photography* and Roland Barthes's *Camera Lucida*. The expressiveness of photography is multiple and exuberant, and in this regard it is similar to the characterization of the expressiveness of the interior.

19. The quotation is from the end of Afaa M. Weaver's stirring "Masters and Master Works: On Black Male Poetics," where he makes a call for a new aesthetic, claiming that "the choice now for black male poets is to embrace this space where they can ask themselves this question of what constitutes beauty and ask it in terms of their own lives, and not those lives weighed down by the suppositions of identity. . . . Black male poets must explore the beauty of the quality of being human."

20. I am borrowing language here (and in the beginning of the paragraph) from Anna Julia Cooper's statement that "only the BLACK WOMAN can say 'when and where I enter, in the quiet, undisputed dignity of my womanhood, without violence and without suing or special patronage, then and there the whole Negro race enters with me'" (*A Voice from the South*, 31).

CHAPTER 2 — NOT DOUBLE CONSCIOUSNESS BUT
THE CONSCIOUSNESS OF SURRENDER

1. The comment is from an essay in *A Voice from the South* and reflects Cooper's overall argument about the importance of black people to discussions of American national culture. Cooper's work is especially important because it reflects the racial and gendered anxieties of a postwar America in the 1890s, where the role and potential of black citizens was a question linked to larger concerns about technology, civil rights, and modernity.

2. The term "surrender" is used often in religious discourses, but for the concept of quiet, the more compelling use is in psychoanalytic writing; see especially Dennis Miehls's "Surrender as Developmental Achievement in Couple Systems" and Emmanuel Ghent's "Masochism, Submission, Surrender." I am grateful to Miehls for the references here.

3. Not much has been written about Bonner's connection to Du Bois, though her work, especially this essay, is often characterized as being immersed in his notion of

the "talented tenth." And yet many of Bonner's plays and stories deal with the experience of working-class people, as Judith Musser astutely notes. For further discussion and a good general introduction to Bonner, see Joyce Flynn's introduction to *Frye Street and Environs: The Collected Works of Marita Bonner.*

Bonner's essay is similar to others written during the Harlem Renaissance that assert the idea of a "new negro" but that also note the contradictions between the promises of modernity and the realities of black life, although Bonner is particular in her attention to sexism. For example, see Alain Locke's "The Negro Takes His Place in American Art" as well as his anthology *The New Negro*, James Weldon Johnson's *Black Manhattan*, Du Bois's "Criteria of Negro Art," and especially E. Franklin Frazier's "La Bourgeoise Noire."

4. Letters have long been considered a gendered form, and even the literary and cultural domain of women. See various discussions in Elizabeth Cook's *Epistolary Bodies* (especially chapter 1 on letters as a negotiation of the gendered binary of public/private), Rebecca Earle's edited collection *Epistolary Selves* (especially Carolyn Steedman's broad-minded "A Woman Writing a Letter"), and Caroline Bland and Máire Cross's *Gender and Politics in the Age of Letter Writing.* Sharon Marcus's discussion of letters in *Between Women* (especially pages 32–43) offers conceptual support for thinking of Bonner's essay as a diary entry, as if the narrator is speaking of herself explicitly in the second person. The fact that the essay's epistolary nature avoids the first person except on one occasion will be addressed later in the chapter.

5. Since Bonner's essay is not well known, it is important to be careful in characterizing the nuance of her arguments, especially when working with excerpts. For example, in critiquing the capacity of people to judge not on the basis of color or gender, but of something finer, something more astute, Bonner writes, "And what has become of discrimination? Discrimination of the right sort ... [that] weighs shadows and nuances and spiritual differences before it catalogues ... that looks clearly past generalization and past appearance to dissect, to dig down to the real heart of matters" ("On Being Young," 5). This passage, when isolated, might suggest that Bonner is ignorant of the material consequences of racism, or for that matter, sexism, which is hardly the case.

6. This is the essence of intersectionality, as first described and defined by Kimberlé Crenshaw; see her essay "Mapping the Margins: Intersectionality, Identity Politics, and Violence against Women of Color." Lorraine Roses and Ruth Randolph, in their essay that considers many of Bonner's unpublished works between 1941 and her death in 1971 ("Marita Bonner: In Search of Other Mothers' Gardens"), note the intersectional character of her ideas; see especially page 179 as well as their entry on Bonner in *Harlem Renaissance and Beyond: Literary Biographies of 100 Black Women Writers 1900–1945.*

7. Patricia Hill Collins makes an attempt in *Black Feminist Thought* to recover silence from its pejorative and enfeebled position: "Silence is not to be interpreted as submission in this collective, self-defined Black women's consciousness" (98). Collins then goes on to cite the end of Bonner's essay, writing that "U.S. Black women intellectuals have long explored this private, hidden space of Black women's consciousness, the 'inside' ideas that allow Black women to cope with and, in many

cases, transcend the confines of intersecting oppressions of race, class, gender, and sexuality" (98). Also see Evelynn Hammonds's discussion of a politics of silence and a politics of articulation in "Black (W)holes." It is notable how much the concept of silence has been a part of black women's cultural work, particularly the consideration of voice.

Bonner's use of silence in this essay has garnered some scholarly attention. Zetta Elliott ("Writing the Black [W]hole: Facing the Feminist Void") wants to make a distinction between silence and quiet, though she claims quiet as a synonym for decorum. Cheryl Wall reads the essay's ending as "a cluster of images of silence, entrapment and paralysis" (*Women of the Harlem Renaissance*, 8), a reading that makes sense in the context of Wall's larger argument about the second-class status of women in the Harlem Renaissance. But one is hard pressed to miss the wild and reckless arrogance implied by Bonner's Buddha metaphor as well as the motion and agency of her use of stillness. In one of the only other scholarly comments on the essay, Joyce Flynn compares its ideology to Bonner's other early piece, "The Hands: A Story," noting that "in 'The Hands' Bonner seems to be expressing skepticism about romantic racialism of either kind" (introduction to *Frye Street and Environs*, xiv). Flynn goes on to argue that "On Being Young" "explores a dichotomy seen in many works by Afro-American writers: the dichotomy between inner reality and socially sanctioned racial and gender roles" (xv). Also see Margo Crawford's essay in *The Cambridge Companion to the Harlem Renaissance*, which notes Bonner's use of Buddha as a location of agency.

8. Bonner's use of idioms of domesticity and femininity, noted by most scholars who have written about this essay, can be somewhat perplexing, given her critique of identity as a whole. Part of her argument engages the principles of womanhood that are embedded in a Victorian gender binary and that still shape our common stereotypes about gender. In phrases like "the softness that makes you a woman," Bonner is engaging this binary deliberately, using the notion of women's inherent interiority as a location of agency, even using the category of woman as a metaphor for the interior. But it is interesting to note that Bonner's argument here is about wisdom and understanding—about people's capacity to experience each other not through categories of identity, but through paying attention. She notes that despite all of the progress civilizations have made, there remain profound gaps in the capacity to understand the humanity of another person. For Bonner, this intimate and simple practice—the capacity to pay attention to another—is the real gauge of social progress, and in this regard, it is women's assumed attentiveness that gives them access to this insight. Bonner is keen to elevate woman's insight to the level of social meaningfulness, personifying their particular "understanding" as the snubbed twin sister of "wisdom." And as she describes the failure of civilization since the Greeks to appreciate the wisdom that comes from being a woman, she maintains the sense that being a woman is, or could be, the location of considerable power.

9. This refusal of the terms of publicness is especially notable. Bonner's stance is not a moment of "Diva Citizenship" which, as Lauren Berlant defines it, is "when a person stages a dramatic coup in a public sphere in which she does not have privilege" (*Queen of America*, 223). Berlant goes on to comment that "the centrality of

publicity to Diva Citizenship cannot be underestimated" (223), and her arguments make sense as a timely critique of the way that a politically conservative discourse of privacy and intimacy overshadows a consideration of the public dimensions of citizenship. But imbedded in Berlant's comments is an unquestioned celebration of the liberating potential of publicness, a potential that is counter to the case that Bonner's essay makes. In fact, against Berlant's larger claims, one could argue, as Robyn Wiegman does, that "to be excluded from the public sphere of citizenship [is] not to be uniformly cast as inhuman" (*American Anatomies*, 45). Also see Kimberly Nichele Brown's arguments about the "revolutionary diva," which include a consideration of audience and publicness as a part of the dynamic of Du Boisian double consciousness.

10. For a general discussion of the limits of autobiography, see especially Paul Jay's reading of the anxiety of the autobiographical subject ("Posing") and Sidonie Smith's discussion of the trouble of the body ("Identity's Body"). Both Jay's and Smith's works are part of a larger body of criticism that explores the politics of representation and truth in autobiography, including work by Leigh Gilmore (especially the introduction and chapter 1 of *The Limits of Autobiography*, chapters 1 and 2 as well as the conclusion of *Autobiographics*, and her discussion of the "mark of autobiography" in the introductory essay in *Autobiography and Postmodernism*); see also Paul John Eakin (*Fictions in Autobiography*) and Timothy Dow Adams (*Telling Lies in Modern American Autobiography*). There is also a useful analysis of "the politics of representative identity" in Robert Levine's book on Martin Delany and Frederick Douglass (see especially the introduction). Part of what is being engaged here is the way that autobiography, as a public genre, replicates the same troubling capacities of publicness as discussed in chapter 1. And yet another aspect is the way that the dynamics of race impose an expectation of truth or authenticity on the representations of black subjectivity, even in fictional genres; see Robin Kelley's *Yo Mama's Disfunktional* (especially chapter 1), bell hooks's "Postmodern Blackness," and Ann duCille's *Skin Trade* (especially "The Occult of True Black Womanhood").

More specific to Bonner is Judith Musser's essay on Bonner's response to the "talented tenth" ("African American Women and Education"). Though Musser's essay is about Bonner's fiction, it is valuable in thinking about the use of voice in "On Being Young." Musser argues that Bonner "avoids any autobiographical elements from her distinctive childhood" (73). While "On Being Young" is clearly autobiographical, it is interesting that Bonner resisted the imposition of autobiography in her writing in general. Finally, to consider Bonner's biography in relation to the essay, see Roses and Randolph, "Marita Bonner: In Search of Other Mothers' Gardens."

11. Elizabeth Hardwick makes a keen argument about authorial agency in letters; for her, the "letter is, by its natural shape, self-justifying; it is one's own evidence, deposition, a self-serving testimony. In a letter the writer holds all the cards" (*Seduction and Betrayal: Women and Literature*, 198). Hardwick is talking about Samuel Richardson's *Clarissa*, but her insights here are applicable to Bonner's narrator (and perhaps even to Bonner herself). Certainly, Bonner's narrator is

controlling, narrating her anxieties as if they are precisely those of the reader. But this exchange is part of the intimacy that is so fascinating in the essay, that the narrator uses this control to create an argument that sustains interiority. It was bell hooks's essay "Writing the Subject: Reading *The Color Purple*" that led me to Hardwick's book.

12. The issue of audience is one that every writer faces, yet it manifests as a particular issue for the black writer. The debate about audience is central to the discourse of the Harlem Renaissance (and it is from here that we get Langston Hughes's defining essay on the topic, "The Negro Artist and the Racial Mountain") as well as the black arts/aesthetic movement (for example, the aesthetic declarations by Amiri Baraka, "Black Art" and "The Revolutionary Theatre"; Hoyt Fuller, "Towards a Black Aesthetic"; and Addison Gayle, "The Black Aesthetic"). The matter of audience is most often framed as an anxiety of what it means to write "for" a white audience or readership; see Sherley Anne Williams's *Give Birth to Brightness* and John Young's *Black Writers, White Publishers*. It is worth noting that Young's title and premise borrow somewhat from another iconic Harlem Renaissance essay, Zora Neale Hurston's "What White Publishers Won't Print," though Hurston's argument is more dynamic than Young's.

But, as Hughes notes, there is also the anxiety caused by the expectation that black writers will write for black readers and in service of the ideas/arguments of cultural nationalism and civil rights. Perhaps the best scholarly discussion of these matters of audience is in Hazel Carby's *Race Men*, particularly the introduction and first chapter. Carby is right to consider audience alongside the notion of the (black) public intellectual. Similarly, Eric Lott, in *The Disappearing Liberal Intellectual*, is astute in noting the "double consciousness" of audience for the black public intellectual; also see Thomas Holt's "The Political Uses of Alienation," Robert Reid-Pharr's *Black Gay Man* (especially chapter 2), Corrie Claiborne's "Quiet Brown Buddha(s)," William M. Banks's *Black Intellectuals*, Elizabeth Alexander's *The Black Interior* (especially the introduction), Shelley Eversley's *The Real Negro*, and Henry Louis Gates, Jr.'s "The Black Man's Burden" and "Criticism in the Jungle." In terms of gender as a part of the discussion of audience and black public intellectualism, see Carby (*Race Men*), Kimberly Nichele Brown (*Writing the Black Revolutionary Diva*), Susan Willis (*Specifying*), and Marlene Nourbese Philip (*She Tries Her Tongue, Her Silence Softly Breaks*). Finally, many black writers have spoken eloquently about this dilemma; see M. Afaa Weaver's "Masters and Master Works," Earl Ingersol's *Conversations with Rita Dove*, and Carl Phillips's *Coin of the Realm*, as three quick examples, as well as David Lionel Smith's astute essay "What Is Black Culture?" which explores the impositions that nationalism makes on the black artist.

13. In his famous essay "Ideology and Ideological State Apparatuses," Althusser offers this efficient summary of the dynamics of interpellation: "The subject acts insofar as he is acted on by the . . . system" (170). Many scholars have engaged Althusser's notion, especially to consider the limits of identity, most famously Judith Butler in *Bodies That Matter*.

14. Carby, in her chapter on Du Bois in *Race Men*, makes a very convincing argument about his engagement of the dynamics of public intellectualism: "Within the

opening pages . . . Du Bois establishes his ability to speak as a race leader and grants himself the authority to evoke a convincing portrayal of the black folk by integrating his own commanding narrative voice, as a black intellectual, with the life of the folk" (20–21). This point is enhanced by Holt's argument that Du Bois's ideas in "The Conservation of the Races" seem to be recalibrated for a white audience when the essay is revised as the first chapter of *Souls* (see especially 238–239 of "The Political Uses of Alienation"). Emily Bernard, in *Remember Me to Harlem*, captures the issue of public intellectualism and its importance to Du Bois: speaking in regard to his stewardship of *The Crisis*, Bernard notes that "*The Crisis* was his pulpit . . . No word was published in *The Crisis* that didn't meet Du Bois' standards. Because art has the potential to liberate black people from social bondage, Du Bois believed it should be approached with gravity, even reverence. Every time a writer put pen to paper, he was taking the future of the race in his hands" (xvi). The case for the public-mindedness of *Souls* is also supported by Robert Stepto's chapter in *From Behind the Veil*, especially pages 53–66, and Henry Louis Gates, Jr., and Terri Oliver's introduction to the Norton edition of *The Souls of Black Folk*. None of this attention to publicness as a valence of Du Bois's work is intended to dismiss the way that *The Souls of Black Folk* is also introspective (as Arnold Rampersad terms it in *The Art and Imagination of W.E.B. Du Bois*); in fact, Nellie McKay goes as far as celebrating Du Bois's engagement of idioms of the private sphere in his writings. Still, the larger point is the way that the exigencies of being a public intellectual manifest in Du Bois's articulation of black consciousness, and how this sits in contrast to Bonner's idiom of consciousness.

15. I am using the term "metalanguage" after Evelyn Higginbotham to refer to the ways that race becomes its own language system and accrues totalitarian significance, even to the exclusion of other aspects of identity. This claim about Du Bois's thinking in *Souls* (and elsewhere) is intended to support the idea that Du Bois was committed to racial difference in a way that Bonner was not; as Holt notes, "the utility of racial difference for social progress [is] a theme to which Du Bois would frequently return" ("Political Uses of Alienation," 237). K. Anthony Appiah, in "The Uncompleted Argument," goes further, arguing that Du Bois's ideas are marred by their acceptance of race as a biologically meaningful construct. Appiah's claim has been contested by many scholars, notably Lucius Outlaw ("'Conserve' Races?: In Defense of W.E.B. Du Bois"), Robert Gooding-Williams ("Outlaw, Appiah, and Du Bois)," and Bernard Boxill ("Du Bois on Cultural Pluralism"). What is clear, and largely undisputed, is that Du Bois was interested in race as a political and social construct, that he was committed to exploring the way that a notion of race and racial difference could be used to mobilize black progress (this is Holt's point and it is supported by Bernard W. Bell's essay tracing the evolution of double consciousness in Du Bois's thought, "Genealogical Shifts in Du Bois' Discourse"; also see Dickson Bruce, Jr., "W.E.B. Du Bois and the Idea of Double Consciousness"). Feminist scholars like Darlene Clark Hine have noted the limitations of Du Bois's idea because it is so singularly focused on race; see her essay "In the Kingdom of Culture."

16. See Joyce Flynn (introduction to *Frye Street and Environs*), Will Harris ("Early Black Women Playwrights"), and Judith Musser ("African American Women and Education") for a discussion of Bonner's nuanced engagement of race,

a consideration that foreshadows the ideas of black women in the 1970s and 1980s (for example, the Combahee River Collective) as well as the articulations of a postmodern blackness or a new black aesthetic in the early 1990s (for example, Trey Ellis, Nelson George, Greg Tate).

17. Imagination is often described as a balance between the interior (internal acts, deliberations, constructions) and external objects, behaviors, states of affairs: "the power of forming mental images or other concepts not directly derived from sensation" (Manser, "Imagination," 596). In philosophy, the term is also discussed in relationship to aesthetics and phenomenology (see, for example Sartre's *Imagination*). More specific to black culture, Elizabeth Alexander sees imagination as key to thinking about black interiority, asking "Where is our abstract space?" (*Black Interior*, 7).

18. This is the argument that many scholars make about black identity; see, for example, Michele Wallace, "Variations on Negation and the Heresy of Black Female Creativity"; Evelynn Hammonds, "Black (W)holes and the Geometry of Black Female Sexuality"; Hortense Spillers, *Black, White, and in Color*; and Corrie Claiborne, "Leaving Abjection: Where 'Black' Meets Theory"; as well as Roderick Ferguson's discussion of aberration. This is also implied in Du Bois's double consciousness—that the black subject is not recognized as a human being—and is the motivation for his gathering evidence of aspects of black life that had previously been understudied or unacknowledged (in *Souls* but also in his Atlanta University Studies). The idea of "blackness as negation" is also legible in Avery Gordon's study of ghosts and the phantasmic (*Ghostly Matters*), Sharon Holland's *Raising the Dead*, as well as novels like Morrison's *Beloved* and Ellison's *Invisible Man*.

19. This notion of consciousness as a sphere of freedom has been central to my very early thinking about black women's contributions to cultural studies, and eventually to the concept of quiet.

20. The point about triumph is echoed in Judith Musser's essay on Bonner's fiction, "African American Women and Education"; Musser writes, "Although [Bonner] follows the African American women's writing tradition in portraying women as her main characters, these women are not independently strong, nor individualized and not triumphant" (73). The idiom "self-measure" is influenced by Nikki Giovanni who, in *Gemini*, notes "I think it's been rather unconscious but we [black women] measure ourselves by ourselves" (144).

21. Jamaica Kincaid has a lovely passage in her novel *The Autobiography of My Mother* that resonates with the idea of quiet: the protagonist Xuela is remembering her father's death and notices that "then a great peace came over me, a quietness that was not silence and not acceptance, just a feeling of peace, a resolve. I was alone and I was not afraid . . . The man to whom I was married, my husband, was alone, too, but he did not accept it, he did not have the strength to do so. He drew upon the noisiness of the world into which he was born, conquests, the successful disruption of other peoples' worlds . . ." (223–224).

CHAPTER 3 — *MAUD MARTHA* AND THE PRACTICE OF PAYING ATTENTION

1. This era of writing between 1940 and 1960 has been called urban or social realism, though Ellison is most often described as being modernist and the terms

"modernism" and "naturalism" are used with "realism" in the section heading of *The Norton Anthology of African American Literature*. Some scholars also refer to it as the era of protest literature. For a discussion here, see Stacy I. Morgan's *Rethinking Social Realism: African American Art and Literature, 1930–1953*; James E. Smethurst's *The New Red Negro: The American Left and African-American Poetry, 1930–1946*; and Stephanie Brown's *The Postwar African American Novel: Protest and Discontent, 1945–1950*. Also see B. J. Bolden, "The Rhetorical Power of Gwendolyn Brooks' *Maud Martha*"; Mary Helen Washington, "'Taming All That Anger Down': Rage and Silence in Gwendolyn Brooks' *Maud Martha*"; Barbara Christian, *Black Feminist Criticism: Perspectives on Black Women Writers*; Malin Lavon Walther, "Re-Wrighting *Native Son*: Gwendolyn Brooks's Domestic Aesthetic in *Maud Martha*" (especially good on Brooks and Wright); Patricia H. Lattin and Vernon E. Lattin, "Dual Vision in Gwendolyn Brooks's *Maud Martha*"; and George Kent, *A Life of Gwendolyn Brooks*, for a discussion of Brooks's historical relation to the black writers of her time.

2. Much of the scholarly discussion of *Maud Martha* acknowledges its attention to the inner world, though it is Barbara Christian in *Black Feminist Criticism* (especially chapters 9 and 15) who is most astute. My own appreciation of the novel is shaped undeniably by the work of Christian and other black feminist scholars from the 1990s, particularly Susan Willis, Karla F. C. Holloway, Trudier Harris, Patricia Hill Collins, and Mary Helen Washington. Also see discussions of the novel by Shelley Eversley (*The Real Negro*) and Hortense Spillers (*Black, White, and in Color*).

Part of thinking about the characterization of the interior in this novel is the concept of imagination explored in the previous chapter. In discussing "Kitchenette Building," Elizabeth Alexander notes that Brooks names "the imagination as a site worth tending" (*Black Interior*, 49). This is consistent with Brooks's oeuvre, which pays particular attention to dreaming and imagination. Also see Julia Leyda's discussion (in "Space, Class, City: Gwendolyn Brooks's *Maud Martha*") of Felix Driver's concept "imaginative geography" in regard to the novel, and Karla Holloway's discussion of imagination in black women's writing (in *Moorings and Metaphors*).

3. The term "existentialism" did not come into wide use until the 1940s to describe some of the writings of the nineteenth-century philosopher Søren Kierkegaard. Though existentialism is organized around the idea of consciousness and the interior, the philosophy rejects the idea of an essential inner self. Among the works that have been most useful to my understanding existentialism are those by Lewis Gordon, *Existence in Black* and *Existentia Africana*; Mark Tanzer, *On Existentialism*; George Cotkin, *Existential America*; and Charles Guignon, "Existentialism." The principles of existentialism are quite relevant to some common ideas in African American culture and thought, especially the notion of consciousness and freedom. In many ways, living a life that is without social and other freedoms makes the question of freedom essential; see especially Gordon. It is not an accident, then, that many of the existentialist writers in France in the twentieth century found aspects of black experience useful to their thinking.

4. Few scholars of the novel use the term "existentialism" (Dorothy Tsuruta mentions it in her essay, "Regional and Regal: Chicago's Extraordinary Maud Martha"), though many implicitly engage existentialist concepts; see Larry Andrews's discussion of the notion of "persistence of a life force amid instability and destruction" as part of his overall discussion of nature ("The Aliveness of Things: Nature in *Maud Martha*," 69) and B. J. Bolden's discussion of ethics and morality ("The Rhetorical Power of Gwendolyn Brooks' *Maud Martha*").

5. The novel has been compared to Sherwood Anderson's *Winesburg, Ohio*, Jean Toomer's *Cane*, Gertrude Stein's *Three Lives*, and Ernest Hemingway's *In Our Time*; see D. H. Melham, *Gwendolyn Brooks: Poetry and the Heroic Voice*, and Bolden, "Rhetorical Power." Some critics consider the novel autobiographical, while others note the parallels between Brooks's life and that of her protagonist but maintain it as a work of fiction; see Melham, *Gwendolyn Brooks*, and Kent, *A Life of Gwendolyn Brooks* (the former offers a useful account of the history of genesis of the novel). Finally, in her discussion of the novel, Hortense Spillers notices the lack of consecutiveness.

6. Just about every chapter begins in mid-thought, as if in stream of consciousness: "What she liked was candy buttons" (chapter 1), "The school looked solid" (chapter 2), "So the gorilla really did escape!" (chapter 3), and so on. The idea of *Maud Martha* as characterizing the mind of a black woman is informed by discussion with the students in my seminar in spring 2010, especially Kimberly Drew and Geraldine Richards.

7. See Julia Leyda, "Space, Class, City," for an excellent extended close reading of these two chapters.

8. The hyphenation in the chapter title is interesting, as if to distinguish this solace from consolation that comes from outside the self.

9. In defending the novel against charges of passivity in relationship to racism, Andrews cites "aliveness" as a characteristic of Maud Martha's agency and notes the novel's attention to matters of power. The most notable criticism of *Maud Martha*'s passivity comes from Mary Helen Washington's classic essay "Taming All That Anger Down," though Washington is not alone in her point of view; see Andrews, "The Aliveness of Things," for a good review of these arguments, and Lattin and Lattin, "Dual Vision in Gwendolyn Brooks's *Maud Martha*," for an engagement of Washington (interestingly, their discussion finds the vignette in the salon to be significant). Notable here is Valerie Frazier's engaging reading of the novel as a chronicle of domestic warfare ("Domestic Epic Warfare in *Maud Martha*"), for though Frazier notes Maud Martha's agency, the argument for a notion of warfare is situated within and against the anxiety of passivity. This is all part of a larger question about the characterization of resistance that readers come to expect from black women's writing, a point that Adrienne McCormick notes in her essay "Is This Resistance?" (though McCormick reads Maud Martha's character as part of the pantheon of resistant black women).

10. Baldwin's comment is from his discussion of the protest novel, and ends with "The failure of the protest novel lies in its rejection of life, the human being, the denial of his beauty, dread, power, in its insistence that it is his categorization

alone which is real and which cannot be transcended" ("Everybody's Protest Novel," 23).

It is worth commenting briefly on Brooks's novel in relationship to Ellison's *Invisible Man*, another work that is characterized by the interior consciousness of its protagonist. As brilliant as *Invisible Man* is, its interiority is engaged with the riddle of race—the protagonist struggles to understand what race means, to avoid and then engage race as a performance. In fact his invisibility, a social condition that becomes psychological, is a metaphor of maskedness. Though the character Invisible Man is not engaged in resistance, all of his thinking is toward the dynamics of race. He is fascinated, appalled, intrigued, dumbfounded, resentful of race and its implications in his life. *Invisible Man* really is a novel of double consciousness, as the character's innocence about racial difference develops, by the novel's end, into a kind of schizophrenia, where he is suspicious of the implications race has in his life. There are many scholarly essays that engage Ellison's novel, though William Lyne's argument in "The Signifying Modernist" about double consciousness is especially relevant to the point above.

11. For further consideration, see Peggy Phelan's *Unmarked* and Michael Warner's "The Mass Public and the Mass Subject."

12. The quotation is from page 6 of Robert Reid-Pharr's introduction to *Once You Go Black*, which offers an interesting discussion of agency and black culture. There is a similar meditation on humanity in another chapter in *Maud Martha*, the one entitled "posts." Also see Tsuruta ("Regional and Regal") and Christian (*Black Feminist Criticism*) for further discussion of Maud Martha's universalism.

13. The term "desire" is most often considered in psychoanalytic thinking, but also in philosophy and aesthetics. See Judith Butler's efficient summary essay, "Desire," which traces the term from Plato to Freud to contemporary poststructuralist/ postmodern thought. Of particular note is Butler's statement that "For Plato, then, it is not that a desire emerges from a body, but that a body emerges *from* a desire" (372, emphasis in original). This claim seems to support the idea that desire constitutes the subject, and Butler goes on to note that this Platonic equation is not far from how desire is engaged in psychoanalytic thinking, where a "libidinal investment gives rise to an imaginary body" (372). Also see Elizabeth Grosz's construction of desire as "an intensity, enervation, positivity, or force," productivity (*Space, Time, and Perversion*, 179). This characterization is important because it moves desire, as a psychoanalytic term, beyond the binary of longing and loss. To that end, Grosz composes a long list of synonyms: desire is "energies, excitations, impulses, actions, movements, practices, moments, pulses of feeling" (182). This notion of energies and excitations is where desire implies agency. That is, desire reflects human capacity, the human subject's will to imagine, want, pursue, as well as how the act of wanting, imagining, and pursuing is a meaningful blueprint for one's humanity. And yet, Butler's discussion of desire in *Undoing Gender* suggests that it is also dislocating: "desire places us outside ourselves" (33), she writes, which reminds us that the desiring subject is not necessarily a subject in control. Again, the term is sometimes ambivalent and not always easy to sum up.

Grosz is one of many feminist scholars who have been astute in challenging the Freudian notion that women lack desire. In making this challenge, Grosz pushes the idea of desire beyond the framework of lack or loss and embraces Spinoza's work as a way to expand the consideration of desire as "processes that produce. . . . Desire is the force of positive production, the action that creates things, makes alliances, and forges interactions" (*Space, Time, and Perversion*, 179); for other formulations of desire as productivity, see Grosz's *Jacques Lacan: A Feminist Introduction*, Butler's essay "Desire," and Catherine Belsey's book of the same title. The discussion of desire as a measure of selfhood is indebted to this conceptualization of desire as productivity, and also works against the idea of quiet as a synonym of decorum or propriety or reticence; in this latter regard see L. H. Stallings, *Mutha' Is Half a Word*, for a consideration of desire and black women's folk culture.

14. See Tate's discussion throughout the entire introduction of *Psychoanalysis and Black Novels*, especially pages 5–10, and Belsey's discussion in *Desire* of desire as derivation.

15. Soon after speaking of the ways women are taught to suppress or distrust the power of this interiority, Lorde notes that men fear "this same depth too much to examine the possibilities of it within themselves" ("Uses of the Erotic," 54).

16. The term "pleasure" is used here as a companion to the notion of desire that Lorde and Grosz have described, though pleasure has its own complicated history. Indeed, in black cultural discourse, the notion of pleasure is sometimes disfavored because of its overlap with the long history of hypersexualization in racial discourse. Cornel West has described pleasure as being counter to joy, a term that he thinks is more ethical and less material. Gina Dent also elevates joy above pleasure; for her, joy is the collective and achieved manifestation of pleasure. See Dent's introduction in *Black Popular Culture* (which notes the comment by West). On the other hand, Robin Kelley offers a useful resuscitation of the usefulness of pleasure and play as concepts in black culture; see chapter 1 of *Yo Mama's Disfunktional.*

17. The notion of feeling and sensation is relevant to Brooks's use of literary synesthesia in the novel. Some examples here include the narrator's description of the Playhouse movie as "classical music that silvered its way into you and made your back cold" (77), or later in the same chapter, when Maud Martha contrasts the beauty and elegance of a rich person's home with the ordinariness of her own kitch-enette apartment with "the gray sound of little gray feet scratching away" (77). Synesthesia reorganizes how one thinks about the experience of the world, especially the sensory world, and even implies that experience cannot be contained to one sense or another—it is too voluptuous for that.

The opening of *Maud Martha* and its reference to dandelions calls to mind another novel about a young dark-skinned black girl where dandelions manifest as an interiority—Toni Morrison's *The Bluest Eye*, which was published nearly twenty years after Brooks's work. Morrison's novel is itself a meditation on interiority, and the dandelion again serves as a metaphor for underappreciated black girlhood. Soon after Pecola is shown desiring blue eyes for the first time, blues eyes that she surmises would convince others of her natural and tender beauty,

she walks down Garden Avenue to a small grocery store which sells penny candy . . . an avenue gently buffeted by the familiar and therefore loved images. The dandelions at the base of the telephone pole. Why, she wonders, do people call them weeds? She thought they were pretty. But grown-ups say "Miss Dunion keeps her yard so nice. Not a dandelion anywhere." Hunkie women in black babushkas go into fields with baskets to pull them up. But they do not want they yellow heads—only the jagged leaves. They make dandelion soup. Dandelion wine. Nobody loves the head of dandelion. Maybe because they are so many, strong, and soon. (47)

In this instance, as it was with Maud Martha, the dandelions here are seen by others as disposable, held in low regard, certainly not a pretty flower to be cherished. To Pecola, the dandelions, like the crack in the street on which she trips, are "inanimate things she saw and experienced. They were real to her. She knew them. They were the codes and touchstones of the world" (47). This is a rare moment of consciousness for Pecola as she identifies the small (and sometimes inanimate) as what she knows, as if by knowing them, she then knows herself. It is a remarkable parallel to Maud Martha's articulation of desire as an ethic of self, though Pecola does not claim these things (dandelions, the cracks in the sidewalks) as what she liked. Still, these are literally emblems of her humanity, albeit less fanciful and dynamic than Maud Martha's.

As Pecola enters the candy store, she is accosted by the gruff demeanor of Mr. Yacobowski, who barely wastes any effort to welcome her or attend to her needs. Though she has the money for candy and therefore has a kind of purchasing power, what she really wants is to be seen, to be a cherishable little girl. Of course, this does not happen and, leaving the store, her assessment of the dandelions changes: "Dandelions. A dart of affection leaps out from her to them. But they do not look at her and do not send love back. She thinks, 'They *are* ugly. They *are* weeds'" (50). Whatever capacity Pecola had to look at the dandelions or the crack in the pavement and to see beauty—the capacity to identify something ordinary as worthwhile and deserving of recognition—has dissipated. Her interior has become conflated with the exterior world and its harsh judgments, and as such, her interior is no longer a place of solace or agency.

It is exactly this dynamic between interior and exterior that *Maud Martha* highlights, the possibility that the public world will overdetermine the meaning of one's interior. This argument is exemplified partly by the attention to beauty in both novels, since beauty is at once exterior and interior, and a particular struggle for women, especially those who are black. Morrison herself is brilliant in talking about this aspect of her novel. In the "Afterword" to the 1994 edition, she admits that the "reclamation of racial beauty in the sixties stirred" thoughts about the social (and external) forces that could create such a strong sense of ugliness in a person, such a sense that one is "wanting, so small a weight on the beauty scale." "Why, although reviled by others, could this beauty not be taken for granted within the community? Why did it need wide public articulation to exist. . . . The assertion of racial beauty was not a reaction to the self-mocking, humorous critique of cultural/racial foibles common in all groups, but against the damaging internalization of assumptions of immutable inferiority originating in an outside gaze" (210). See Adele Newson-Horst ("Maud Martha Brown") and Patrice Cormier-Hamilton ("Black Naturalism and Toni Morrison"), who make some interesting connections between these two works.

18. This seems like a different version of being unmarked from the way Peggy Phelan uses the term.

19. Lorde's discussion of the erotic is useful in thinking about desire and collectivity; in "Uses of the Erotic," Lorde links the erotic to the possibility for collective action (see especially 58–59). In his brief but excellent essay "Queer Theory: Unstating Desire," Lee Edelman writes beautifully about desire and contact, which also calls to mind Grosz's discussion of surfaces in "Refiguring Lesbian Desire."Also see Samuel Delany's consideration of contact and desire in *Times Square Red, Times Square Blue*, especially pages 123–128 as well as the entire second essay, where he argues that contact is more important to maintaining interclass relationships that yield more humanity.

20. The poem here is "The Second Sermon on the Warpland," and I am grateful for Larry Andrews's essay "The Aliveness of Things," which alerted me to this piece.

21. Though Maud Martha the character seems to represent an idiomatic way of being, or even an idiomatic representation of interiority, it also seems counter to the novel to describe Maud Martha as idiomatic. She is not an iconic black female character along the likes of Janie from Hurston's *Their Eyes Were Watching God* or Sula from Morrison's novel of the same name. She, Maud Martha, is not audacious and she does not enjoy the renaissance that comes with black feminism in the 1970s. In terms of its place in the literary canon, the novel *Maud Martha* is almost undermined by its quiet as much as it is animated by it—indeed, this might be why it is little studied or remembered. As Barbara Christian notes, "Perhaps because *Maud Martha* was such a departure from the usual characterizations of Afro-American women in previous fiction, the novel went out of print almost immediately after it appeared" (*Black Feminist Criticism*, 176).

CHAPTER 4 — QUIET, VULNERABILITY, AND NATIONALISM

1. Like almost any critical term, nationalism is defined differently by different people, and is called different things—Pan Africanism, black cultural nationalism, Afro-centricism, for example. At the heart of some of the debate over the term is what constitutes nationalism. Some scholars such as Wilson Moses and Dean Robinson argue that nationalism should only apply to arguments in favor of a separate state, but most scholars of politics and history see the utility of using the term more broadly. This latter point of view is sometimes called "black cultural nationalism," the idea of advocacy for black empowerment based on collective self-definition and self-determination. In short, black cultural nationalism recognizes racial difference—either as an essence or as a legacy of racist practices—and aims to assert and advocate that difference. For clarity's sake, this chapter will use nationalism or black nationalism to refer to the broad idea, rather than to a specific or historical ideological viewpoint.

For an excellent discussion of the historical and conceptual complexities of nationalism, see *Is It Nation Time?*, edited by Eddie Glaude, Jr. This work is indispensible because, unlike engagements of nationalism that are either celebratory or critical, *Is It Nation Time?* studies the ambiguities and nuances; see especially the argument that Glaude makes in the introduction. The attempt to engage the nuances of nationalism is also taken up by James Smethurst, who gives a terrific definition of cultural nationalism in the context of the 1960s: cultural nationalism "involves a concept of liberation and self-determination. . . . It also often entails some notion of the development or recovery of a true 'national' culture" (*The Black Arts Movement*, 17). Throughout his study, Smethurst does well to complicate the superficial ways in which the black arts movement, and black cultural nationalism, have been read. Wahneema Lubiano asserts the same thing, arguing that black nationalism is "plural, flexible and contested" ("Black Nationalism and Black Common Sense" 232). As in Lubiano's work, part of seeing breadth in black/cultural nationalism has been to consider gender in the discourse; in this regard, see Nikol Alexander-Floyd's *Gender, Race and Nationalism in Contemporary Black Politics* and Madhu Dubey's *Black Women Novelists and the Nationalist Aesthetic*. On nationalism in general, see the introductions of Moses's *Classical Black Nationalism* and William L. Van Deburg's *Modern Black Nationalism*; see also Lubiano ("Standing in for the State"), James Cone (*Black Theology and Black Power*), Jeffrey Ogbar (*Black Power*), and Philip Brian Harper (*Are We Not Men?*).

2. Again, the work in Eddie Glaude's *Is It Nation Time?* is especially helpful in thinking through the complicated relevance and challenges of nationalism; see especially essays by Cornel West and Adolph Reed. Also see Lubiano's "Black Nationalism and Black Common Sense," which makes an attempt to rehabilitate nationalism against criticisms of narrowness. Though I agree with Lubiano's overall premise—that, in practice, nationalism is heterogeneous—I am interested still in the ways that the dominant representations of the nationalist subject reinforce the notion of blackness as resistance. Part of the matter here is that nationalism gives birth to the identity it aims to advocate for, as implied in Dexter Gordon's book *Black Identity*, which asserts that nationalism is "the birth of the black subject" (69).

3. Some scholars would question the use of the civil rights movement as an example of nationalism, as remarked in the first note. I am convinced by Peniel Joseph's work that questions the neat separation between the civil rights and the black power movements, as well as his capacity to see nationalist impulses in the civil rights movement's articulation of self-identity, self-determination, and liberation (see *The Black Power Movement*). In many ways, the term "the civil rights movement" has come to stand for both the specific movement as well as the longer decade of black liberation struggle; and though Clayborne Carson makes a strong case for using the general term "black freedom movement" ("Civil Rights Reform and the Black Freedom Struggle"), this idiom does not have the popular resonance of the former term.

4. See Charles Payne's "The View from the Trenches" and T. V. Reed's *The Art of Protest*, which discuss the flawed master narrative of the civil rights movement; also see Payne's beautiful *I've Got the Light of Freedom*. See especially section 3 of Renee Romano and Leigh Raifford, *The Civil Rights Movement in American Memory*. Also see critiques of the representation of Rosa Parks and of the South in Susan Schramm-Pate and Rhonda Jeffries's *Grappling with Diversity*. Indeed, nearly every scholarly work on the movement, especially historical accounts, make some reference to the trouble that dominant icons pose to telling a more supple history.

5. King's work exists along with others that address the ways that the individuality and humanity of black bodies is hidden "beneath devastating racial markings" (*African Americans and the Culture of Pain*, 17), though it is especially important to be clear that King is not questioning the legitimacy of the pain or violence that black people experience—nor am I. The question is to consider the ways in which that pain is engaged discursively, what it comes to mean about black identity. For further discussions of pain, injury, and collectivity, see Robin Wiegman (*American Anatomies*), Dorothy Roberts (*Killing the Black Body*), Judith Butler (*Undoing Gender*), Wendy Brown (*States of Injury*), Karla Holloway (*Passed On*), Harriet Washington (*Medical Apartheid*), and Jennifer Brody (*Impossible Purities*), all of whom describe various states of (black) injury and the impact such has on collective identity. There has been much work done in queer studies on the notion of shame, and some of it is relevant to thinking about black culture and nationalism; see especially Robert Reid-Pharr's *Gay Black Man* and Kathryn Bond Stockton's *Beautiful Bottom, Beautiful Shame*. It is worth noting that King discusses silence in chapters 3 and 4 of her book, though her use of the term is not parallel to my engagement of quiet.

It is also important to clarify that the argument here is not that nationalism creates the consciousness of injury—the legacy and persistence of violence does that; neither does nationalism perpetuate unnecessary anxiety or alertness. The question is about the way that this consciousness of injury dominates how we think about black humanity, the way that it limits the understanding of vulnerability. It is the impact of these limits that Ralph Ellison rejects so eloquently in his essay "The World and the Jug," where he dismisses Irving Howe's assessment that Richard Wright's Bigger Thomas is a more accurate black character because he exemplifies black victimization. And Ellison is not alone in his discomfort with the limits of nationalism— James Baldwin also discusses the limits of the idiom "victim": in *The Evidence of Things Not Seen*, he writes, "I refuse to speak from the point of view of the victim. The victim can have no point of view for precisely so long as he thinks of himself as a victim" (78); also see *Notes of a Native Son* (especially page 102).

6. See my discussion of interiority in Malcolm X's autobiography in "Black Feminisms and *The Autobiography of Malcolm X*," as well as the consideration of photography as a "quiet" medium in chapter 1. Also, the exploration of quiet in the context of the civil rights movement should not be collapsed with the ideology of nonviolence, especially because of the way that nonviolence is often a political and public practice.

7. For a broader discussion of Baldwin through this period, see David Leeming's biography. Various scholars have discussed Baldwin's status as a race man; see E. Frances White's "The Evidence of Things Not Seen" (which suggests that Baldwin negotiated his sexuality to protect this status), Henry Louis Gates, Jr.'s "The Welcome Table," C.W.E. Bigsby's "The Divided Mind of James Baldwin," and Benjamin DeMott's "James Baldwin on the Sixties." Relatedly, much has been written about Baldwin's engagement of identity; most useful to my thinking have been two exceptional essays: Will Walker's "After *The Fire Next Time*" and Jeffrey Stout's "Theses on Black Nationalism." Also see Robert Corber's terrific review

essay, Dwight A. McBride's edited *James Baldwin Now* (especially essays by Rebecca Aanerud and Lawrie Balfour), Andrew Shin and Barbara Judson's essay on his novels ("Beneath the Black Aesthetic"), and Rodney Coates and Sandra Lee Browning's consideration of intellectualism ("James Baldwin: *The Fire Next Time* and Black Intellectuals").

8. See the discussion in chapter 2 of the letter as an aesthetic in general and in relation to Marita Bonner's essay.

9. In aligning himself with nurturing, Baldwin offers a subtle challenge to American conceptualizations of black masculinity. Domesticity as a trope is foreign to black masculinity, for though black men might be characterized theoretically as emasculated, even as markers of a kind of failed or partially effeminized maleness, the *virtues* of domesticity—the power of love and nurturing, of the ethical agency of what is domestic—are rarely attributed to or claimed for/by black men.

10. The way that Baldwin navigates audience and address is reminiscent of Bonner in "On Being Young." Like Baldwin's, Bonner's essay reads like a letter of caution and advice, uses direct address, and refers to the larger social discourse through third-person narration ("They have locked up wisdom"). Both essays are sensitive to the dynamics of audience in the "race" essay, which means speaking to a black audience and against/about a white one. Baldwin's negotiation of this imposition is particularly expert, not only because he is able to contain the necessity of speaking against a white majority but especially because of the way that his writing to his nephew allows him to engage the idiom of black collectivity, while still maintaining the intimacy of the exchange between one person and another. That is, Baldwin uses the intimate to reflect and stand in for the black collective.

11. The tensions here are reminiscent of Baldwin's first novel, the semiautobiographical *Go Tell It on the Mountain*; see Peter Powers's essay on the novel ("The Treacherous Body "), as well as Lawrie Balfour's discussion of terror in Baldwin's work ("Finding the Words").

12. It is important to remember that this second essay is a letter Baldwin writes to and about himself, and therefore can be read as a reprisal of the first letter, also to a fourteen-year-old black boy, also about the perils of coming of age in America. In this regard, Baldwin is both mentee and is mentor, at once the narrator and protagonist and audience; and in light of the aesthetic of interiority, his use of the first person is not authority or arrogance, but self-interrogation. That is, it is not first-person narration that creates the interiority, but rather Baldwin's idioms, the letter form, and the use of direct address that sustain a quality of intimacy.

13. This characterization is similar to the notion of "self-connection shared," Audre Lorde's description of the erotic capacity to feel deeply. Lorde notes that this capacity is not a retreat from the exterior but a deepening of the possibility that one might recognize a greater humanity in another. Baldwin's second essay explores sensuality in a way that connects with Lorde's notion of the erotic. He writes: "To be sensual, I think, is to respect and rejoice in the force of life, of life itself, and to be *present* in all that one does" (43, emphasis in original).

14. Names and renaming are important tropes in black cultural discourse; see Kimberly Benston's classic essay ("I Yam What I Am"), as well as the discussion of

interpellation in chapter 2. Some of the ideas here are inspired partly by Denise Riley's book on feminism and postmodernism, *"Am I That Name?"* as well as Judith Butler's *Undoing Gender*. Of course, the larger idea, about the conceptual limits of racial blackness, has been discussed by many, including Michelle Wright (*Becoming Black*), Robert Reid-Pharr (*Once You Go Black*), Paul Gilroy (*Against Race*), bell hooks ("Postmodern Blackness"), Thomas Holt (*The Problem of Race*), David Lionel Smith ("What Is Black Culture?"), Cornel West (*Race Matters*), Greg Tate (*Flyboy in the Buttermilk*), Barbara Smith ("Towards a Black Feminist Criticism"), Trey Ellis ("The New Black Aesthetic"), Thelma Golden (her notion of "post-black" in *Freestyle*), to name a few. Their ideas are part of the discussion of collectivity that follows.

15. *Black Is* was the seventh and final screen production of Riggs's career, which included celebrated works like *Ethnic Notions*, *Tongues Untied*, and *Color Adjustment*. As with his previous work, Riggs was interested in documenting various aspects of black identity—from the legacies of racist representations, to the creativity of black artistic contributions, to the negotiation of homophobia and sexism. This final film, then, is something of a culmination of Riggs's ambition in his earlier works. See E. Patrick Johnson's excellent consideration of the film in chapter 1 of *Appropriating Blackness*; also see Phillip Brian Harper's "Marlon Riggs: The Subjective Position of Documentary Video" for a brief discussion of Riggs's seminal films, Amy Abugo Ongiri's "We Are Family" for its engagement of nationalism in relationship to Riggs and Issac Julien, and Maurice Stevens's "The Power to Trans(per)form" in *Troubled Beginnings*.

16. As his work in *Ethnic Notions* suggests, the lack of focus might reflect Riggs's distrust of the primitivist implications of a naked black person in the woods, even as he finds the image to be a powerful metaphor. But the scene also works to reclaim the capacity of black nakedness from the narrow boundaries of primitivism; that is, the scene gives us another visual image for thinking about black nakedness in the woods besides racist caricatures of people in African countries. See E. Patrick Johnson's chapter in *Appropriating Blackness* for further consideration of this scene.

17. The film is not without its own inconsistencies, as Riggs's homosexuality is taken for granted but not mentioned explicitly in the film. The discussion of homosexuality and homophobia is left to others in the film. Of course, it is also the case that Riggs the narrator avoids championing any single issue or perspective in the film, and it is also true that his homosexuality is well known; in that light, this position does not seem so inconsistent.

18. This quality of collectivity is evident in Baldwin's approach in *The Fire Next Time*, particularly his attention to intimacy. It is striking to behold that the essay collection begins with a note of failure—"Dear James, I have started this letter five times and torn it up five times." Even as a moment of rhetorical flourish, that Baldwin begins his book with this sense of incompleteness and impossibility is refreshing, an implicit acknowledgment of a nationalism that finds value in what is irresolute. And like Baldwin, Riggs's film embraces failure and incompleteness.

19. See Brian Norman's thorough discussion of the Statement, including an extended consideration of collectivity ("'We' in Redux"); also see Kimberly Springer's discussion in the essential *Living for the Revolution*.

20. This implication is supported by Crenshaw when she argues that "intersectionality provides a basis for reconceptualizing race as a coalition between men and women of color . . . race can also be a coalition of straight and gay people of color" ("Mapping the Margins," 1299). In this regard, race is no longer singularly or even centrally about race, which is one of the real contributions of Crenshaw's construct to cultural theory.

21. There has been extensive discussion of the term "womanism"; see, for example, Layli Phillips's edited *The Womanist Reader*, especially her terrific introduction and overview of "five overarching characteristics" of womanism (xxiv) and her comment on its relevance to postmodernism. Phillips's collection also includes Walker's 1979 short story "Coming Apart," where she first used and defined the term. Also see Patricia Hill Collins's "What's in a Name" and Nikol G. Alexander-Floyd and Evelyn M. Simien's "Revisiting 'What's in a Name," Katie Cannon's excellent exploration of the wisdom in black women's culture (*Katie's Canon*), and Clenora Hudson-Weems's notion of "Africana womanism," which she considers to be distinct from Walker's.

22. Layli Phillips, in discussing race and Walker's term, writes "Womanism detests race but loves ethnicity and culture, because the concept of race is rooted in the relations of domination and oppression, whereas ethnicity and culture are storehouses of human knowledge" (xxxvi).

23. This comment was inspired by one from Merce Cunningham on the nature of dance: "You have to love dancing to stick to it. It gives you nothing back, no manuscripts to store away, no paintings to show on walls and maybe hang in museums, no poems to be printed and sold, nothing but that single fleeting moment when you feel alive." The quotation is from an obituary by Elizabeth Zimmer.

24. Part of the discourses that surrounded Obama's election and inauguration—and therefore Alexander's reading—was the notion of a post-racial or post-black America. And yet in some ways, it seemed that Alexander's poem was not black enough and did not demonstrate in ways that were legible as authentic cultural blackness.

25. This question about the nature of freedom should not be read as anti-activism, especially considering Baldwin's role in the black freedom struggle. Another activist, Audre Lorde, provides a useful metaphor in her description of the erotic, where she discusses the possibility that the interior can be a source of activism. Having cautioned against living by "external directives only rather than from our internal knowledge and needs," Lorde continues, "But when we begin to live from within outward, and allowing that power to inform and illuminate our actions upon the world around us, then we begin to recognize our deepest feelings, we begin to give up, of necessity, being satisfied with suffering and self-negation, and with the numbness which so often seems like their only alternative in our society. Our acts against oppression become integral with self, motivated and empowered from within" (58). Her argument is that a sense of interior should guide our interactions with the world, even our acts of protest. Part of what is useful in Lorde's description is that it depends on redefining the notion of freedom, at least the ways that freedom has been established as the goal of nationalism. Lorde almost suggests that there is a

capacity of freedom within, untethered to the world outside and its hateful gestures, a freedom that can inspire a more meaningful relationship to activism.

26. The idea of love as "the prize" is inspired by Baby Suggs's language during her speech in the Clearing in Toni Morrison's *Beloved*.

CHAPTER 5 — THE CAPACITIES OF WAITING,
THE EXPRESSIVENESS OF PRAYER

1. The nature of language is studied in various scholarly traditions, though the comments here are informed by Ferdinand de Sauserre's work in linguistics and Jacques Lacan's in psychoanalysis. Also see José Medina's book *Language: Key Concepts in Philosophy*. McLaughlin's essay "Figurative Language" is useful because it is related to literature and also because he suggests that language is, in part, interior.

2. It is in this regard that language and literacy are part of the celebrated nature of black expressiveness; see, for example, Henry Louis Gates Jr.'s *Figures in Black*. Many writers have engaged the idea of language as ambivalence; see my discussion in chapters 6 and 7 of *(Un)Becoming the Subject*.

3. Many poets have written about the nature of poetic language; see, for example, Mary Oliver's excellent *A Poetry Handbook*. In her poem "Morgan Harris," Cheryl Clarke notices the interior of poetic language: "To her, poetry is the smallest thing,/ her greater depth" (*Experimental Love: Poems*, 14). This sense of what is small, what is tender and fragile, is the aim of poetry; as Rita Dove notes, poetry is a form that "connects you to yourself, to the self that doesn't know how to talk or negotiate. We have emotions that we can't really talk about, and they're very strong" (quoted in Clarence Major's *The Garden Thrives*, xxvi). Dove goes on to suggest that "I really don't think of poetry as being an intellectual activity. I think of it as a very visceral activity." The claim that is being made about the language of poetry is also relevant to the short story, which works with limited space and therefore relies on brevity and symbolism, at least as much as the novel (see note 11 below). This is even truer of music, where pieces are made up of gaps and silence as much as they are of notes played, a point that is especially legible in listening to jazz. I am grateful to L. H. Stallings for the reference to Clarke's poem.

4. For a consideration of the tension between form and content in black litera-ture, see Gates's *Figures in Black* (especially "Introduction" and "Literary Theory and the Black Tradition"), "Criticism in the Jungle," and his introduction to *The Signifying Monkey*; also see Madelyn Jablon (*Black Metafiction*) and Keith E. Byerman (*Fingering the Jagged Grain*). Additionally, see William Andrews's formu-lation of "posing as artless" (*To Tell a Free Story*), John Michael Vlach's *By the Work of Their Hands* (especially the introduction and chapter 1), and Robin Kelley's *Yo Mama's Disfunktional* (especially chapter 1). An anxiety about form fuels many of the aesthetic debates of the Harlem Renaissance (including varying essays by Romare Bearden ["The Negro Artist and Modern Art"], W.E.B. Du Bois ["Criteria of Negro Art"], Langston Hughes ["The Negro Artist and the Racial Mountain"], Zora Neale Hurston ["What White Publishers Won't Print"], Alain Locke ["The Negro Takes His Place in American Art"], and George Schyuler ["The Negro-Art

Hokum"]), and of the Black Arts Movement in the 1960s (for example, Amiri Baraka's "Black Art," Addison Gayle's "The Black Aesthetic," and Hoyt Fuller's "Towards a Black Aesthetic"). For a more general consideration of form, see Hayden White's *The Content of the Form*, and Michael Boccia's *Form as Content and Rhetoric in the Modern Novel*.

5. Of repetition, James Snead writes, "whenever we encounter repetition in cultural forms, we are indeed not viewing 'the same thing' but its transformation." Snead's comment is from his truly excellent essay "Repetition as a Figure of Black Culture," 59.

6. In keeping with the aesthetic of the entire collection, Trethewey uses the intimacy of family (mother/daughter relationship; biracial child's relationship to the South; interracial family; black men's relationship to the national family) to explore big narratives of race, loyalty, war.

7. In this regard, realism is authority, as Wahneema Lubiano has phrased it in "'But Compared to What?' Reading Realism, Representation, and Essentialism," and has often been advocated, implicitly or explicitly, by cultural leaders. The intent of authoritative realism is to document, a goal that means being attuned to a public audience as well as committed to a notion of truth that necessarily compromises the representation of complexity. The best overall work on realism and black culture is Gene Andrew Jarrett's *Deans and Truants*. Some key examples of the advocacy of realism by cultural leaders include Alain Locke's "The Saving Grace of Realism," Richard Wright's "Blueprint for Negro Writing," Amiri Baraka's poem "Black Art," and Addison Gayle's "The Black Aesthetic." Also see Gates's discussion of the politics of realism in his introduction to *Figures in Black*, especially pages xxvi–xxvii. For other discussions of the presence and limits of "racial realism," see Dubey's *Signs and Cities*, Tate's *Psychoanalysis* (especially the introduction), Jablon's *Black Metafiction,* and Eversley's *The Real Negro*; as well as the general discussions of realism by Michael Elliott (*The Culture Concept*, especially chapters 2 and 3), Kenneth Warren (*Black and White Strangers*), Amy Kaplan (*The Social Construction of American Realism*), and Michael Bell (*The Problem of American Realism*).

8. Part of the consideration of surrealism must include its political inclinations— that many proponents of the aesthetic saw it as a way to advocate progressive, even revolutionary, ideas. This merger of the political and the imaginative made surrealism attractive to the Negritude poets and other black writers; see Jean-Claude Michel's *The Black Surrealists* and Robin Kelley's *Freedom Dreams*, especially the chapter "Keepin' It (Sur)real: Dreams of the Marvelous." Some scholars suggest that surrealism, conceptually, is natural to black experience, as Kelley does in discussing Richard Wright: "For Wright, black people did not have to go out and find surrealism, for their lives were already surreal" (183). One challenge in thinking about surrealism is its use of primitivism, which seems similar to racist notions about black identity; as T. Denean Sharpley-Whiting notes: "Reason, Absolute Truth, Logic— ideals held as unique to the European Enlightenment—are denounced by Césaire in favor of the madness, the illogical, uncivilized, cannibalistic tendencies ascribed to blacks by Europeans" (*Negritude Women*, 9). Sharpley-Whiting goes on to argue

that the primitivism of surrealism was not exclusive to black people, though there was general acceptance of the idea that "people of color . . . were more in touch with the id" (85). Some of these ideas about surrealism are also relevant to other ideologies of fantastical expression, for example magical realism.

Another example in thinking about the quality of language described here is Mark Rothko's late works, those brilliant paintings of two or three blocks of colors. These pieces evoke terrific fluidity and intensity, a sense of being overwhelmed by the ocean of feeling. That such simple and abstract blocks of color could produce such abundance and intimacy arises from the poetic capacity of Rothko's language. His aesthetic is not minimalist or even economical, and is not merely beyond what is real (or hyper-real); instead, it is accessible and supple, expressive as well as ambiguous, a bigness of feeling. See Jeffrey Weiss, who quotes Rothko's claim that his work is about intimacy (*Mark Rothko*, 262). Rothko's work has been described as abstract expressionism, though he never embraced the term. He has also been described as minimalist, though minimalism—which is sometimes based on objectivity—is different from the capacity being described here. On minimalism, see Kirk Curnutt's *Wise Economies* (especially pages 205–216) and Cynthia Whitney Hallett's *Minimalism and the Short Story*.

9. Here I am referring largely to pieces like *Same, Time Pieces, Easy for Who to Say, Guarded Conditions* and *Dividing Lines*. These pieces and further discussion of Simpson's work can be found in Beryl Wright and Saidya Hartman's *Lorna Simpson: For the Sake of the Viewer*, Deborah Willis's *Lorna Simpson*, and Coco Fusco's *English Is Broken Here* and "Uncanny Dissonance"; also see my discussion of Simpson in chapter 1 of *Black Women, Identity, and Cultural Theory*.

10. André Bazin claims that "The photographic image is the object itself, the object freed from the conditions of time and space that govern it" ("The Ontology of the Photographic Image," 8). This claim might be too bold to be entirely true (for example, Smith and Carlos's image is informed by time and space), but it does speak to the way that Simpson plays with timelessness.

11. There is a predicament of expression with the sublime that makes it an interesting framework for thinking about quiet. Historically, as a part of the discourse of aesthetics, the term "sublime" has been used to describe an excellent and awesome quality of experience, a sense of transcendence. The sublime is a revelation of what is beyond our social understanding of humanness, an awe that is divine; in its capacity to take us beyond what is human, the sublime is a disturbance or even loss of identity. The sublime has been used interchangeably with the beautiful, though beginning in the Enlightenment, the sublime was theorized as superior to the beautiful. The distinction between the two lies in the argument that the sublime is beyond nature, while the beautiful is limited to and by nature; the sublime is "the inhuman, the realm of things beyond ourselves, the dimension of otherness we can never know" (Mary Arensberg, *The American Sublime*, 1). This is all part of the long intellectual history of aesthetics, a discourse that has shaped thinking from ancient Greece to the Enlightenment to postmodernism and has been central to philosophy, religion, art, psychology, and sociology. Most interesting to thinking about quiet is the notion of beauty as a human capacity to perceive, experience, judge—beauty as

a quality of being or measure of being human. Some useful general resources here include Jeremy Gilbert-Rolfe's *Beauty and the Contemporary Sublime* (especially pages 1–10, where he argues that the expressiveness of the sublime is freedom), Umberto Eco and Alastair McEwen's *History of Beauty*, and Jerome Stolnitz's essay "'Beauty': Some Stages in the History of an Idea." Also see Stolnitz's and Stephen Ross's encyclopedia entries on "beauty." Of course, the concept of beauty also has historical relevance to racist ideas about black inferiority, especially physically; see Maxine Craig's *Ain't I a Beauty Queen?* and Noliwe Rooks's *Hair Raising*. In terms of thinking about the sublime as a loss of identity, see Donald Pease's "Sublime Politics," Helen Regueiro's "Dickinson and the Haunting of the Self," and Frances Ferguson's *Solitude and the Sublime* (which argues that the beautiful is social and the sublime is isolation); also see Barbara Freeman's construction of the "feminine sublime" as an engagement of otherness. For other discussions of the sublime and beauty, see Marc Conner (*The Aesthetics of Toni Morrison*, especially pages 49–76), Dolan Hubbard's "W.E.B. Du Bois and the Invention of the Sublime in *The Souls of Black Folk*," and Gilbert-Rolfe's discussion of Schiller in *Beauty and the Contemporary Sublime*.

Another way of describing this kind of language is to notice its gaps and hesitations, as if it were working "by some more intuitive method of communication, by rhythm, or as the structuralists would say, by a deep structure that lies beneath the conscious level of concept" (Charles May, *The New Short Story Theories*, xx), a level of human capacity and understanding that exists beneath what is conscious. This is Charles May's way of thinking about the language of short story, and it seems to be consonant with the idea of interiority. Discussions of the aesthetic of the short story as a genre have informed the consideration of language in this chapter; see, for example, May's and Julio Cortazar's essays in *The New Short Story Theories*, Michael Wood's *Children of Silence*, Curnutt's *Wise Economies*, Raymond Carver's "On Writing," Valerie Shaw's *The Short Story, a Critical Introduction*, and Susan Lohafer and Jo Ellyn Clarey's *Short Story Theory at a Crossroads* (especially Lohafer's excellent introduction to part one and Austin Wright's essay). Also see Suzanne Ferguson's argument about interior action ("Defining the Short Story").

12. Prayer is a vast concept, hardly representing a defined set of notions. Philip and Carol Zaleski, in their highly readable and comprehensive book *Prayer: A History*, note that prayer merges "the absurd and the sublime . . . the fantastic and the banal," action and contemplation, the material and the imaginative, being and becoming (3–6). Furthermore, it may be interior, even a sense of stillness, but it is concerned with the world of things and is also motion (as in the African proverb "when you pray, you move your feet"). For further references on prayer, see Patricia Carrington's *Freedom in Meditation*, George Maloney's *Inward Stillness*, and D. Z. Phillips's *The Concept of Prayer*.

13. Within various religious traditions, the discussion of audience and even double consciousness would be different from that above. The discussion here is predicated on the concept of prayer drawn from its general practice. No distinction is being made here between ritual and personal prayer, for example, or the ways that religious communities can serve as an external audience; instead, prayer is being spoken of in its most essential and idealized sense.

14. The quotation is from Natalie Goldberg's distinction between procrastination and waiting (*Wild Mind*, 211).

15. Hurston herself notices the gendered difference between men and women's concept of adventure in the opening paragraphs of the novel, which starts "Ships at a distance carry every man's wish on board." In contemporary literature, works like Sena Naslund's *Ahab's Wife* challenge the construct of women who wait for men's return from epic adventure. And of course Mary Helen Washington famously critiqued the characterization of black men's adventures as being more meaningful than black women's stories of interior journeys (see the introduction of *Invented Lives*).

16. This is part of the magic that Brand's narrator is able to manifest. Magic is a part of the Zaleskis' history of prayer: "prayer partakes of magic and sacrifice yet reserves to itself something altogether more mysterious, more difficult to define" (90); see especially chapters 2 and 3. Also, in thinking about prayer as a means to connection, see D. Z. Phillips, who makes a convincing argument about the tenuousness of such connection (*The Concept of Prayer*, especially chapters 1 and 4).

CONCLUSION

1. In philosophy, oneness is often discussed in conjunction with Spinoza's notion of monism, though the two terms are not synonyms. A notion of oneness is also legible in the medieval concept of beauty via the doctrine of the "transcendentia"; see Jan Aresten's "Beauty in the Middle Ages" as well as his encyclopedia essay "Beauty." The term is also relevant to psychoanalysis (for example, Jacques Lacan and Luce Irigaray), psychotherapy, and religion.

2. For Spillers, the "one" is a perfect name for the remarkable ambivalence of human potential: "the 'one' is both conceded and not-oneself; it is not to be doubted as its sureness is tentative" (*Black, White, and in Color*, 395). She, the "one," is a being but she is also becoming, her existence in flux as much as it is also assured and definite. In this way, oneness reflects the idea of cosmopolitanism, the sense of being not a citizen of a state or a particular community but of the world. Cosmopolitanism, as Anthony Appiah notes, "rejects the conventional view that every . . . person belong[s] to a community" (*Cosmopolitanism*, xiv) as well as the conclusion that a person is the same as his or her community. This idea is not the same as universalism, since cosmopolitanism does not ignore the differences of human experience or the cultural or economic particularities of specific communities. Instead, cosmopolitanism is based on the notion of broad humanity—that any person can belong to or be connected with any experience or possibility, that a person's humanity is not confined to the particularity of his or her social or communal identity. As the North African playwright Terence writes in one of his comedies from antiquity, "I am human: nothing human is alien to me." Appiah reads Terence's statement as the principle of cosmopolitanism (see 101–113) and also discusses the role of difference (see xv). For a further consideration of cosmopolitanism and black racial identity, see Ifeoma Nwankwo's *Black Cosmopolitanism* and Robert Reid-Pharr's essay in *Black Gay Man*; also see the excellent work in Pheng Cheah and Bruce Robbins's edited *Cosmopolitics*.

More broadly, in light of Spillers's claim about the lack of attention to "oneness," it is interesting to notice how regularly concepts like individualism and selfhood appear in black cultural criticism, especially since both—as terms of publicness— are more legible than the idea of oneness.

3. This notion of everything and nothing is a feature of meditation practices, as well as many religions; see Zaleski and Zaleski's *Prayer: A History*, as well as Carrington's *Freedom in Meditation*. There is a moving example of this notion in Kenneth Rexroth's poem "Quietly," collected in the book *Sacramental Acts*. Though Rexroth is not black and does not seem to have any explicit connection to black culture, the poem is still useful in thinking about the everything of quiet. Most significant here is the fact that the poem uses the word "quiet" ten times in its short fourteen lines, each use expanding and undoing the one before. The cumulative effect of the repetition is that quiet becomes everything and nothing, a plenitude of human experience.

4. See, for example, Paul Gilroy's *The Black Atlantic*, Carole Boyce Davies's *Black Women, Writing, Identity*, Brent Edwards's *The Practice of Diaspora*, and Michelle Wright's *Becoming Black*, as well as Henry Louis Gates, Jr.'s *The Signifying Monkey*.

5. These ideas about wandering are shaped partly by the thinking of Anne McClintock (*Imperial Leather*) and Saidya Hartman (*Lose Your Mother*). And the discussion of freedom is influenced, as my ideas often are, by James Baldwin, particularly the essay "Everybody's Protest Novel."

6. For a further discussion of this dynamic, see Eric Lott's *Love and Theft*.

7. For a further discussion of these ideas, see chapters 3, 6, and 7 of my book *(Un)Becoming the Subject*.

8. Mary Helen Washington has famously noticed this attention to the interior as the key difference between the writing tradition of black men and black women. And though Washington's comment might run too close to essentialism, what it does highlight is the way that the concerns of black women have often extended beyond the struggle for the privileges of maleness in the larger culture, to an interest in the life that happens in small places (in relationships or interactions between people, in the mind, in the doing of everyday tasks). See Washington's argument on black female literary tradition in *Invented Lives*.

9. What follows is a brief engagement of other texts or moments that relate to quiet as it has been discussed thus far. These "snapshots" are admittedly random, though they reflect ideas that were part of the early writing of this book. They are included because they help support the case that a concept of quiet could be useful to many aspects of black culture.

10. This is one of the ways that gumbo functions as a metaphor in Marlon Riggs's film *Black Is . . . Black Ain't*.

11. I am grateful to Beverly Morgan-Welch for the phrase "full-orbed life."

Bibliography

Adams, Timothy Dow. *Telling Lies in Modern American Autobiography*. Chapel Hill: University of North Carolina Press, 1990.

Alexander, Elizabeth. *The Black Interior: Essays*. Saint Paul, Minn.: Graywolf, 2004.

———. *Praise Song for the Day: A Poem for Barack Obama's Presidential Inauguration, January 20, 2009*. Saint Paul, Minn.: Graywolf, 2009.

Alexander-Floyd, Nikol G. *Gender, Race and Nationalism in Contemporary Black Politics*. Basingstoke, England: Palgrave Macmillan, 2007.

Alexander-Floyd, Nikol G., and Evelyn M. Simien. "Revisiting 'What's in a Name?': Exploring the Contours of Africana Womanist Thought." *Frontiers—A Journal of Women's Studies* 27, no. 1 (January 2006): 67–89.

Allen, Ernest. "Du Boisian Double Consciousness: The Unsustainable Argument." *Black Scholar* 33, no. 2 (2003): 25–43.

Als, Hilton. "Family Secrets." *PEN America* 2 (2007). http://www.pen.org/viewmedia .php/prmMID/1080/prmID/525.

Althusser, Louis. "Ideology and Ideological State Apparatuses: Notes toward an Investigation." In Althusser, *Lenin and Philosophy, and Other Essays*, translated by Ben Brewster, 127–186. New York: Monthly Review Press, 1971.

Andrews, Larry. "The Aliveness of Things: Nature in *Maud Martha*." In *Gwendolyn Brooks' Maud Martha: A Critical Collection*, edited by Jacqueline Bryant, 69–89. Chicago: Third World Press, 2002.

Andrews, William L. *To Tell a Free Story: The First Century of Afro-American Autobiography 1760–1865*. Urbana: University of Illinois, 1986.

Appiah, K. Anthony. *Cosmopolitanism: Ethics in a World of Strangers*. New York: W.W. Norton, 2006.

———. "The Uncompleted Argument: Du Bois and the Illusion of Race." In *"Race," Writing and Difference*, edited by Henry Louis Gates, Jr., 21–67. Chicago: University of Chicago Press, 1986.

Arensberg, Mary, ed. *The American Sublime*. Albany: State University of New York Press, 1986.

Armstrong, Nancy. *Desire and Domestic Fiction: A Political History of the Novel.* New York: Oxford University Press, 1987.

Arsten, Jan A. "Beauty." In *Encyclopedia of Aesthetics*, 4 vols., edited by Michael Kelly, vol. 1, 237–251. New York: Oxford University Press, 1998.

———. "Beauty in the Middle Ages: A Forgotten Transcendental?" *Medieval Philosophy and Theology* 1 (1991): 68–97.

Attali, Jacques. *Noise: The Political Economy of Music.* Translated by Brian Massumi. Minneapolis: University of Minnesota Press, 1985.

Baker, Houston A. *Blues, Ideology, and Afro-American Literature: A Vernacular Theory.* Chicago: University of Chicago Press, 1987.

———. "Critical Memory and the Black Public Sphere." In *The Black Public Sphere: A Public Culture Book*, edited by the Black Public Sphere Collective, 5–38. Chicago: University of Chicago Press, 1995.

Baldwin, James. "Everybody's Protest Novel." In Baldwin, *Notes of a Native Son*, 13–23. [1955] Boston: Beacon, 1984.

———. *The Evidence of Things Not Seen.* New York: Holt, Rinehart and Winston, 1985.

———. *The Fire Next Time.* [1962] New York: Vintage, 1993.

Balfour, Lawrie. "Finding the Words: Baldwin, Race Consciousness and Democratic Theory." In *James Baldwin Now*, edited by Dwight A. McBride, 75–99. New York: New York University Press, 1999.

Banks, William M. *Black Intellectuals: Race and Responsibility in American Life.* New York: W. W. Norton, 1996.

Baraka, Amiri. "Black Art" and "The Revolutionary Theatre." In *The Norton Anthology of African American Literature*, edited by Henry Louis Gates, Jr., and Nellie Y. McKay, 1883, and 1899–1902. New York: W. W. Norton, 1996.

Barthes, Roland. *Camera Lucida: Reflections on Photography.* New York: Hill and Wang, 1981.

Bass, Amy. *Not the Triumph but the Struggle: The 1968 Olympics and the Making of the Black Athlete.* Minneapolis: University of Minnesota Press, 2002.

Bazin, André. "The Ontology of the Photographic Image." In *What Is Cinema?*, edited and translated by Hugh Gray, 9–16. Berkeley: University of California Press, 1971.

Bearden, Romare. "The Negro Artist and Modern Art." In *The Portable Harlem Renaissance Reader*, edited by David L. Lewis, 138–141. New York: Penguin, 1995.

Bell, Bernard W. "Genealogical Shifts in Du Bois' Discourse on Double Consciousness as the Sign of African American Difference." In *W.E.B. Du Bois on Race and Culture: Philosophy, Politics, and Poetics*, edited by Emily Grosholz Bell and James B. Stewart, 87–108. New York: Routledge, 1996.

Bell, Michael Davitt. *The Problem of American Realism: Studies in the Cultural History of a Literary Idea.* Chicago: University of Chicago, 1993.

Belsey, Catherine. *Desire: Love Stories in Western Culture.* Cambridge, Mass.: Blackwell, 1994.

Benhabib, Seyla. "Models of Public Space: Hannah Arendt, the Liberal Tradition, and Jurgen Habermas." In *Habermas and the Public Sphere*, edited by Craig Calhoun, 73–98. Cambridge: MIT Press, 1992.

Benston, Kimberly W. "I Yam What I Am: The Topos of (un)naming in Afro-American Literature." In *Black Literature and Literary Theory*, edited by Henry Louis Gates, Jr., 151–172. New York: Methuen, 1984.

Berlant, Lauren. *The Queen of America Goes to Washington City: Essays on Sex and Citizenship*. Durham: Duke University Press, 1997.

Bernard, Emily. Introduction to *Remember Me to Harlem: The Letters of Langston Hughes and Carl Van Vechten, 1925–1964*, edited by Bernard, xiii–xxvii. New York: Knopf, 2001.

Bigsby, C.W.E. "The Divided Mind of James Baldwin." *Journal of American Studies* 13, no. 3 (1979): 325–342.

Black, Daniel P. "Literary Subterfuge: Early African American Writing and the Trope of the Mask." *CLA Journal* 48, no. 4 (2005): 387–403.

Black Is, Black Ain't. Directed by Marlon Riggs. San Francisco: California Newsreel, 1995.

Bland, Caroline, and Máire Cross, eds. *Gender and Politics in the Age of Letter Writing, 1750–2000*. Aldershot, England: Ashgate, 2004.

Boccia, Michael. *Form as Content and Rhetoric in the Modern Novel*. New York: Lang, 1989.

Bolden, B. J. "The Rhetorical Power of Gwendolyn Brooks' *Maud Martha*." In *Gwendolyn Brooks' Maud Martha*, edited by Jacqueline Bryant, 90–104. Chicago: Third World Press, 2002.

Bonner, Marita. "On Being Young—a Woman—and Colored." In *Frye Street and Other Environs: The Collected Works of Marita Bonner*, edited by Joyce Flynn and Joyce Occomy Sticklin, 3–8. Boston: Beacon, 1987.

Boxill, Bernard R. "Du Bois on Cultural Pluralism." In *W.E.B. Du Bois on Race and Culture*, edited by Bernard W. Bell, Emily Grosholz, and James B. Stewart, 57–85. New York: Routledge, 1996.

Brand, Dionne. "Blues Spiritual for Mammy Prater." In Brand, *No Language Is Neutral*, 14–16. [1990] Toronto: McClelland & Stewart, 1998.

Brody, Jennifer DeVere. *Impossible Purities: Blackness, Femininity and Victorian Culture*. Durham: Duke University Press, 1998.

Brooks, Gwendolyn. *In the Mecca*. New York: Harper and Row, 1964.

———. *Maud Martha*. [1953] Chicago: Third World Press, 1993.

Brown, Kimberly Nichele. *Writing the Black Revolutionary Diva: Women's Subjectivity and the Decolonizing Text*. Bloomington: Indiana University Press, 2010.

Brown, Stephanie. *The Postwar African American Novel: Protest and Discontent, 1945–1950*. Jackson: University Press of Mississippi, 2011.

Brown, Wendy. *States of Injury: Power and Freedom in Late Modernity*. Princeton: Princeton University Press, 1995.

Bruce, Dickson D., Jr., "W.E.B. Du Bois and the Idea of Double Consciousness." *American Literature* 64 (June 1992): 299–309.

Butler, Judith. *Bodies That Matter: On the Discursive Limits of "Sex."* New York: Routledge, 1993.

———. "Desire." In *Critical Terms for Literary Study*, edited by Frank Lentricchia and Thomas McLaughlin, 369–389. Chicago: University of Chicago Press, 1995.

———. *Undoing Gender.* New York: Routledge, 2004.

Byerman, Keith Eldon. *Fingering the Jagged Grain: Tradition and Form in Recent Black Fiction.* Athens: University of Georgia Press, 1985.

Cage, John. *Silence: Lectures and Writings.* [1961] Cambridge: MIT Press, 1969.

Calhoun, Craig, ed. *Habermas and the Public Sphere.* Cambridge: MIT Press, 1992.

Camp, Stephanie. *Closer to Freedom: Enslaved Women and Everyday Resistance in the Plantation South.* Chapel Hill: University of North Carolina Press, 2004.

Cannon, Katie G. *Katie's Canon: Womanism and the Soul of the Black Community.* New York: Continuum, 1995.

Carby, Hazel V. *Race Men.* Cambridge: Harvard University Press, 1998.

Carrington, Patricia. *Freedom in Meditation.* Garden City, N.Y.: Anchor, 1977.

Carson, Clayborne. "Civil Rights Reform and the Black Freedom Struggle." In *The Civil Rights Movement in America*, edited by Charles W. Eagles, 19–32. Jackson: University Press of Mississippi, 1986.

Carver, Raymond. "On Writing." In *Fires: Essays, Poems, Stories*, 13–18. New York: Vintage, 1984.

Césaire, Aimé. "Poetry and Knowledge." In *Refusal of the Shadow: Surrealism and the Caribbean*, edited by Michael Richardson, translated by Richardson and Krysztof Fijalkowski, 134–146. London: Verso, 1996.

Cheah, Pheng, and Bruce Robbins, eds. *Cosmopolitics: Thinking and Feeling beyond the Nation.* Minneapolis: University of Minnesota Press, 1998.

Cheung, King-Kok. *Articulate Silences: Hisaye Yamamoato, Maxine Hong Kingston, Joy Kogawa.* Ithaca: Cornell University Press, 1993.

Christian, Barbara. *Black Feminist Criticism: Perspectives on Black Women Writers.* New York: Pergamon Press, 1985.

Claiborne, Corrie. "Leaving Abjection: Where 'Black' Meets Theory." *Modern Fiction Studies* 26, no. 4 (Autumn 1996): 27–36.

———. "Quiet Brown Buddha(s): Black Women Intellectuals, Silence and American Culture." PhD dissertation, Ohio State University, 2000.

Clarke, Cheryl. *Experimental Love: Poems.* Ithaca, N.Y.: Firebrand Books, 1993.

Coates, Rodney, and Sandra Lee Browning. "James Baldwin: *The Fire Next Time* and Black Intellectuals." In *Research in Race and Ethnic Relations: The Black Intellectuals*, edited by Rutledge M. Dennis, 87–114. Greenwich, Conn.: JAI Press, 1997.

Collins, Patricia Hill. *Black Feminist Thought: Knowledge, Consciousness, and the Politics of Empowerment.* New York: Routledge, 1991.

———. "What's in a Name?: Womanism, Black Feminism, and Beyond." *Black Scholar* 26, no. 1 (1996): 9–17.

The Combahee River Collective Statement: Black Feminist Organizing in the Seventies and Eighties. New York: Kitchen Table Press, 1986.

Cone, James H. *Black Theology and Black Power.* New York: Seabury, 1969.

Conner, Marc C. *The Aesthetics of Toni Morrison: Speaking the Unspeakable.* Jackson: University Press of Mississippi, 2000.

Cook, Elizabeth Heckendorn. *Epistolary Bodies: Gender and Genre in the Eighteenth-Century Republic of Letters.* Stanford: Stanford University Press, 1996.

Cooper, Anna Julia. *A Voice from the South.* [1892] New York: Oxford University Press, 1988.

Corber, Robert J. "Review. Everybody Knew His Name: Reassessing James Baldwin." *Contemporary Literature* 42, no. 1 (2001): 166–175.

Cormier-Hamilton, Patrice. "Black Naturalism and Toni Morrison: The Journey away from Self-Love in *The Bluest Eye.*" *MELUS* 19, no. 4 (Winter 1994): 109–127.

Cortazar, Julio. "Some Aspects of the Short Story." In *The New Short Story Theories,* edited by Charles E. May, 245–255. Athens: Ohio University Press, 1994.

Cotkin, George. *Existential America.* Baltimore: Johns Hopkins University Press, 2003.

Cotter, Holland. "Lorna Simpson, Gathered." *New York Times,* July 1, 2011.

Craig, Maxine Leeds. *Ain't I a Beauty Queen? Black Women, Beauty, and the Politics of Race.* New York: Oxford University Press, 2002.

Crawford, Margo. "'Perhaps Buddha Is a Woman': Women's Poetry in the Harlem Renaissance." In *The Cambridge Companion to the Harlem Renaissance,* edited by George Hutchinson, 126–140. New York: Cambridge University Press, 2007.

Crenshaw, Kimberle. "Mapping the Margins: Intersectionality, Identity Politics, and Violence against Women of Color." *Stanford Law Review* 43, no. 6 (July 1991): 1241–1299.

Curnutt, Kirk. *Wise Economies: Brevity and Storytelling in American Short Stories.* Moscow: University of Idaho Press, 1997.

Davies, Carole Boyce. *Black Women, Writing, Identity: Migrations of the Subject.* New York: Routledge, 1994.

Davis, Angela. "The Legacy of Slavery: Standards for a New Womanhood." In Davis, *Women, Race and Class,* 3–29. New York: Random House, 1981.

Delany, Samuel. *Times Square Red, Times Square Blue.* New York: New York University Press, 1999.

DeMott, Benjamin. "James Baldwin on the Sixties: Acts and Revelations." In *James Baldwin: A Collection of Critical Essays,* edited by Kenneth Kinnamon, 155–162. Englewood Cliffs, N.J.: Prentice Hall, 1974.

Dent, Gina, ed. *Black Popular Culture.* New York: New Press, 1998.

Dove, Rita. *Thomas and Beulah.* Pittsburgh: Carnegie-Mellon University Press, 1986.

Dove, Rita, and Earl G. Ingersoll. *Conversations with Rita Dove.* Jackson: University Press of Mississippi, 2003.

Dubey, Madhu. *Black Women Novelists and the Nationalist Aesthetic.* Bloomington: Indiana University Press, 1994.

———. *Signs and Cities: Black Literary Postmodernism.* Chicago: University of Chicago Press, 2003.

Du Bois, W.E.B. "Criteria of Negro Art." In *The Portable Harlem Renaissance Reader,* edited by David L. Lewis, 100–105. New York: Penguin, 1995.

———. *Souls of Black Folk.* [1903] New York: W. W. Norton, 1999.

DuCille, Ann. *Skin Trade.* Cambridge: Harvard University Press, 1996.

Dunbar, Paul Laurence. "We Wear the Mask." In Dunbar, *The Complete Poems of Paul Laurence Dunbar,* 112–113. New York: Dodd, 1913.

Eakin, John Paul. *Fictions in Autobiography: Studies in the Art of Self-Invention.* Princeton: Princeton University Press, 1985.

Earle, Rebecca, ed. *Epistolary Selves: Letters and Letter-writers, 1600–1945.* Aldershot, England: Ashgate, 1999.

Early, Gerald, ed. *Lure and Loathing: Essays on Race, Identity, and the Ambivalence of Assimilation.* New York: Penguin, 1993.

Eco, Umberto, and Alastair McEwen. *History of Beauty.* New York: Rizzoli, 2004.

Edelman, Lee. "Queer Theory: Unstating Desire." *GLQ: A Journal of Lesbian and Gay Studies* 2 (1995): 343–346.

Edwards, Brent. *The Practice of Diaspora: Literature, Translation, and the Rise of Black Internationalism.* Cambridge: Harvard University Press, 2003.

Elliott, Michael A. *The Culture Concept: Writing and Difference in the Age of Realism.* Minneapolis: University of Minnesota Press, 2002.

Elliott, Zetta. "Writing the Black (W)hole: Facing the Feminist Void." *Thirdspace* 5, no. 2 (Winter 2006). http://www.thirdspace.ca/journal/article/view/elliott/135

Ellis, Trey. "The New Black Aesthetic." *Callaloo* 38 (Winter 1989): 233–243.

Ellison, Ralph. *Invisible Man.* [1952] New York: Vintage International. 1995.

———. "The World and the Jug." In Ellison, *Shadow and Act,* 107–143. [1964] New York: Vintage 1995.

Eversley, Shelly. *The Real Negro: The Question of Authenticity in Twentieth-Century African American Literature.* New York: Routledge, 2004.

Fanon, Frantz. *Black Skin, White Masks.* Translated by Charles Markmann. [1967] New York: Grove, 1991.

Ferguson, Frances. *Solitude and the Sublime: Romanticism and the Aesthetics of Individuation.* New York: Routledge, 1992.

Ferguson, Roderick A. *Aberrations in Black: Toward a Queer of Color Critique.* Minneapolis: University of Minnesota Press, 2004.

Ferguson, Suzanne. "Defining the Short Story: Impressionism and Form." In *The New Short Story Theories,* edited by Charles E. May, 218–230. Athens: Ohio University Press, 1994.

Finney, Nikky. *Head Off & Split: Poems.* Evanston, Ill: TriQuarterly Books/ Northwestern University Press, 2011.

Flynn, Joyce. "Introduction" to *Frye Street and Environs: The Collected Works of Marita Bonner,* edited by Flynn and Joyce Occomy Sticklin, xi–xxvii. Boston: Beacon, 1987.

Fraser, Nancy. "Rethinking the Public Sphere: A Contribution to the Critique of Actually Existing Democracy." In *Habermas and the Public Sphere,* edited by Craig Calhoun, 109–142. Cambridge: MIT Press, 1992.

Frazier, E. Franklin. "La Bourgeoise Noire." In *The Portable Harlem Renaissance Reader,* edited by David L. Lewis, 173–181. New York: Penguin, 1995

Frazier, Valerie. "Domestic Epic Warfare in *Maud Martha.*" *African American Review* 39, nos. 1–2 (Spring/Summer 2005): 133–141.

Freeman, Barbara Claire. *The Feminine Sublime: Gender and Excess in Women's Fiction.* Berkeley: University of California Press, 1995.

Fuller, Hoyt. "Towards a Black Aesthetic." In *The Norton Anthology of African American Literature*, edited by Henry Louis Gates, Jr., and Nellie Y. McKay, 1810–1816. New York: W. W. Norton, 1996.

Fusco, Coco. *English Is Broken Here: Notes on Cultural Fusion in the Americas.* New York: New Press, 1995.

———. "Uncanny Dissonance: The Work of Lorna Simpson." *Third Text* 22 (Spring 1993): 27–32.

Gates, Henry Louis, Jr. "The Black Man's Burden." In *Fear of a Queer Planet: Queer Politics and Social Theory*, edited by Michael Warner, 230–238. Minneapolis: University of Minneapolis Press, 1993.

———. "Criticism in the Jungle." In *Black Literature and Literary Theory*, edited by Gates, 1–24. New York: Methuen, 1984.

———. *Figures in Black: Words, Signs, and the "Racial" Self.* New York: Oxford University Press, 1987.

———, ed. *Reading Black, Reading Feminist: A Critical Anthology.* New York: Meridian, 1990.

———. *The Signifying Monkey: A Theory of African-American Literary Criticism.* New York: Oxford University Press, 1988.

———. "The Welcome Table." In Gates, *Thirteen Ways of Looking at a Black Man*, 3–20. New York: Random House, 1997.

Gates, Henry Louis, Jr., and Terri Oliver. Introduction to *The Souls of Black Folk*, Norton critical edition, edited by Gates and Oliver, xi–xxxvii. New York: W. W. Norton, 1999.

Gay, Geneva, and Willie Baber. *Expressively Black: The Cultural Basis of Ethnic Identity.* New York: Praeger, 1987.

Gayle, Addison. "The Black Aesthetic." In *The Norton Anthology of African American Literature*, edited by Henry Louis Gates, Jr., and Nellie Y. McKay, 1870–1877. New York: W.W. Norton, 1996.

George, Nelson. *Buppies, B-boys, Baps and Bohos: Notes on Post-Soul Black Culture.* New York: Harper Collins, 1992.

Ghent, Emmanuel. "Masochism, Submission, Surrender: Masochism as a Perversion of Surrender." *Contemporary Psychoanalysis* 26 (1990): 108–136.

Gilbert-Rolfe, Jeremy. *Beauty and the Contemporary Sublime.* New York: Allworth Press, 1999.

Gilmore, Leigh. *Autobiographics: A Feminist Theory of Women's Self-Representation.* Ithaca: Cornell University Press, 1994.

———. *The Limits of Autobiography: Trauma and Testimony.* Ithaca: Cornell University Press, 2001.

———. "The Mark of Autobiography: Postmodernism, Autobiography, and Genre." In *Autobiography and Postmodernism*, edited by Kathleen Ashley, Leigh Gilmore, and Gerald Peters, 3–18. Amherst: University of Massachusetts Press, 1994.

Gilroy, Paul. *Against Race: Imagining Political Culture beyond the Color Line.* Cambridge: Harvard University Press, 2000.

———. *The Black Atlantic: Modernity and Double Consciousness*. Cambridge: Harvard University Press, 1993.

Giovanni, Nikki. *Gemini*. New York: Penguin, 1971.

———. "Revolutionary Dreams." In Giovanni, *Re:Creation*, 20. Detroit: Broadside Press, 1972.

Glaude, Eddie S., Jr., ed. *Is It Nation Time?: Contemporary Essays on Black Power and Black Nationalism*. Chicago: University of Chicago Press, 2002.

Goldberg, Natalie. *Wild Mind: Living the Writer's Life*. New York: Bantam, 1990.

Golden, Thelma. *Freestyle: The Studio Museum in Harlem*. New York: Studio Museum in Harlem, 2001.

Gooding-Williams, Robert. "Outlaw, Appiah, and Du Bois' 'The Conservation of Races.'" In *W.E.B. Du Bois on Race and Culture*, edited by Bernard W. Bell, Emily Grosholz, and James B. Stewart, 39–56. New York: Routledge, 1996.

Gordon, Avery. *Ghostly Matters: Haunting and the Sociological Imagination*. Minneapolis: University of Minnesota Press, 1996.

Gordon, Dexter. *Black Identity: Rhetoric, Ideology, and Nineteenth-Century Black Nationalism*. Carbondale: Southern Illinois University Press, 2003.

Gordon, Lewis, ed. *Existence in Black: An Anthology of Black Existential Philosophy*. New York: Routledge, 1997.

———. *Existentia Africana: Understanding Africana Existential Thought*. New York: Routledge, 2000.

Grosz, Elizabeth. *Jacques Lacan: A Feminist Introduction*. London: Routledge, 1990.

———. "Refiguring Lesbian Desire." In Grosz, *Space, Time, and Perversion: Essays on the Politics of Bodies*, 173–186. New York: Routledge, 1995.

———. *Space, Time, and Perversion: Essays on the Politics of Bodies*. New York: Routledge, 1995.

———. *Volatile Bodies: Towards a Corporeal Feminism*. Bloomington: Indiana University Press, 1994.

Guignon, Charles B. "Existentialism." In *Routledge Encyclopedia of Philosophy*, edited by Edward Craig, 493–502. New York: Routledge, 2000.

Guillory, Monique, and Richard Green, eds. *Soul: Black Power, Politics, and Pleasure*. New York: New York University Press, 1998.

Gwaltney, John Langston. *Drylongso: A Self-Portrait of Black America*. [1980] New York: New Press, 1993.

Habermas, Jürgen. *The Structural Transformation of the Public Sphere*. [1962] Cambridge: MIT Press, 1989.

Hallett, Cynthia Whitney. *Minimalism and the Short Story: Raymond Carver, Amy Hempel, and Mary Robison*. Lewiston, N.Y.: Edwin Mellen, 2003.

Hammonds, Evelynn. "Black (W)holes and the Geometry of Black Female Sexuality." *Differences: A Journal of Feminist Cultural Studies* 6 (1994): 126–145.

Hardwick, Elizabeth. *Seduction and Betrayal: Women and Literature*. New York: Random House, 1974.

Harper, Phillip Brian. *Are We Not Men?: Masculine Anxiety and the Problem of African-American Identity*. New York: Oxford University Press, 1996.

———. "Marlon Riggs: The Subjective Position in Documentary Video." *Art Journal* 54, no. 4 (Winter 1995): 69–72.

Harris, Trudier. *From Mammies to Militants: Domestics in Black American Literature.* Philadelphia: Temple University Press, 1982.

Harris, Will. "Early Black Women Playwrights and the Dual Liberation Motif." *African American Review* 28, no. 2 (Summer 1994): 205–221.

Hartman, Saidiya V. *Lose Your Mother: A Journey along the Atlantic Slave Route.* New York: Farrar, Straus and Giroux, 2007.

Higginbotham, Evelyn Brooks. *Righteous Discontent: The Women's Movement in the Black Baptist Church, 1880–1920.* Cambridge: Harvard University Press, 1993.

Hine, Darlene Clark. "In the Kingdom of Culture: Black Women and the Intersection of Race, Gender and Class." In *Lure and Loathing*, edited by Gerald Early, 337–351. New York: Penguin, 1993.

———. "Rape and the Inner Lives of Black Women in the Middle West." *Signs* 14 (1989): 912–920.

Holland, Sharon. *Raising the Dead: Readings of Death and (Black) Subjectivity.* Durham: Duke University Press, 2000.

Holloway, Karla F. C. *Moorings and Metaphors: Figures of Culture and Gender in Black Women's Literature.* New Brunswick: Rutgers University Press, 1992.

———. *Passed On: African American Mourning Stories, A Memorial.* Durham: Duke University Press, 2002.

Holt, Thomas C. "The Political Uses of Alienation: W.E.B. Du Bois on Politics, Race, and Culture, 1903–1940." In *Intellectuals and Public Life: Between Radicalism and Reform*, edited by Leon Fink, Stephen T. Leonard, Donald M. Reid, 236–256. Ithaca: Cornell University Press, 1996.

———. *The Problem of Race in the Twenty-first Century.* Cambridge: Harvard University Press, 2000.

hooks, bell. "Postmodern Blackness." In hooks, *Yearning: Race, Gender and Cultural Politics*, 23–31. Boston: South End Press. 1990.

———. *Talking Back: Thinking Feminist, Thinking Black.* Boston: South End Press, 1989.

———. "Writing the Subject: Reading *The Color Purple*." In *Reading Black, Reading Feminist*, edited by Henry Louis Gates, Jr., 454–470. New York: Meridian, 1990.

Hubbard, Dolan, ed. *The Souls of Black Folk: One Hundred Years Later.* Columbia: University of Missouri Press, 2003.

———. "W.E.B. Du Bois and the Invention of the Sublime in *The Souls of Black Folk*," in *The Souls of Black Folk: One Hundred Years Later*, 298–322. Columbia: University of Missouri Press, 2003.

Hudson-Weems, Clenora. *Africana Womanism: Reclaiming Ourselves.* Troy, Mich.: Bedford, 2004.

Huggins, Nathan Irvin. *Harlem Renaissance.* New York: Oxford University Press, 1971.

Hughes, Langston. "The Negro Artist and the Racial Mountain." In *The Portable Harlem Renaissance Reader*, edited by David L. Lewis, 91–95. New York: Penguin, 1995.

Hurston, Zora Neale. *Their Eyes Were Watching God.* [1937] New York: Harper & Row, 1990.

——. "What White Publishers Won't Print." In *I Love Myself When I Am Laughing . . . and Then Again When I Am Looking Mean and Impressive: A Zora Neale Hurston Reader,* edited by Alice Walker, 169–173. New York: Feminist Press, 1979.

Jablon, Madelyn. *Black Metafiction: Self-consciousness in African American Literature.* Iowa City: University of Iowa Press, 1997.

Jarrett, Gene Andrew, ed. *African American Literature beyond Race: An Alternative Reader.* New York: New York University Press, 2000.

——. *Deans and Truants: Race and Realism in African American Literature.* Philadelphia: University of Pennsylvania Press, 2007.

Jay, Paul. "Posing: Autobiography and the Subject of Photography." In *Autobiography and Postmodernism,* edited by Kathleen Ashley, Leigh Gilmore, and Gerald Peters, 191–211. Amherst: University of Massachusetts Press, 1994.

Johnson, Barbara. "Metaphor, Metonymy and Voice in *Their Eyes Were Watching God.*" In *Black Literature & Literary Theory,* edited by Henry Louis Gates, Jr., 205–220. New York: Methuen, 1984.

Johnson, Barbara, and Henry Louis Gates, Jr. "A Black and Idiomatic Free Indirect Discourse." In *Zora Neale Hurston's "Their Eyes Were Watching God,"* edited by Harold Bloom, 73–85. New York: Chelsea House Publishers, 1987.

Johnson, E. Patrick. *Appropriating Blackness: Performance and the Politics of Authenticity.* Durham: Duke University Press, 2003.

Johnson, Galen A. "Inside and Outside: Ontological Considerations." In *Merleau-Ponty, Interiority and Exteriority, Psychic Life and the World,* edited by Dorothea Olkowski and James Morley, 25–34. Albany: State University of New York Press, 1999.

Johnson, James Weldon. *Black Manhattan.* [1930] New York: Da Capo, 1991.

Johnson, Walter. "On Agency." *Journal of Social History* 37, no. 1 (Autumn 2003): 113–124.

Jones, Joni L. "'Making Holy': Love and the Novel as Ritual Transformation." Introduction to *Love Conjure/Blues,* by Sharon Bridgforth, xiii–xix. Washington, D.C.: RedBone Press, 2004.

Joseph, Peniel E., ed. *The Black Power Movement: Rethinking the Civil Rights-Black Power Era.* New York: Routledge, 2006.

Kaplan, Amy. *The Social Construction of American Realism.* Chicago: University of Chicago Press, 1988.

Kaplan, Carla. *The Erotics of Talk: Women's Writing and Feminist Paradigms.* New York: Oxford University Press, 1996.

Kasher, Steven. *The Civil Rights Movement: A Photographic History, 1954–68.* New York: Abbeville, 1996.

Katz, Tamar. *Impressionist Subjects: Gender, Interiority and Modernity Fiction in England.* Urbana: University of Illinois Press, 2000.

Keeling, John. "Paul Dunbar and the Mask of Dialect." *Southern Literary Journal* 25, no. 2 (1993): 24–38.

Kelley, Robin D. G. *Freedom Dreams: The Black Radical Imagination*. Boston: Beacon, 2002.

———. "Looking for the Real Nigga." In Kelley, *Yo Mama's Disfunktional: Fighting the Culture Wars in Urban America*, 15–42. Boston: Beacon, 1997.

———. *Yo Mama's Disfunktional: Fighting the Culture Wars in Urban America*. Boston: Beacon, 1997.

Kenan, Randall. *Let the Dead Bury Their Dead, and Other Stories*. San Diego: Harcourt Brace, 1992.

Kent, George E. *A Life of Gwendolyn Brooks*. Lexington: University of Kentucky Press, 1990.

Kincaid, Jamaica. *The Autobiography of My Mother*. New York: Farrar Straus Giroux, 1996.

———. *A Small Place*. New York: Penguin, 1988.

King, Debra Walker. *African Americans and the Culture of Pain*. Charlottesville: University of Virginia Press, 2008.

Kocher, Ruth Ellen. *When the Moon Knows You're Wandering*. Kalamazoo: Western Michigan University, 2002.

Lattin, Paticia H., and Vernon Lattin E. "Dual Vision in Gwendolyn Brooks's *Maud Martha*." *Critique: Studies in Contemporary Fiction* 25 no. 4 (1984): 180–188.

Leeming, David. *James Baldwin, A Biography*. New York: Henry Holt, 1995.

Levine, Robert S. *Martin Delany, Frederick Douglass, and the Politics of Representative Identity*. Chapel Hill: University of North Carolina Press, 1997.

Leyda, Julia. "Space, Class, City: Gwendolyn Brooks's *Maud Martha*." *Japanese Journal of American Studies* 19 (2008): 123–137.

Lieber, Todd M. "Ralph Ellison and the Metaphor of Invisibility in Black Literary Tradition." *American Quarterly* 24, no. 1 (1972): 86–100.

Lively, Adam. *Masks: Blackness, Race and the Imagination*. Oxford: Oxford University Press, 1998.

Locke, Alain. "The Negro Takes His Place in American Art," and "The New Negro." In *The Portable Harlem Renaissance Reader*, edited by David L. Lewis, 134–137, and 46–51. New York: Penguin, 1995.

———, ed. *The New Negro*. [1925] New York: Simon and Schuster, 1997.

———. "The Saving Grace of Realism: Retrospective Review of the Negro Literature of 1933." In *The Critical Temper of Alain Locke: A Selection of His Essays on Art and Culture*, edited by Locke and Jeffrey C. Stewart, 221–223. New York: Garland, 1983.

Lohafer, Susan, and Jo Ellyn Clarey. *Short Story Theory at a Crossroads*. Baton Rouge: Louisiana State University Press, 1989.

Lorde, Audre. "Uses of the Erotic: The Erotic as Power." In Lorde, *Sister Outsider: Essays and Speeches*, 53–59. Freedom, Cal.: Crossing Press, 1984.

Lott, Eric. *The Disappearing Liberal Intellectual*. New York: Basic Books, 2006.

———. *Love and Theft: Blackface Minstrelsy and the American Working Class*. New York: Oxford University Press, 1993.

Lubiano, Wahneema. "Black Nationalism and Black Common Sense: Policing Ourselves and Others." In *The House that Race Built*, edited by Lubiano, 232–252. New York: Vintage, 1998.

———. "'But Compared to What?' Reading Realism, Representation, and Essentialism." *Black American Literature Forum* 25, no. 2 (1992): 253–282.

———. "Standing in for the State: Black Nationalism and 'Writing' the Black Subject." In *Is It Nation Time?*, edited by Eddie S. Glaude, 156–164. Chicago: University of Chicago Press, 2002.

Lyne, William. "The Signifying Modernist: Ralph Ellison and the Limits of the Double Consciousness." *PMLA* 107, no. 2 (March 1992): 318–330.

Major, Clarence, ed. *The Garden Thrives: Twentieth-Century African-American Poetry*. New York: Harper Perennial, 1996.

Maloney, George A. *Inward Stillness*. Denville, N.J.: Dimension, 1976.

Manser, A. R. "Imagination." In *Encyclopedia of Philosophy*, 2nd ed., edited by Donald M. Borchert, 596–599. New York: Thomson-Gale, 2006.

Marcus, Sharon. *Between Women: Friendship, Desire, and Marriage in Victorian England*. Princeton: Princeton University Press, 2007.

Marriott, David. *On Black Men*. New York: Columbia University Press, 2000.

May, Charles E. "The Nature of Knowledge in Short Fiction." In *The New Short Story Theories*, edited by May, 131–143. Athens: Ohio University Press, 1994.

———, ed. *The New Short Story Theories*. Athens: Ohio University Press, 1994.

McBride, Dwight A., ed. *James Baldwin Now*. New York: New York University Press, 1999.

McClintock, Anne. *Imperial Leather: Race, Gender, and Sexuality in the Colonial Contest*. New York: Routledge, 1995.

McCormick, Adrienne. "Is This Resistance?: African-American Postmodernism in *Sarah Philips*." *Callaloo* 27, no. 3 (2004): 808–828.

McKay, Nellie Y. "The Souls of Black Women in the Folk Writing of W.E.B. Du Bois." In *Reading Black, Reading Feminist*, edited by Henry Louis Gates, Jr., 227–243. New York: Meridian, 1990.

McLaughlin, Thomas. "Figurative Language." In *Critical Terms for Literary Study*, edited by Frank Lentricchia and McLaughlin, 80–90. Chicago: University of Chicago Press, 1995.

McWhorter, John H. *Losing the Race: Self-sabotage in Black America*. New York: Free Press, 2000.

Medina, José. *Language: Key Concepts in Philosophy*. New York: Continuum, 2005.

Melham, D. H. *Gwendolyn Brooks: Poetry and the Heroic Voice*. Lexington: University of Kentucky Press, 1997.

Michel, Jean-Claude. *The Black Surrealists*. New York: Peter Lang, 2000.

Miehls, Dennis. "Surrender as a Developmental Achievement in Couple Systems." *Psychoanalytic Social Work* 18, no. 1 (2011): 39–53.

Miller, Monica. *Slaves to Fashion: Black Dandyism and the Styling of Black Diasporic Identity*. Durham: Duke University Press, 2009.

Mocombe, Paul C. *The Soul-less Souls of Black Folk: A Sociological Reconsideration of Black Consciousness as Du Boisian Double Consciousness*. Lanham, Md.: University Press of America, 2009.

Morgan, Stacy I. *Rethinking Social Realism: African American Art and Literature, 1930–1953*. Athens: University of Georgia Press, 2004.

Morrison, Toni. *Beloved*. 1986. New York: Vintage International, 2004.

———. *The Bluest Eye*. 1970. New York: Penguin, 1994.

———. "The Site of Memory." In *What Moves at the Margin: Selected Nonfiction*, edited by Carolyn C. Denard, 65–80. Jackson: University Press of Mississippi, 2008.

———. *Sula*. [1973] New York: Plume, 1982.

Moses, Wilson J. *The Golden Age of Black Nationalism, 1850–1925*. Hamden, Conn.: Archon, 1978.

———, ed. *Classical Black Nationalism: From the American Revolution to Marcus Garvey*. New York: New York University Press, 1996.

Moten, Fred. *In the Break: The Aesthetics of the Black Radical Tradition*. Minneapolis: University of Minnesota Press, 2003.

Musser, Judith. "African American Women and Education: Marita Bonner's Response to the 'Talented Tenth.'" *Studies in Short Fiction* 34, no. 1 (Winter 1997): 73–85.

Naslund, Sena. *Ahab's Wife, or the Star-Gazer*. New York: William Morrow, 1999.

Newson-Horst, Adele. "Maud Martha Brown: A Study in Emergence." In *Gwendolyn Brooks' Maud Martha*, edited by Jacqueline Bryant, 161–181. Chicago: Third World Press, 2002.

Norman, Brian. "'We' in Redux: The Combahee River Collective's 'Black Feminist Statement.'" *Differences: A Journal of Feminist Cultural Studies* 18, no. 2 (Summer 2007): 103–132.

Nwankwo, Ifeoma Kiddoe. *Black Cosmopolitanism: Racial Consciousness and Transnational Identity in the Nineteenth-century Americas*. Philadelphia: University of Pennsylvania Press, 2005.

Ogbar, Jeffrey Ogbonna Green. *Black Power: Radical Politics and African American Identity*. Baltimore: Johns Hopkins University Press, 2004.

Oliver, Mary. *A Poetry Handbook*. San Diego: Harcourt, 1994.

Olkowski, Dorothea. "The Continuum of Interiority and Exteriority in the Thought of Merleau Ponty." In *Merleau-Ponty, Interiority and Exteriority, Psychic Life and the World*, edited by Olkowski and James Morley, 1–21. Albany: State University of New York Press, 1999.

Ongiri, Amy Abugo. "We Are Family: Black Nationalism, Black Masculinity, and the Black Gay Cultural Imagination." *College Literature* 24, no. 1 (February 1997): 280–294.

Outlaw, Lucius. "'Conserve' Races?: In Defense of W.E.B. Du Bois." In *W.E.B. Du Bois on Race and Culture*, edited by Bernard W. Bell, Emily Grosholz, and James B. Stewart, 15–37. New York: Routledge, 1996.

Parker, Pat. "For the White Person Who Wants to Know How to Be My Friend." In Parker, *Movement in Black: The Collected Poetry of Pat Parker, 1961–1978*, 99. [1978] Ithaca, N.Y.: Firebrand, 1989.

Payne, Charles M. *I've Got the Light of Freedom: The Organizing Tradition and the Mississippi Freedom Struggle*. Berkeley: University of California Press, 1995.

———. "The View from the Trenches." In *Debating the Civil Rights Movement, 1945–1968*, 2nd ed., edited by Steven F. Lawson and Payne, 115–155. Lanham, Md.: Rowman & Littlefield, 2006.

Pease, Donald. "Sublime Politics." In *The American Sublime*, edited by Mary Arenberg, 21–50. Albany: State University of New York Press, 1986.

Phelan, Peggy. *Unmarked: The Politics of Performance*. London: Routledge, 1993.

Philip, Marlene Nourbese. *She Tries Her Tongue, Her Silence Softly Breaks*. Ontario: Ragweed Press, 1989.

Phillips, Carl. *Coin of the Realm: Essays on the Life and Art of Poetry*. Saint Paul, Minn.: Graywolf, 2004.

Phillips, D. Z. *The Concept of Prayer*. New York: Seabury, 1981.

Phillips, Layli, ed. *The Womanist Reader*. New York: Routledge, 2006.

Powers, Peter Kerry. "The Treacherous Body: Isolation, Confession, and Community in James Baldwin." *American Literature* 77, no. 4 (2005): 787–813.

Quashie, Kevin. "Black Feminisms and *The Autobiography of Malcolm X*." *Journal X* 4, no. 1 (Autumn 1991): 42–69.

———. *Black Women, Identity, and Cultural Theory: (Un)Becoming the Subject*. New Brunswick: Rutgers University Press, 2004.

———. "The Trouble with Publicness: Toward a Theory of Black Quiet." *African American Review* 42, nos. 2–3 (Summer/Fall 2009): 329–343.

Racine, Maria J. "Voice and Interiority in Zora Neale Hurston's *Their Eyes Were Watching God*." *African American Review* 28, no. 2 (Summer 1994): 283–292.

Raiford, Leigh. "The Consumption of Lynching Images." In *Only Skin Deep: Changing Visions of the American Self*, edited by Coco Fusco and Brian Wallis, 267–273. New York: Harry Abrams, 2003.

———. "Restaging Revolution: Black Power, *Vibe* Magazine, and Photographic Memory." In *The Civil Rights Movement in American Memory*, edited by Renee C. Romano and Leigh Raiford, 220–249. Athens: University of Georgia Press, 2006.

Rampersad, Arnold. *The Art and Imagination of W.E.B Du Bois*. Cambridge: Harvard University Press, 1976.

Reed, T. V. *The Art of Protest: Culture and Activism from the Civil Rights Movement to the Streets of Seattle*. Minneapolis: University of Minnesota Press, 2005.

Regueiro, Helen. "Dickinson and the Haunting of the Self." In *The American Sublime*, edited by Mary Arensberg, 83–100. Albany: State University of New York Press, 1986.

Reid-Pharr, Robert. *Black Gay Man: Essays*. New York: New York University Press, 2001.

———. *Once You Go Black: Choice, Desire, and the Black American Intellectual*. New York: New York University Press, 2007.

Rexroth, Kenneth. *Sacramental Acts: The Love Poems of Kenneth Rexroth*, edited by Sam Hamill and Elaine Laura Kleiner. Townsend, Wash.: Copper Canyon Press, 1997.

Riley, Denise. *"Am I That Name?": Feminism and the Category of "Women" in History*. Minneapolis: University of Minnesota Press, 1988.

Roberts, Dorothy E. *Killing the Black Body: Race, Reproduction and the Meaning of Liberty*. New York: Vintage, 1997.

Robinson, Dean E. *Black Nationalism in American Politics and Thought*. Cambridge: Cambridge University Press, 2001.

Rody, Caroline. "Toni Morrison's *Beloved*: History, 'Rememory,' and a 'Clamor for a Kiss.'" *American Literary History* 7, no. 1 (1995): 92–119.

Romano, Renee C., and Leigh Raiford, eds. *The Civil Rights Movement in American Memory*. Athens: University of Georgia Press, 2006.

Rooks, Noliwe M. *Hair Raising: Beauty, Culture, and African American Women*. New Brunswick: Rutgers University Press, 1996.

Rose, Tricia. *Longing to Tell: Black Women Talk about Sexuality and Intimacy*. New York: Farrar, Straus and Giroux, 2004.

Roses, Lorraine Elena, and Ruth E. Randolph. "Marita Bonner." In *Harlem Renaissance and Beyond: Literary Biographies of 100 Black Women Writers 1900–1945*, 18–21. Boston: G. K. Hall, 1990.

———. "Marita Bonner: In Search of Other Mothers' Gardens." *Black American Literature Forum* 21, nos. 1–2 (Spring, Summer 1987): 165–183.

Ross, Stephen. "Beauty." In *Encyclopedia of Aesthetics*, edited by Michael Kelly, 237–244. New York: Oxford University Press, 1998.

Rugg, Harold. *Imagination*. New York: Harper and Row, 1963.

Sartre, Jean-Paul. *Imagination*. Translated by Forrest Williams. Ann Arbor: University of Michigan Press, 1962.

Schramm-Pate, Susan, and Rhonda B. Jeffries, eds. *Grappling with Diversity: Readings on Civil Rights Pedagogy and Critical Multiculturalism*. Albany: State University of New York Press, 2008.

Schuyler, George. "The Negro-Art Hokum." In *The Portable Harlem Renaissance Reader*, edited by David L. Lewis, 96–99. New York: Penguin, 1995.

Scott, James C. *Domination and the Arts of Resistance: Hidden Transcripts*. New Haven: Yale University Press, 1990.

Sharpley-Whiting, T. Denean. *Negritude Women*. Minneapolis: University of Minnesota Press, 2002.

Shaw, Valerie. *The Short Story, a Critical Introduction*. London: Longman, 1983.

Shin, Andrew, and Barbara Judson. "Beneath the Black Aesthetic: James Baldwin's Primer of Black American Masculinity." *African American Review* 32, no. 2 (1998): 247–261.

Smethurst, James E. *The Black Arts Movement: Literary Nationalism in the 1960s and 1970s*. Chapel Hill: University of North Carolina Press, 2005.

———. *The New Red Negro: The American Left and African-American Poetry, 1930–1946*. New York: Oxford University Press, 1999.

Smith, Barbara. "Towards a Black Feminist Criticism." In *All the Women Are White, All the Blacks Are Men, But Some of Us Are Brave: Black Women's Studies*, edited by Gloria T. Hull, Patricia Bell Scott, and Barbara Smith, 157–175. New York: Feminist Press, 1982.

Smith, David Lionel. "What Is Black Culture?" In *The House That Race Built*, edited by Wahneema Lubiano, 178–194. New York: Vintage, 1998.

Smith, Sidonie. "Identity's Body." In *Autobiography and Postmodernism*, edited by Kathleen Ashley, Leigh Gilmore, and Gerald Peters. 266–292. Amherst: University of Massachusetts Press, 1994.

Smith, Tommie, with David Steele. *Silent Gesture: The Autobiography of Tommie Smith.* Philadelphia: Temple University Press, 2007.

Smitherman, Geneva. *Black Talk: Words and Phrases from the Hood to the Amen Corner.* New York: Houghton Mifflin, 1994.

———. *Talkin That Talk: Language, Culture, and Education in African America.* London: Routledge, 2000.

Snead, James. "Repetition as a Figure of Black Culture." In *Black Literature and Literary Theory,* edited by Henry Louis Gates, Jr., 59–79. New York: Methuen, 1984.

Sontag, Susan. *On Photography.* New York: Picador USA, 2001.

Spillers, Hortense. *Black, White, and in Color: Essays on American Literature and Culture.* Chicago: University of Chicago Press, 2003.

Springer, Kimberly. *Living for the Revolution: Black Feminist Organizations, 1968–1980.* Durham: Duke University Press, 2005.

Stallings, L. H. *Mutha' Is Half a Word: Intersections of Folklore, Vernacular, Myth, and Queerness in Black Female Culture.* Columbus: Ohio State University Press, 2007.

Steedman, Carolyn. "A Woman Writing a Letter." In *Epistolary Selves: Letters and Letter-writers, 1600–1945,* edited by Rebecca Earle, 111–133. Aldershot, England: Ashgate, 1999.

Stepto, Robert. *From behind the Veil: A Study of Afro-American Narrative.* [1979] Urbana: University of Illinois Press, 1991.

Stevens, Maurice. *Troubled Beginnings: Trans(per)forming African American History and Identity.* New York: Routledge, 2003.

Stockton, Kathryn Bond. *Beautiful Bottom, Beautiful Shame: Where "Black" Meets "Queer."* Durham: Duke University Press, 2006.

Stolnitz, Jerome. "Beauty." In *Encyclopedia of Philosophy,* 2nd ed., edited by Donald M. Borchert, 511–515. Detroit: Macmillan Reference USA, 2006.

———. "'Beauty': Some Stages in the History of an Idea." *Journal of the History of Ideas* 22, no. 2 (1961): 185–204.

Stout, Jeffrey. "Theses on Black Nationalism." In *Is It Nation Time?,* edited by Eddie S. Glaude, 234–256. Chicago: University of Chicago Press, 2002.

Sundquist, Eric J. *King's Dream.* New Haven: Yale University Press, 2009.

Tanzer, Mark. *On Existentialism.* Belmont, Cal.: Thomson Wadsworth, 2008.

Tate, Claudia. *Psychoanalysis and Black Novels: Desire and the Protocols of Race.* New York: Oxford University Press, 1998.

Tate, Greg. *Flyboy in the Buttermilk: Essays on Contemporary America.* New York: Simon and Schuster, 1992.

Thompson, Robert Farris. *Flash of the Spirit: African and Afro-American Art and Philosophy.* New York: Vintage Books, 1983.

Toibin, Colm. "A Gesture Life." *New York Times Magazine,* April 10, 2005. http://www.nytimes.com/2005/04/06/magazine/10wwln.html?scp=1&sq=colm%20toibin%20a%20gesture%20life&st=cse

Trethewey, Natasha D. *Native Guard.* Boston: Houghton Mifflin, 2007.

Trinh T. Minh-ha. *Woman. Native. Other: Writing Postcoloniality and Feminism.* Bloomington: Indiana University Press, 1997.

Tsuruta, Dorothy Randall. "Regional and Regal: Chicago's Extraordinary Maud Martha." In *Gwendolyn Brooks' Maud Martha*, edited by Jacqueline Bryant, 41–68. Chicago: University of Chicago Press, 2002.

Van Deburg, William, ed. *Modern Black Nationalism from Marcus Garvey to Louis Farrakhan*. New York: New York University Press, 1997.

Vlach, John Michael. *By the Work of Their Hands: Studies in Afro-American Folklife*. Ann Arbor: University of Michigan Research Press, 1991.

Walker, Alice. "Coming Apart." In *The Womanist Reader*, edited by Layli Phillips, 3–11. New York: Routledge, 2006.

———. *In Search of Our Mothers' Gardens: Womanist Prose*. San Diego: Harcourt Brace Jovanovich, 1983.

Walker, Will. "After *The Fire Next Time*: James Baldwin's Postconsensus Double Bind." In *Is It Nation Time?*, edited by Eddie S. Glaude, 225–233. Chicago: University of Chicago Press, 2002.

Wall, Cheryl. *Women of the Harlem Renaissance*. Bloomington: Indiana University Press, 1995.

Wallace, Michele. "Variations on Negation and the Heresy of Black Female Creativity." In *Women's Creativity and the Arts: Critical and Autobiographical Perspectives*, edited by Diane Apostolos-Capadonna and Lucinda Ebersole, 124–138. New York: Continuum, 1995.

Walther, Malin Lavon. "Re-Wrighting *Native Son*: Gwendolyn Brooks's Domestic Aesthetic in *Maud Martha*. *Tulsa Studies in Women's Literature* 13, no. 1 (Spring 1994): 143-145.

Warner, Michael. *Publics and Counterpublics*. New York: Zone Books, 2002.

———. "The Mass Public and the Mass Subject." In *Habermas and the Public Sphere*, edited by Craig Calhoun, 377–401. Cambridge: MIT Press, 1992.

Warren, Kenneth W. *Black and White Strangers: Race and American Literary Realism*. Chicago: University of Chicago Press, 1993.

———. "The End(s) of African American Studies." *American Literary History* 12, no. 3 (2000): 637–655.

Washington, Booker T. *Up from Slavery*. [1901] New York: Penguin, 1986.

Washington, Harriet A. *Medical Apartheid: The Dark History of Medical Experimentation on Black Americans from Colonial Times to the Present*. New York: Doubleday, 2006.

Washington, Mary Helen, ed. *Invented Lives: Narratives of Black Women Writers, 1860–1960*. New York: Anchor Books, 1987.

———. "'Taming All That Anger Down': Rage and Silence in Gwendolyn Brooks' *Maud Martha*." In *Black Literature and Literary Theory*, edited by Henry Louis Gates, Jr., 249–262. New York: Methuen, 1984.

Weaver, Afaa. M. "Masters and Master Works: On Black Male Poetics." Poets.Org 2005. http://www.poets.org/viewmedia.php/prmMID/18987.

Weiss, Jeffrey S., and John Gage. *Mark Rothko*. Washington, D.C.: National Gallery of Art, 1998.

Wells, Liz. *Photography: A Critical Introduction*. 2nd edition. London: Routledge, 2000.

West, Cornel. *Race Matters*. Boston: Beacon, 1993.

White, Deborah Gray. *Ar'n't I a Woman?: Female Slaves in the Plantation South*. New York: W.W. Norton, 1985.

White, E. Frances. "The Evidence of Things Not Seen: The Alchemy of Race and Sexuality." In *James Baldwin and Toni Morrison: Comparative Critical and Theoretical Essays*, edited by Lovalerie King and Lynn Orilla Scott, 239–260. New York: Palgrave Macmillan, 2006.

White, Hayden V. *The Content of the Form: Narrative Discourse and Historical Representation*. Baltimore: Johns Hopkins University Press, 1987.

White, Shane, and Graham White. *Stylin': African American Expressive Culture from its Beginnings to the Zoot Suit*. Ithaca: Cornell University Press, 1998.

Wiegman, Robyn. *American Anatomies: Theorizing Race and Gender*. Durham: Duke University Press, 1995.

Williams, Sherley Anne. *Give Birth to Brightness: A Thematic Study in Neo-Black Literature*. New York: Dial, 1972.

Willis, Deborah. *Lorna Simpson*. San Francisco: Friends of Photography, 1992.

Willis, Susan. *Specifying: Black Women Writing the American Experience*. Madison: University of Wisconsin Press, 1987.

Wood, Michael. *Children of Silence: On Contemporary Fiction*. New York: Columbia University Press, 1998.

Wright, Beryl J., and Saidiya V. Hartman. *Lorna Simpson: For the Sake of the Viewer*. New York: Universe, 1992.

Wright, Michelle M. *Becoming Black: Creating Identity in the African Diaspora*. Durham: Duke University Press, 2004.

Wright, Richard. "Blueprint for Negro Writing." In *Portable Harlem Renaissance Reader*, edited by David L. Lewis, 194–205. New York: Penguin, 1995.

———. *White Man Listen!* New York: Doubleday, 1957.

Young, John. *Black Writers, White Publishers: Marketplace Politics in Twentieth-Century African American Literature*. Jackson: University Press of Mississippi. 2006.

Zafar, Rafia. *We Wear the Mask: African Americans Write American Literature, 1760–1870*. New York: Columbia University Press, 1997.

Zaleski, Philip, and Carol Zaleski. *Prayer: A History*. Boston: Houghton Mifflin, 2005.

Zimmer, Elizabeth. "Merce Cunningham's 'Fleeting Moment When You Feel Alive.'" Obit Magazine.com, July 28, 2009. http://obit-mag.com/articles/merce-cunninghams-fleeting-moment-when-you-feel-alive.

Index

aesthetics, 143n9, 149n2, 160n8, 165–166n11

agency, 11, 14, 57, 60, 63, 71, 114, 115, 124, 129

Alexander, Elizabeth, 10, 21, 122, 144n11, 151n17, 152n2, 162n24; "Praise Song for the Day" (poem), 97–99

Alexander-Floyd, Nikol, 158n1, 162n21

Allen, Ernest, Jr., 140n2

Als, Hilton, 84

Althusser, Louis, 149n13; and interpellation, 39–40

Anderson, Marian, 25

Anderson, Sherwood, 153n5

Andrews, Larry, 153n9, 157n20

Andrews, William, 37, 163n4

Appiah, Anthony, 150n15, 167n2

Arensberg, Mary, 165n11

Armstrong, Nancy, 143n11

Arsten, Jan, 167n1

Auden, W. H., 97

audience: in black art and literature, 39, 43, 81, 82, 84, 88, 149n12; and double consciousness, 148n9

authenticity, 37, 66, 144n14

autobiography, 37, 141n3, 148n10

Baber, Willie, 143n9

Baker, Houston, 140n1, 142n5, 142n6

Baldwin, James, 25, 48, 62, 80–86, 139–140n4, 153–154n10, 159n5, 159n7, 160n11; *The Fire Next Time*, 10, 79–88, 100–101, 132, 161n18; love, concept of, 101–102

Balfour, Laurie, 160n11

Ballard, Florence, 25

Banks, William M., 149n12

Baraka, Amiri, 149n12, 163–164n4

Barthes, Roland, 145n18

Bass, Amy, 139n2

Bazin, Andre, 165n10

Bearden, Romare, 163n4

beauty: in black art and literature, 50, 156n17, 165–166n11; and black women, 155–156n17; as discussed in James Baldwin, 100, 101–102; and the sublime, 165–166n11

Bell, Bernard W., 141n2, 150n15

Bell, Michael, 164n7

Belsey, Catherine, 155n14

Benhabib, Seyla, 143n11

Benston, Kimberly, 160n14

Berlant, Lauren, 143n10, 147–148n9,

Bernard, Emily, 150n14

Bernstein, Leonard, 25

Bigsby, C.W.E., 159n7

Black, Daniel P., 142n6

black arts movement, 149n12, 157–158n1, 164n4

black culture, 4, 11, 140n1; and contemplative tradition, 24, 78, 125; and duplicity, use of, 141n5; and publicness, 8, 11, 18, 23, 27, 30, 40, 116. *See also* black identity

black expressiveness. *See* expressiveness

black female consciousness. *See* black female identity

black female identity, 29–30, 35–36, 50, 53, 64, 67, 70, 93, 124, 130; and beauty, 155–156n17; in black art and literature, 4–5, 33, 37; in Brooks (*Maud Martha*), 53; and desire, 155–156n17; and feminism, 93–96, 139n4; and interiority, 29, 34, 55, 130, 141n4, 143n11

black freedom movement, 84, 100; and nationalism, 74, 158n3

black identity, 26–27, 32–33, 139, 140n1, 141n5, 142n6, 145n17, 161n15; in Bonner, 28, 33, 41; collective, 10, 27, 73–74, 91, 92, 110, 123; and desire, 65, 95, 155n13; and double consciousness, 33, 40, 44, 65, 140n2; in Du Bois, 14, 28, 33; and gender, 35; and interiority, 33, 40, 42, 45, 52, 76, 89; and nationalism, 32, 79; and publicness, 4, 15, 140n1. *See also* identity

black nationalism, 30, 35, 41, 42, 73–102, 157–158n1; and civil rights movement, 74; and concept of victimization, 76. *See also* nationalism

blackness. *See* black identity

black subject, the. *See* black subjectivity

black subjectivity, 1, 11, 24, 31–32, 36, 50, 52; and double consciousness, 11, 36; and interpellation, 39–40

Bland, Caroline, 146n4

Boccia, Michael, 164n4

Bolden, B. J., 152n1

Bonner, Marita, 28–29, 33, 43–44, 73, 145–146n3, 147n7, 150–151n16; "On Being Young, a Woman, and Colored," 9, 28–41, 47, 64, 112, 114, 130, 147n7, 148n10, 160n10

Boxill, Bernard, 150n15

Brand, Dionne, 10, 114–116, 126, 167n16

Brody, Jennifer DeVere, 159n5

Brooks, Gwendolyn, 62, 71, 73, 97; *Maud Martha*, 9, 47, 49–61, 63–64, 67–68, 70–73, 99, 130, 131, 151n1, 154n12, 157n20, 157n21

Brown, Kimberly Nichele, 5, 139n4, 141n2, 148n9, 149n12

Brown, Stephanie, 152n1

Brown, Wendy, 159n5

Bruce, Dickson, Jr., 141n2, 150n15

Butler, Judith, 93, 149n13, 154n13, 159n5, 161n14

Byerman, Keith, 140n2, 163n4

Cage, John, 144n12

Calhoun, Craig, 140n1

Camp, Stephanie, 4–5

Cannon, Katie, 162n21

Carby, Hazel, 5, 139n4, 141n3, 149–150n12

Carlos, John, 1–3, 11, 20, 23–24, 75, 77, 88, 103, 116–117, 134, 139n2, 165n10

Carrington, Patricia, 166n12, 168n3

Carson, Clayborne, 158n3

Carver, Raymond, 166n11

Césaire, Aimé, 104

Cheah, Pheng, 167n2

Cheung, King-Kok, 144n12

Christian, Barbara, 64, 139, 152n1, 152n2, 157n21

civil rights movement, 66, 75, 78, 84, 158n4; in black art and literature, 10; and black nationalism, 74; and interiority, 79; and publicness, 145n16

Claiborne, Corrie, 149n12, 151n18

Clarey, Jo Ellyn, 166n11

Clark, Septima, 78

Clarke, Cheryl, 163n3

Coates, Rodney, 160n7

Collins, Patricia Hill, 139n4, 144n12, 146n7, 152n2, 162n21

Combahee River Collective, 92–93, 151n16

Cone, James, 158n1

Conner, Marc, 166n11

consciousness. *See* black identity

Cook, Elizabeth, 146n4

Cooper, Anna Julia, 27, 141n3, 145n17, 145n20, 145n1

Cormier-Hamilton, Patrice, 155–156n17

Cortazar, Julio, 166n11

cosmopolitanism, 125, 167n2

Cotkin, George, 51, 152n3

Cotter, Holland, 109

Craig, Maxine, 166n11

Crawford, Margo, 146n7

Crenshaw, Kimberlé, 139n4, 146n6, 162n20

Crisis, The (magazine), 28, 150n14

Cross, Maire, 146n4

cultural nationalism. *See* black nationalism

Curnutt, Kirk, 166n11

Davies, Carole Boyce, 168n4

Davis, Angela, 25, 143n11

Delany, Martin, 74, 148n10

Delany, Samuel, 157n19
demonstrativity. *See* performance
DeMott, Benjamin, 159n7
Dent, Gina, 143n9, 155n16
de Sauserre, Ferdinand, 163n1
desire, 64, 70, 157n19; and agency, 154n13;
   and black identity, 65, 95; in Bonner,
   64; and interiority, 65, 66, 71, 115
direct address (in literature), 37, 160n10.
   See also voice: first- and second-person
dissemblance, 15, 20
double consciousness, 9, 12, 13–15, 17, 20,
   27, 28, 30, 32, 39–41, 140n2, 141n2,
   148n9, 149n12, 150n15, 151n18, 154n10,
   166n13; and black identity, 31, 140n2; in
   Bonner, 30, 150n15; defined, 11; in Du
   Bois, 9, 11, 28, 32, 148n9, 151n18; in
   Ellison's *Invisible Man*, 153–154n10; and
   identity, racial, 31, 150n15, 151n18; and
   interiority, 15. *See also* doubleness
doubleness, 4, 7, 9, 12, 40, 44, 140n2,
   141n5. *See also* double consciousness
Douglass, Frederick, 148n10
Dove, Rita, 5, 70, 132, 149n12, 163n3;
   "Daystar" (poem), 9, 68–69, 120
dreaming, act of, 42, 56, 96, 108, 112, 121
Driver, Felix, 152n2
Dubey, Madhu, 158n1, 164n7
Du Bois, W.E.B., 9, 13–14, 30, 33, 39–41,
   145–146n3, 149–150n14, 150n15, 163n4,
   166n11; double consciousness, 11, 28, 32,
   140–141n2, 148n9, 151n18
DuCille, Ann, 139n4, 148n10
Dunbar, Paul Laurence, 9, 15–17, 142n6

Eakin, Paul John, 148n10
Earle, Rebecca, 146n4
Early, Gerald, 141n2
Eco, Umberto, 166n11
Edelman, Lee, 157n19
Edwards, Brent, 168n4
Ellington, Duke, 24
Elliott, Michael, 164n7
Elliott, Zetta, 147n7
Ellis, Trey, 5, 139n4, 151n16, 161n14
Ellison, Ralph, 5, 48, 140n4, 142n6, 151n18,
   151–152n1, 154n10, 159n5
epistolary form, use of, 38, 81, 84, 146n4,
   160n8
erotic, the, 66, 143n8, 157n19, 160n13,
   162n25

Eversley, Shelley, 149n12, 152n2, 164n7
existentialism, 48, 53–55, 70, 120–123, 125,
   129, 145n17, 152n3, 153n4, 168n3
expressiveness, 9–11, 20–27, 34–35, 45, 99,
   103–106, 111, 117, 122, 145n18; as African
   cultural retention, 143n9
exterior world. *See* exteriority
exteriority, 47, 62, 68, 122–123, 144n11,
   155–156n17

Farmer, James, 78
Fanon, Franz, 13, 140n1, 145n17
Ferguson, Francis, 166n11
Ferguson, Roderick, 151n18
Ferguson, Suzanne, 166n11
figurative language, use of, 104, 125,
   163n1, 165n8
Finney, Nikky, 132
first-person, 17, 36–37, 146n4, 160n12
Flynn, Joyce, 146n3, 147n7, 150n16
form, 105, 106–108, 163n4
Fraser, Nancy, 142n6
Frazier, E. Franklin, 146n3
Frazier, Valerie, 153n9
Freedom Riders, 75
Freeman, Barbara, 166n11
Fuller, Hoyt, 163n12
Fusco, Coco, 165n9

Garnet, Henry Highland, 24
Gates, Henry Louis, Jr., 141n2, 141n3,
   141–142n5, 142–143n8, 149n12, 159n7,
   163n2, 163n4, 168n4
Gay, Geneva, 143n9
Gayle, Addison, 149n12, 164n4
George, Nelson, 151n16
Ghent, Emmanuel, 145n2
Gilbert-Rolfe, Jeremy, 166n11
Gilmore, Leigh, 148n10
Gilroy, Paul, 5, 139n4, 161n14, 168n4
Giovanni, Nikki, 96, 151n20;
   "Revolutionary Dreams" (poem),
   96
Glaude, Eddie, Jr., 157n1
Goldberg, Natalie, 26, 66, 167n14
Golden, Thelma, 5, 139n4, 161n14
Gooding-Williams, Robert, 150n14
Gordon, Avery, 151n18
Gordon, Dexter, 158n2
Gordon, Lewis, 145n17, 152n3
Griffin, Farah Jasmine, 139n4

Grosz, Elizabeth, 143–144n11, 154–155n13, 155n16
Guignon, Charles, 152n3
Guillory, Monique, 143n9
Gwaltney, John L., 142n5

Habermas, Jürgen, 140n1
Hallett, Cynthia Whitney, 164–165n8
Hammonds, Evelynn, 141n4, 144n12, 147n9, 151n17
Hardwick, Elizabeth, 148–149n11
Harlem Renaissance, 28, 37, 143n9, 146n3, 146n6, 147n7, 149n12, 163n4
Harper, Michael, 122
Harper, Philip Brian, 158n1, 161n15
Harris, Shanette, 140n2
Harris, Trudier, 152n2
Harris, Will, 150n16
Hartman, Saidiya, 165n9, 168n4
Hemingway, Ernest, 153n4
Henderson, Mae, 139n4
Higginbotham, Evelyn, 141n4, 150n14
Hine, Darlene Clark, 15, 141n4, 150n15
Hines, Chester, 48
Holiday, Billie, 7
Holland, Sharon, 151n18
Holloway, Karla F. C., 152n2, 159n5
Holt, Thomas, 5, 139n4, 149n12, 150n15, 161n14
hooks, bell, 139n4, 144n12, 148n10, 149n11, 161n14
Hubbard, Dolan, 140n2, 166n11
Hudson-Weems, Clenora, 162n21
Huggins, Nathan, 129
Hughes, Langston, 5, 145n17, 149n12, 163n4
Hull, Gloria, 140n4
Hurston, Zora Neale, 5, 28, 144n14, 149n12, 163n4; *Their Eyes Were Watching God*, 9, 18–20, 113–114, 167n15

identity, 11, 41, 69–70, 149n12; collective, 10, 70, 79; and double consciousness, 13. *See also* black identity
imagination, 41–44, 56, 60, 64, 67, 69, 113–114, 151n17, 152n2; and interiority, 41, 69, 116, 151n17
Ingersol, Earl, 149n12
inner life. *See* interiority
interiority, 6–12, 16–18, 21–24, 49, 55, 59, 62, 71, 77, 83–88, 107, 111, 142n8,

143–144n11, 146n2, 149n11, 153n8, 155–156n17, 159n6; in Baldwin, 84, 88; and black female identity, 29, 143n11, 155n17; and black identity, 11, 12, 24, 42, 45, 76, 78–79, 89, 122–123; and black nationalism, 42, 89; in Bonner, 30; defined, 21; and desire, 65; in Du Bois, 13–14; and expressiveness, 52; and exteriority, 47, 62, 66; and language, 64, 166n11; and publicness, 3, 6, 21, 29, 50, 52, 78, 86, 117; and vulnerability, 3, 76, 84, 91, 115, 122
interpellation, 39–40, 62, 149n13, 160–161n14
intersectionality, 32, 41, 92, 93, 130, 146n6, 162n20
intimacy, 3, 20, 29–31, 38, 43, 45, 81–88, 99, 149n12, 165n8; and publicness, 3, 20, 83, 84, 99

Jablon, Madelyn, 163n4
Jarrett, Gene Andrew, 139n4, 164n7
Jay, Paul, 148n10
Jeffries, Rhonda, 158n4
Johnson, Barbara, 142–143n8
Johnson, E. Patrick, 161n16
Johnson, Galen, 144n11
Johnson, James Weldon, 146n3
Johnson, Walter, 139n3
Jones, Loni, 72
Joseph, Peniel, 158n3

Kaplan, Amy, 164n7
Kaplan, Carla, 143n8
Kasher, Steven, 77
Katz, Tamar, 143n11
Keeling, John, 142n6
Kelley, Robin D. G., 42–44, 142n7, 148n10, 155n16, 163n4, 164n8
Kenan, Randall, 130–131
Kent, George, 152n1
Kierkegaard, Soren, 152n3
Kincaid, Jamaica, 132, 151n21
King, Bernice, 25
King, Debra, 76, 159n5
King, Martin Luther, Jr., 25, 75
Kirschke, Amy, 140n2
Kocher, Ruth Ellen, 10, 126–128

Lacan, Jacques, 163n1, 167n1
language: in black art and literature, 104, 125, 145n17, 150n15; and expressiveness,

103, 112; figurative vs. literal, 103; and interiority, 163n3, 166n11, 166n12; politics of, 114
Larsen, Nella, 28
Lattin, Patricia, 152n1, 153n9
Leeming, David, 159n7
Let Your Motto Be Resistance (exhibit), 9, 24
Levine, Robert, 148n10
Leyda, Julia, 152n2, 153n7
Lieber, Todd, 142n6
Lively, Adam, 142n6, 145n17
Locke, Alain, 146n3, 163n4, 164n7
Lohafer, Susan, 166n11
Lorde, Audre, 65, 66, 155n15, 157n19, 160n13, 162n25
Lott, Eric, 149n12, 168n6
love, 98, 101, 128
Lovell, Whitfield, 6–8, 110
Lubiano, Wahneema, 158n2, 164n7
lynching, 23, 144n15
Lyne, William, 154n10
Lyon, Danny, 78, 79

Major, Clarence, 163n3
Malcolm X, 25, 75, 78, 159n6
Maloney, George, 166n12
Manser, A. R., 151n17
Marcus, Sharon, 146n4
Marriott, David, 144n15
mask, the, 11, 15, 20, 142n6, 154n10
masking. See mask, the
May, Charles, 166n11
McBride, Dwight A., 160n7
McClintock, Anne, 168n5
McCormick, Adrienne, 153n9
McEwan, Alastair, 166n11
McKay, Nellie, 139n4, 141n3
McLaughlin, Thomas, 103–104, 165n1
McWorther, John, 140n4
Medina, José, 163n1
Melham, D. H., 153n5
metalanguage, 41, 150n15
Michel, Jean-Claude, 164n8
Miehls, Dennis, 145n2
Miller, Monica, 142n6
Mocombe, Paul, 140–141n2
Montgomery bus boycott, 75
Morgan, Stacy I., 151–152n1
Morrison, Toni, 128, 132–133, 145n17, 151n18, 155–156n17, 163n26, 166n11; *Sula*, 10, 120–125, 157n21

Moses, Wilson J., 73, 74, 158n1
Moten, Fred, 144n12
Muhammed, Elijah, 84–88
Musser, Judith, 148n10, 150–151n16

naming, act of, 88, 89, 94, 95, 160n14
Naslun, Sena, 167n15
National Museum of African American History and Culture, 9, 24
nationalism, 73–102, 105, 150n15, 157–158n1; and black cultural identity, 10, 79, 100, 159n5; and black freedom movement, 74, 158n3; and black nationalism, as distinct from, 83; defined, 73, 88; and gender, 158n1; and injury, 159n5. See also black nationalism
Negritude movement, 164n8
Newsom-Horst, Adele, 155–156n17
noise, in relation to quiet, 144n12, 151n21
Norman, Brian, 161n19
Norman, Peter, 1–2
Nwankwo, Ifeoma, 167n2

Obama, Barack, 97, 162n24
Ogbar, Jeffrey, 158n1
Oliver, Mary, 163n3
Oliver, Terri, 150n14
Olkowski, Dorothea, 144n11
Olympics (Mexico City, 1968), 1–3, 11, 103, 104, 139
oneness, concept of, 119–126, 129, 130, 167n1, 168n2
Ongiri, Amy Abugo, 161n15
OPHR (Olympic Project for Human Rights), 1, 3
Outlaw, Lucius, 150n15
Owens, Jesse, 25

Parker, Pat, 132
Parks, Gordon, 25
Parks, Rosa, 75, 158n4
Payne, Charles, 158n4
Pease, Donald, 166n11
Petry, Ann, 48
Phelan, Peggy, 154n11
Philip, Marlene Nourbese, 144n12, 149n12
Phillips, Carl, 149n12
Phillips, D. Z., 166n12, 167n16
Phillips, Layli, 162n21, 162n22

photography, 26, 139n2, 145n18, 159n6, 165n10. *See also* social movement photography

pleasure: and black identity, 66–68, 70, 155n16

poetry: and form, 16–17, 94–108, 114–115, 126–128, 168n3; and language, 103, 105, 111, 145n45, 163n3

Powers, Peter, 160n11

prayer, 10, 61, 103, 112–113, 116–117, 166n12, 167n16, 168n3

public expressiveness. *See* publicness

publicness, 150n14; in black art and literature, 7, 31, 39; and black identity, 8, 11, 23, 30, 36, 40, 116, 122; in Bonner, 31, 35, 36, 40, 147n9; and interiority, 31–32, 36, 143n11

Quashie, Kevin, 140n1, 144n11, 159n6, 163n2, 165n9, 168n7

quiet, 145n20, 151n21, 157n21, 168n3; as action, 56, 63; and audience, 22; defined, 6, 21; and existentialism, 48, 51, 70; and exteriority, 70; and interiority, 9, 21, 26, 35, 57, 60, 70, 116; and noise, 144n12; and silence, 6, 21, 35, 146n7; and surrender, 9, 24, 27, 28, 44–47, 112, 129, 134; and vulnerability, 24; and waiting, 35

Racine, Maria, 143n8

racism, 1, 14, 30–31, 54, 80–83; and publicness, 32, 57, 83

Raiford, Leigh, 75, 139n2, 144n15, 158n4

realism, limitations of, 108–109, 164n7

Rampersad, Arnold, 149–150n14

Reed, Adolph, 158n2

Reed, T. V., 77, 158n4

Regueiro, Helen, 166n11

Reid-Pharr, Robert, 5, 139n4, 149n12, 154n12, 159n5, 161n14, 167n2

representation, 4, 5, 37, 39, 41, 47, 62, 148n10

resistance: in black art and literature, 23–25, 31, 105; and black freedom movement, 4; and black identity, 1–5, 8, 11, 15, 34, 122, 129, 139n4, 158n1

Rexroth, Kenneth, 168n3

Riggs, Marlon, 90, 161n15; *Black Is, Black Ain't* (film), 10, 89–92, 161n15, 168n10

Riley, Denise, 161n14

Robbins, Bruce, 167n2

Roberts, Dorothy, 159n5

Robinson, Dean E., 157n1

Rody, Caroline, 133

Romano, Renee, 75, 158n4

Rooks, Noliwe, 166n11

Rose, Tricia, 141n4

Roses, Lorraine, 146n6, 148n10

Ross, Diana, 25

Ross, Stephen, 166n11

Rothko, Mark, 165n10

Rugg, Harold, 42

Sartre, Jean-Paul, 151n17

Schramm-Pate, Susan, 158n4

Schyuler, George, 163–164n4

Scott, James C., 141n5

self-consciousness, 4, 31–32, 36–39, 48, 54, 77, 86

sexism, 31–32, 54, 146n3

Sharpley-Whiting, T. Denean, 164n8

Shaw, Valerie, 166n12

Shin, Andres, 160n7

signifying, 9, 11, 15–20

silence, 22, 35, 146n7; and gender, 147n7; and quiet, 34, 144n12

Simpson, Lorna (visual artist), 10, 108–110, 165n9; *Waterbearer*, 10, 108–110

Smethurst, James E., 152n1, 158n1

Smith, Barbara, 139–140n4, 161n14

Smith, David Lionel, 5, 149n12, 161n14

Smith, Sidonie, 148n10

Smith, Tommie, 1–3, 11, 20, 23–24, 75, 77, 99, 103, 116–117, 134, 139n2, 165n10

Smith, Zadie, 5

Smitherman, Geneva, 17, 142n7

Snead, James, 164n5

social movement photography, 139n2

Sontag, Susan, 145n18

Spillers, Hortense, 23, 40, 124, 126, 139n4, 144n11, 151n18, 153n5, 167–168n2

Springer, Kimberly, 161n19

Stallings, L. H., 155n13

Steedman, Carolyn, 146n4

Stein, Gertrude, 153n5

Stepto, Robert, 141n3, 150n14

Stevens, Maurice, 161n15

Stockton, Kathryn Bond, 159n5

Stolnitz, Jerome, 166n11

Stout, Jeffrey, 74, 159n7

stream of consciousness, 153n6

subjectivity, 39–40, 67; and interiority, 36; and surrender, 36. *See also* black subjectivity

sublime, the, 165–166n11

Sundquist, Eric, 79

surrealism, 108, 164–165n8

surrender, 24, 27–28, 34, 38, 41, 59, 66, 68; as action, 28, 114; and black identity, 36, 41; consciousness of, 35, 41; and double consciousness, 41; and interiority, 72; and quiet, 9, 24, 28, 47, 112, 129, 134, 145n2; and resistance, 32

"talented tenth," 146n3, 148n10

Tanzer, Mark, 152n3

Tate, Claudia, 64–56, 66, 139n4, 155n14, 164n7

Tate, Greg, 151n16, 161n14

Thompson, Robert Farris, 142n9

Till, Emmett, 75

Toibin, Colm, 116–117

Toomer, Jean, 153n5

Trethewey, Natasha, 10, 106–108, 164n6; "Incident" (poem), 106–108

Trinh T. Minh-ha, 45, 71, 139n4, 144n12

Tsuruta, Dorothy, 153n4

univeralism, 154n12. *See also* cosmopolitanism

Van Deburg, William L., 158n1

voice: in black art and literature, 143n11, 148n10; first- and second-person, 17, 36–40, 146n4, 160n12. *See also* direct address

Vlach, John Michael, 143n9, 163n4

vulnerability, 3, 80, 82, 103; in Baldwin, 85–87; in black art and literature, 85, 111, 122; and black identity, 76–79, 86; and interiority, 76, 84, 91, 115, 122; and nationalism, 77; and quiet, 24

waiting, 10, 50, 56, 87, 103; as action, 41, 44, 113, 114, 167n14; and prayer, 113–116; and quiet, 35

Walker, Alice, 10, 93, 162n21; "Womanist," 93–96

Walker, Kara, 145n17

Walker, Will, 159n7

Wall, Cheryl, 139n4, 147n7

Wallace, Michele, 151n18

Walther, Malin Lavon, 152n1

wandering, 125–128, 152n2, 168n5; and interiority, 125–128; in Ruth Ellen Kocher, 126–128

Warner, Michael, 142n6, 154n11

Warren, Kenneth, 5, 139n4, 164n7

Washington, Booker T., 25, 141n3

Washington, Harriet, 159n5

Washington, Mary Helen, 139n4, 152n1, 153n9, 167n14, 168n8

Weaver, Afaa M., 5, 100–101, 145n19, 149n12

Weiss, Jeffrey, 165n8

Wells, Liz, 145n18

West, Cornel, 155n16, 158n2, 161n14

White, Deborah Gray, 5

White, E. Frances, 159n7

White, Hayden, 164n4

White, Shane, 143n9

Whitney, Cynthia, 165n8

Wiegman, Robyn, 148n9, 159n5

Williams, Sherley Anne, 149n12

Willis, Deborah, 165n9

Willis, Susan, 139n4, 152n2

Wilson, Mary, 35

womanism, 10, 93–96, 162n21, 162n22

Wood, Michael, 166n11

Wright, Beryl, 165n9

Wright, Michelle, 5, 139n4, 161n14, 168n4

Wright, Richard, 3–4, 48, 159n5, 164n7

Young, John, 149n12

Zafar, Rafia, 142n6

Zaleski, Philip and Carol, 166n12, 168n3

About the Author

Kevin Quashie is an associate professor at Smith College, where he teaches in the department of Afro-American Studies and the program for the Study of Women and Gender. He is coeditor of the anthology *New Bones: Contemporary Black Writers in America*, and is author of *Black Women, Identity and Cultural Theory: (Un)Becoming the Subject.*

CPSIA information can be obtained
at www.ICGtesting.com
Printed in the USA
LVHW011544240722
723806LV00002B/7

9 780813 553108